INVENTING AGENCY

INVENTING AGENCY

Essays on the literary and philosophical production of the modern subject

Edited by
Claudia Brodsky
Eloy LaBrada

Bloomsbury Academic
An imprint of Bloomsbury Publishing Inc

B L O O M S B U R Y
NEW YORK · LONDON · OXFORD · NEW DELHI · SYDNEY

Bloomsbury Academic
An imprint of Bloomsbury Publishing Inc

1385 Broadway	50 Bedford Square
New York	London
NY 10018	WC1B 3DP
USA	UK

www.bloomsbury.com

BLOOMSBURY and the Diana logo are trademarks of Bloomsbury Publishing Plc

First published 2017

© Claudia Brodsky, Eloy LaBrada, and Contributors, 2017

All rights reserved. No part of this publication may be reproduced or transmitted in any form or by any means, electronic or mechanical, including photocopying, recording, or any information storage or retrieval system, without prior permission in writing from the publishers.

No responsibility for loss caused to any individual or organization acting on or refraining from action as a result of the material in this publication can be accepted by Bloomsbury or the editors.

Library of Congress Cataloging-in-Publication Data
Names: Brodsky, Claudia, 1955- editor. | LaBrada, Eloy, editor.
Title: Inventing agency: essays on the literary and philosophical production of the modern subject / edited by Claudia Brodsky, Eloy LaBrada.
Other titles: Literary and philosophical production of the modern subject
Description: New York: Bloomsbury Academic, 2016. | Includes bibliographical references and index.
Identifiers: LCCN 2016019089 (print) | LCCN 2016035441 (ebook) | ISBN 9781501317149 (hardback) | ISBN 9781501317156 (ePub) | ISBN 9781501317163 (ePDF)
Subjects: LCSH: Subject (Philosophy) | Subjectivity in literature. | Literature–Philosophy. | Criticism. | BISAC: LITERARY CRITICISM / General. | LITERARY CRITICISM / Semiotics & Theory. | PHILOSOPHY / General.
Classification: LCC PN56.S7414 I58 2016 (print) | LCC PN56.S7414 (ebook) | DDC 126–dc23
LC record available at https://lccn.loc.gov/2016019089

ISBN: HB: 978-1-5013-1714-9
PB: 978-1-5013-1713-2
ePDF: 978-1-5013-1716-3
ePub: 978-1-5013-1715-6

Cover design: Eleanor Rose
Cover image © Guggenheim Museum, New York, Gift, Mr Irving Blum, 1982

Typeset by Deanta Global Publishing Services, Chennai, India

CONTENTS

Introduction
Claudia Brodsky 1

PART ONE SUBJECTS 15

1 I think, therefore I feel
   Marshall Brown 17

2 Some dark interiority: A brief conceptual history
   Eduardo Lerro 28

3 Unsexing subjects: Marie de Gournay's philosophy of sex eliminativism
   Eloy LaBrada 51

PART TWO CAUSALITIES 81

4 Shadows on the wall of reason: Diderot before Fragonard
   David Ferris 83

5 Timely plot and unplotted time: Action and experience before and after Hegel
   John Park 109

6 Unexpected yet connected: On Aristotle's *Poetics* and its heterodox receptions
   Karen Feldman 134

7   The causal economy of the subject in Kant, Hegel, and Marx: Being in time and externalization
    Irina Simova   148

PART THREE   JUDGMENT   171

8   The man within the breast: Sympathy, deformity, and moral subjectivity in Adam Smith's *The Theory of Moral Sentiments*
    Paul Kelleher   173

9   Judging, inevitably: Aesthetic judgment and novelistic form in Fielding's *Joseph Andrews*
    Vivasvan Soni   201

10 The linguistic condition of judgment: Kant's "common sense"
    Claudia Brodsky   225

Index   255

INTRODUCTION

What happens when the subject matter called the "subject" is removed from the "picture" of human history—of previously undetermined and unpredictable actions and events—overall? Both that question and the quotation marks within it speak to the origin of the present book. It is no coincidence that contemporary literary studies appealing to a "materialist" "theory" of history have remained stuck in the same spatializing—anti-"literary," anti-"theoretical," and anti-historical-materialist—paradigms that pitted "new" historicisms against "old," which is to say, hermeneutical "new criticism." For, whether quantitative or anecdotal, explicitly or implicitly "magical" in method, such unselfconsciously visualist, selectively curatorial, metaphorically "archaeological," taxonomically pictorial approaches to past events and texts exclude, by definition, the fundamentally non-static conditions from which actions spring: contradiction, negation, difference and differentiation, temporal and causal reversal, re-evaluation and re-signification—in brief, the processes of change that are the subjectively and objectively transforming work of life itself. If, as literary and theoretical writers from Cervantes and Goethe to Baudelaire and Borges, Plato and Thucydides to Nietzsche, Freud, and Husserl, have observed, history is made as much of forgetting as remembering, then against the new monism, or monadologism calling itself "ontology," of subjective depictions of subjectively perceived givens, the twin question of the *critical subject* may be seen to arise with renewed urgency, from the positivist spell of oblivion, again. This book brings together new analyses of pivotal modern theories and fictions of agency written during the period, generally viewed as extending from the mid-seventeenth through the early nineteenth centuries, that Kant nonchronologically dubbed "the Age of Critique," when the concepts of the human and the defining possibility of agency were interrogated as never before.

Instead of presenting a homogenous depiction purporting to define "what" subjects "were" at a certain "time," each of the essays solicited and edited for this book demonstrates what *happens* when pictures of the human production of history no longer suffice. The diverse political, aesthetic, ethical, and epistemological implications of the literary and philosophical works the following essays examine, and understandings of personhood, subjecthood, and sexual, ideological and social difference and identity they represent and explore, are not only deeply, if often unconsciously reflected in current thinking on these issues, but, perhaps most significantly, in the very fact of our conception of them, *as* interrelated, critical issues, in the first place. At the same time, many of the theoretical questions examined in the book rest on reinterpretations and recastings of classical literary models, forms and genres whose representations remain central to our sense of both the possibility and diversity of human action. That individuation is represented in turn by the breadth of authors of different linguistic and cultural traditions on which the individual essays focus, including Plato, Aristotle, Gournay, Descartes, Diderot, Rousseau, and Flaubert; Shaftesbury, Smith, Richardson, Fielding, Keats, Wordsworth, and William James; and Lessing, Kant, Goethe, Kleist, Hegel, Marx, Arendt, Wittig, and Althusser in their comparative scope.

All the authorial subjects studied complicate depictions substituting (ontological) "substances" or (ideological) presumptions for the self-critical capacities of subjects, just as they effectively question neo-"materialist" and new "biologist" exclusions of the occurrence of action overall, no less than the mysterious impartation of the "energies" of bygone eras to "new" historicist *tableaux*. Submitting their own arguments and representations to the overlapping logic linking critique and imagination, interrogation and irony, the works analyzed in the following essays act to negate mystical assertions of a "being" supervening human agency upon which, ironically enough, only human beings have the capacity to report. Like the purposefully incomplete syllogism at the origin of the modern understanding of "thinking" examined in this book's opening essay by Marshall Brown—a "cogito" whose stated subject is first generated by thinking itself—the authors of *Inventing Agency* represent actions that constitute the subject, rather than the reverse.

The contributions are organized according to three conceptual axes—Judgment, Causalities, Subjects—whose co-emergence in early modernity rendered the ages of "critique" and "revolution" at once cotemporaneous and "irreversible" (Kant, *Critique of Pure Reason*, B XII–XXII; *Contest of*

Faculties, A 147–48, 150). In examining these and related conceptions of agency, including, perhaps most importantly, the capacity to "negate" the supposed necessity of the given (Kant, *Critique of Pure Reason*, B XXIV), one of the book's critical aims is to demystify the portrayal of autotelic domination that has dominated historicist literary and cultural criticism over the past decades. Conflating "knowledge" with "power" and thereby nullifying the content and consequences of each, and defining history as the chronological inventory of the arts and artifacts employed *by* "knowledge-power" to oversee the objects *of* "knowledge-power," such a tautological description of "history" evacuates history of historicity by conflating it with reification instead. Each of the individual contributions to *Inventing Agency* works to open up this fundamentally closed representation of history as a homologous and homogeneous "space" to the diachronic practices and divergent products of subjects acting in critical interaction with the given, with the very history they make. By the same token, the book works to shift conceptions of the subject away from traditional subject/object dichotomies that, bracketing subjectivity from materiality, rely upon either precritical subjectivist or, what is the same, "postcritical" norms—those that are, or claim to be, "all subjectivity" or all "objective structure" in orientation. As the contributions to the book demonstrate individually, such unilateral approaches must also inevitably suppose an opposition between the subject and subjects, as between the one and the many, that merely devolve into construals of the subject/object dichotomy in time. In raising instead the question of agency, and defining subjects as agents themselves subject to and challenged to action, the analyses offered here come to a different understanding of subjects as constitutively capable of differing critically from themselves.

I Subjects

Few concepts were subjected to more fundamental philosophical and literary criticism during Kant's "Age of Critique" than that of the subject itself. In sharp distinction from the purely formal function assigned it as a grammatical and logical category by Port Royal, the subject conceived as a sentient and particular temporal being, whose experiential existence his *Discourse on Method* and *Meditations* aim to confirm *autobiographically*, was first made a central, self-reflexive subject of philosophy by Descartes. In the opening essay of the book, "I Think, Therefore I Feel," Marshall

Brown presents Descartes' "subject" of "thought" in a significantly new light, describing the dependence of thinking within the circular logic of the *cogito* upon a "feeling" of "being" from which thinking itself must differ. The purposefully incomplete employment of syllogistic form in the *cogito* requires a complement, Brown suggests, something other than or in excess of thinking which, whether preceding or arising from, must, in either temporal event, exist in relation to thought. Cogently and eloquently relating the inherently recursive structure of the *cogito* to the critically delimited existential subject hypothesized by the "Copernican Revolution" of Kant (and, later, the "essentially" "existential being" theorized in Heidegger's *Being and Time*); the "fluid" quality informing the alternation of "thinking" and "feeling" in Rousseau's *Rêveries*; and their inalienable, experiential interdependence in the poetry of Wordsworth, Keats, and Clare and narratives and dramas of *Bildung* and *anagnoresis* of Goethe and Kleist, Brown importantly underscores the heterogeneity inhering in any subject's capacity for cogitation as it is differently represented across periods and genres: the critical understanding arrived at by each of the authors he examines, that "the ground of thinking both is and is not itself a thought."

The replacement of the full range of the subject's internal experience by the notion of an "interior" space furnished with external objects is the focus of "Some Dark Interiority: A Brief Conceptual History," Eduardo Lerro's critical assessment of the subjection of the subject to its objectified depiction by a certain anachronistic tendency in contemporary literary criticism. Lerro expertly traces the specific ways in which early modern philosophical and religious understandings of inwardness and internality, as orientations away from things inhering in the course of conceptual and moral work, were supplanted by turn-of-the-century Anglo-American pragmatic notions of "interiority" as a scene or space populated by the same externalities we recognize as the givens—whether natural or social—of the empirical world. Lerro's philological study contributes a masterful critique, richly supported by early modern fiction, of the reified understanding of both the subject and its prose representation effected and reflected in the—largely figural—replacement of internal processes by external objects on the part of mimetically oriented evaluations of the "realist" novel in particular. Borrowing its view of the "real" from the positivist precepts of behavioral psychology, this ideology of objects, Lerro argues, continues to fall short of and distort the critical understandings of the subject proposed in early modern theory and fiction alike, verbal works whose own ongoing internal processes can be recognized in the concerns, as well as controversies, of theory of realism today.

In "Unsexing Subjects: Marie de Gournay's Philosophy of Sex Eliminativism," Eloy LaBrada incisively analyzes an extraordinary early modern model for thinking through contemporary debates regarding the nature and definition of the subject, the mid-seventeenth-century exposition of the fallacies inherent in sexual categorization by the feminist philosopher, Marie de Gournary. Gournay's pyrrhonic skepticism, LaBrada argues, enables her to reveal not only the preemptively social basis of the category of "sex"—its construction *as* "natural" marker of inferiority or, in Aristotle's canonical view, incompletion—but the logical contradictions at work in any and all categorical ascriptions of "sex"-based "identity" to members of a single "species," the "human," itself unqualified and undivided by "sex." The additional observation that attributions of identity according to "sex" do not in fact occur with regard to all, but the subclass of "female" "humans" alone, effectively renders "female humans," or "women," the embodiment of an ontological contradiction, that of being human and not human simultaneously. To the failures and internal contradictions of "canonical humanism"—its claim to treat and consider all "humans" as equal while categorizing them as unequal—LaBrada opposes "Gournay's [skeptical] methodology" of "philosophically equalizing or neutralizing metaphysical claims about the inherent differences between men and women." Integrating an exacting reading of Gournay's logical critique of the extension of Aristotelian analytic conventions to considerations of "sex" with an in-depth exploration of its contemporary consideration by leading figures in analytic feminist philosophy, LaBrada's essay makes a landmark contribution not only to feminist theory, theory of sex and gender, and historical philosophical criticism, but to current and future understandings of the very terms of this ever-consequential debate.

II Causalities

Any understanding of the subject as agent must include a reconsideration of the bases of causality. While the Newtonian model of mechanical causality rests upon and enforces a strict division between subjects and objects, critical causalities redefine both subjects and objects as occupying temporary positions in any causal progression or chain, and thus able to change historical and grammatical places, effectivity, and meaning. Any subject capable of reflection, of considering its own status *as* subject, is capable of estranging itself into an object, which is to say, of itself undergoing the negative experience of self-consciousness. And with the distance or difference from itself the subject undergoes results a consciousness of other causalities, forces of estrangement it neither enacts nor controls: the actions and resistances of other subjects; the independence, recalcitrance and mutability of objects; the effectivity of historical and systemic norms, as of their accumulation, inevitable internal differentiation, eventual contradiction and disruption; and of the experience of time itself.

In "Shadows on the Wall of Reason: Diderot before Fragonard," David Ferris closely examines the chain of effects without objective causes constitutive of Diderot's verbal representation of a markedly theatrical painting of self-sacrifice that Diderot, by his own report, has not seen. The proper "subject" matter, then, antecedent to—behind or "before"— Diderot's entry on Fragonard in the *Salon of 1765* is not an object but the traces of invisible actions: the effects of discourse, including the discursive capability for impersonating and staging a conversation with a fictive agency not one's own (Diderot's friend and ventriloquized interlocutor in the entry on Fragonard, "Grimm"); of reading and dreaming an allegory staging a play of shadows in a cave from which reader and dreamer do not emerge; of the shadowy origins of painting itself, in a transmitted myth of absence and recollection; and of vision figured in the medium of sound itself refracted into diffuse echoes. Even as it draws out the extenuating causality of effects transmitted without foreseeable limitation by other effects, the sinuous line of argument of Ferris' superb contribution involves the reader in a critical act of understanding the effectivity of shadows over or before the "actual" or "objective" vision they replace. As Ferris relates it, the famed "light" of "Enlightenment" thinking, of which Diderot was a primary source, derives not from the symbolically freighted, natural mechanics of the "sun" but a reflection of and on the chain of representational effects, the "same" staged source of Plato's shadows on the wall.

While Ferris analyzes the play of shadows of which Diderot's pointedly discursive representation of an unseen painting of an imagined narrative dénouement is composed, John Park's elegant comparative analysis of the unprecedented prose styles of Richardson and Flaubert, "Timely plot and unplotted time: Action and experience before and after Hegel," sheds new light on the narrative representation of the relation between temporality and action in specifically "realist" fiction. As Park insightfully demonstrates, the smooth coordination of time with events upon which narrated causality, or plot construction, depends is disrupted by both authors' predominant use of a single, nonnarrative tense. In *Clarissa, or the History of a Young Lady,* Park argues, the present tense of "'writing to the moment'" explicitly described and practiced by both Richardson, in his "Preface" to the novel and creation of its epistolary content, and Lovelace, self-styled arch-"plotter" or prime mover of events within that content, submits the simple story line of this longest of all English novels to the "ignorance, confusion, suspicions, and duplicity" occurring at every present moment of its action, including the purposefully misleading "'Now'" of its allegorically reported *dénouement manqué*. In Flaubert's "Un Coeur Simple" ("A Simple Heart"), by contrast, the present does not appear to occur at all. Flaubert's signature use of the imperfect tense, first singled out by Proust, and near reification of commonly designated units of time, often piled upon each other as if tangible items of interchangeable narrative weight, so vitiates the reader's sense of causal logic in the narrative—the basic qualities and conditions of when, where, why, who, how, and, in Flaubert's case, even what—upon which the perception and understanding of plotted action depends, that the title of Flaubert's story seems to stand not only for its stunningly "simple-minded" main "character" but itself. Both the historical singularity and true causality of these landmark "realist" narratives, then, lie in their active impact upon the reader, the negation of readerly expectations and instantiation of interpretive acts of "mediation" their prose styles effect. These causes and effects are illuminatingly mediated in turn by Park's sparely clarifying discussion of the philosophy of Hegel, in which the necessarily negative conditions of consciousness-formation require foremost that theoretical reflection, too, be composed as a "history" or narrative of the "real," which is to say, of consequential acts of mediation.

Opposite to the question, implicit to Park's essay, of what happens in the course of life, or its representation, when the causality of experience, or of the relation of content to plot, cannot be discerned, the question posed by Karen Feldman's lucid analysis of the historical reception of Aristotle's *Poetics*, "Unexpected yet connected: on Aristotle's *Poetics* and its heterodox reception," might be summarized thus: what happens to our understanding of tragedy, the prototype of plotted action, when causality, divorced from mimesis—from emotional and intellectual content of any kind—is all that can be discerned in our experience of the action? Beginning with Lessing's signal reinterpretation and retranslation of Aristotolian *catharsis* as evocative not of "fear and pity" but of "fearful pity," Feldman examines the identification of the tragic genre with a heightened sense not only of mimetic identification with the subject of tragedy but of our own capacity to identify with all subjects whom unexpected, tragic events may befall. The long-standing view that, in Feldman's words, "tragedy calls on a recognition already present in the emotions themselves of our shared human finitude and proneness to disaster," imbues tragic plot with the "metaphysical" values of "universal truths" as ancient as Aristotle's definition of "poetry" as more "philosophical" than "history," while the causality particular to tragic poetry inevitably aligns it with the larger meanings we read into the causality identified in history itself. As Feldman next analyses in detail, however, other interpretations and retranslations of the terms of the definition of tragedy in the *Poetics*, from Hardison and Golden, to Veloso and, most recently, Ferrari, take an entirely different view. Arguing instead that sheer causality—"the bare connection of tragic events to one another" rather than any "*metaphysical* inevitability"—alone provides us with the heightened, while uninstructive "pleasure" induced by the "'writerly inevitability'" of its crafted "suspense," they question the intersection of philosophy and poetry, or knowledge and representation, long conceived as both basis and force of tragedy itself. Thus tragedy serves in Feldman's historical analysis as a fulcrum for identifying the ways in which content and causality may be interpreted to exclude each other, but also, at the same time, for representing "the impossibility of separating the formal level of critique from the historical object" in view.

The making of history is the subject of Irina Simova's "The Causal Economy of the Subject in Kant, Hegel and Marx," a rigorous "reevaluation of the materialist strain in Enlightenment thought" beginning with Kant's explication of the subject's own formative dependence on externality. Analyzing that formation as the very "relation" between subjects and objects by which the "existence" ("Dasein") of both is constituted "in time" ("in der Zeit"), Simova identifies in the temporal interdependence of the material and intellectual at the foundation of Kant's critical epistemology the precursor to the materially "situated selfhood" and "dialectical paradigm of work *as action*—of object-production and subject-formation" theorized by Hegel. Simova's elucidating analysis links the history of negations informing Hegel's dialectical exposition of "true" sense perception, that is, perceptions whose immediacy is critiqued by the subject in time, to the material rather than ideational basis of the Hegelian "concept," in which the history of perceptions of the material is not supplanted but contained. Like the unlimited extension of Kant's "Dasein in der Zeit," no independent truth arrests the twin history of subject-formation and object-cognition in Hegel, for, as Simova states, in "Hegel, Kant's model of being in time is not only a mode of subject formation, but is also reflected in the structures of cognition" as these, too, unfold, or come into being, in time. The "thwart[ing]" of any "self-sufficient subject position" by Hegel's interpersonal model of the dialectic in the lord-bondsman relation, and his expansion of that model to the state in his exposition of the conflicting bonds of allegiance in *Antigone*, are two such "histories" Simova investigates in depth. Finally, on Simova's view, the critique of "idealism" issued by Marx's dialectical materialism, while following squarely upon Kant's and Hegel's lead, regresses from them in hypothesizing a subject no longer in causal need of externality, "'a complete restoration of man to himself'" signaling the (impossible) end of history as such.

III Judgment

It would be fair to call the "Age of Critique" the "Age of Judgment" as well: the very sense of the ability "to judge" now most commonly held—to separate oneself from both immediate, circumstantial and personal wishes and interests, and routinized, social and cultural expectations and norms—not only "came of age," as Kant was first to remark, with the practice of critique, but first made critique "actual" or practicable to begin with. "Our age is the actual age of *critique*" ("Unser Zeitalter is das eigentliche Zeitalter der *Kritik*" [emphasis in text]), Kant observes in the first Preface to the First Critique (Kant, *Critique of Pure Reason*, A XII), and its origin and identity as such owe, conversely, "to the mature *power of judgment* of the age" ("der gereiften *Urteilskraft* des Zeitalters" [emphasis in text]). Rather than reflecting either theoretically stipulated forms or socially presumed norms of cognition, judgment and critique compose the temporally interactive "mode of thinking of our time" ("Denkungsart unserer Zeit" [Kant, *Critique of Pure Reason*, A XII]), and perhaps first among the positive assumptions they act together to negate is the normative conception of linear or one-directional causality itself. For "thinking" is only possible with the distantiation from preemptive assumptions afforded to it by the negative "power of judgment," and "the power of judgment" already carries with it the very possibility of thoughtful critique. The essays in this final section of the book explore critical philosophical and literary representations of the exploration and enactment of judgment during the "time" in which such exploration and enactment were coeval, not only in their power to define the "age" but to define and constitute at any "age" "the power of judgment" itself.

Paul Kelleher's opening contribution to this section, "'The Man Within the Breast:' Sympathy, Deformity, and Moral Subjectivity in Adam Smith's *The Theory of Moral Sentiments*," importantly refers a formative text of the history of empirically based moral theory and judgment to the inclusion of otherness, not "outside" it but at its specular core. Describing Smith's theory of "sympathy as a form of moral judgment," whose subject, "'the impartial spectator'" or "'great inmate in the breast,'" similar to "the invisible hand" that, first mentioned in *Moral Sentiments*, is famously credited in the later *Wealth of Nations* with guiding capitalist self-interest toward the achievement of the common good, Kelleher analyzes the critical difference upon which moral judgments depend. For, as opposed to an anonymously beneficial, systematic economic force, the "impartial" arbiter of moral judgment is figured by Smith as residing within the subject itself as a second self capable of judging the first. Most importantly, this double or specular interiority of the subject of moral judgment opens subjectivity into a kind of "scene" populated by the visible bodies of others. In basing "self"-perception, self-esteem and the social "calculus" of moral norms on our "perceptions and assessments of others," including those whose apparent distortion or "deformation" of social norms of beauty render them, like the "disabled," incapable of embodying those norms, acts of judgment effectively internalize "others"—those bodies without whom Smith's "abstract," "impartial spectator," Kelleher astutely concludes, "would remain unrealized and, in some sense, so too would the human subject itself." Kelleher ultimately relates Smith's essentially other-oriented moral theory to a similar differential understanding of empirical perception theorized within contemporary disability studies, according to which the act of "staring" at the disabled body, rather than "fixing" it with one's "gaze," opens the "starer" to the possibility of a different "shared experience" of the inevitable "change" all empirical bodies "undergo." Kelleher's moving conclusion, in turn, opens Smith's moral theory of empirical otherness interiorized and normalized by specular, imaginative acts of judgment to the possibility of imagining and judging one's self and other selves by different specular norms.

That such a possibility in fact informs the very foundation of English fiction is the critical premise of Vivasvan Soni's new reading of one of the landmark texts of the realist tradition, "Judging, Inevitably: Aesthetic Judgment and Novelistic Form in Fielding's *Joseph Andrews*." Soni describes judgment as an imaginative mode of agency opposed to interiorizing "sentimental" and mechanistically "sociological" models of the novel and subjecthood alike. Recalling Aristotle's definition of deliberation, in the *Nicomachean Ethics*, as the ability to decide, and so act, differently or in divergence from the appearance of inevitability determined by purely external circumstance, Soni contrasts early-eighteenth-century theories and representations of judgment by "figures like Shaftesbury and Fielding" with "the overwhelming sense of necessity and inevitability that dominates philosophical, psychological, sociological, and scientific accounts in the period." The disruptive socioeconomic developments and ensuing commercialization of personal relations entailed by early modern processes of urbanization and industrialization—"monetization, legalization, professionalization, and mobility"—effectively consolidate, on Soni's view, the "Hobbesian" account of necessarily "agnostic" subjects motivated solely by the pursuit of atomistic "self-interest." In a very different vein, Shaftesbury's apparently anti-Hobbesian theory of the existence of "a shared sense or sense of the common operative [within the social subject] alongside the instinct toward self-preservation"—an instinctual "*Sensus Communis*" "equiprimordial" with self-interest itself—similarly obviates, Soni proposes, the necessity for individuals to form judgments of their own. For while Fielding "openly acknowledged" his "debt " to it in the *Preface* to *Joseph Andrews,* Shaftesburian "common sense," Soni argues persuasively, "is the 'judgment' of society or history or the market, requiring no individual to have undertaken any exercise of judgment along the way." It is the importance Fielding accords in *Joseph Andrews* to the story of the uniquely "hospitable" Wilson, whose "idyllic," self-sustaining life in the country had followed upon a "wayward" urban existence recounted by the narrative in detail, that, Soni argues, introduces an important "utopian" alternative into the fabric of the otherwise Hobbesian world the novel represents. While, by a typical turn or trope of the early modern picaresque, Wilson is later revealed to be Joseph's father, it is "the space of judgment" that "Wilson's utopia opens . . . in the novel," in "allow[ing] us to imagine an alternative to the modernity that seemed so inevitable," that, Soni implies, is his most signal importance and function not only in this particular novel but in the representation of the possibility of judgment within "realist" narrative as a whole.

Finally, an entirely different account of "common sense," as critically essential to the very possibility of judgment, is analyzed in my contribution, "The Linguistic Condition of Judgment: Kant's 'Common Sense'." Just as he defines the capacity to judge as the essential condition of his entire tripartite project—sole and necessary "mediating link" ("Mittelglied") between the otherwise incommunicable "realms" ("Gebiete") of representational cognition and moral action theorized in the First Critique and Second Critique, respectively—Kant designates something he calls "common sense" (in explicit "distinction" from both "common understanding" and the so-called "philosophy of common sense" he routinely critiqued) as the "undetermined condition" ("unbestimmte Bedingung") and "capacity" ("Vermögen") on which the enactment of judgment depends in the Third Critique [Kant, *Critique of Judgment*, B VI, 65–68]. While Kant's referencing of "common sense" later became the basis of Hannah Arendt's turn to his theory of judgment to explore the political potential of aesthetics, an innovative move that largely set the precedent for reconsiderations of the link between the aesthetic and the political today, "The Linguistic Condition" attempts to define Kant's enigmatic referencing of "common sense" according to his definition of what constitutes the "power to judge" in the first place. For while Kant states that, unlike every other internal and sensory capacity he describes, he "neither can nor wants to" define the temporal-experiential origin of "common sense"—that is, whether it is either *a priori* or *a posteriori* to experience in basis—his precise description of acts of judgment is as unorthodox as the notion that judgment depends upon "common sense" itself (Kant, *Critique of Judgment*, B 68). In the exacting terms of Kant's analytic account, "the power to judge" is indistinguishable from the power to speak: consisting in an impersonal and noncognitive statement ("I say, 'it is beautiful,' 'it is sublime'") spoken in a "general voice," judgment, Kant states, must be inherently "communicable" ("mitteilbar") by "anyone" ("jedermann") to "anyone" above all (Kant, *Critique of Judgment*, B 67). Rather than reflect a personal impression or transitory opinion, judgment, according to Kant, makes the other and, just as importantly, others—other subjects and the otherness of unknown sensory objects— the constitutive condition of its enactment, one that traverses the opposition between self and other and subject and object alike. In defining aesthetic judgment as indissociable from its specifically verbal form, Kant implies that the "common" "condition" on which it is based is the particularly human condition of linguistic agency itself. In this, perhaps more than any other theorist, Kant fundamentally links rather than opposes language and action, "The Linguistic Condition" suggests. Integral, by his own explanation, to both the overarching project of his Critique and individual, interrelated practices it describes, Kant's pathbreaking theory of judgment unites the action enabled by language with the possibility of critical agency of every kind.

While the individual contributions to *Inventing Agency* are diverse in topic and approach, their rejection of reductive views of what constitutes a subject and, as a result of these, an object, may be defined as their own "common" mode of "communicability," or "sense." Rather than oracular in mode, each essay is text-specific, analytic, and engaged in producing rather than curtailing further examination. And while oracular foreclosures of attempts to conceive the subject will return wherever and whenever a positive return on their promulgation is guaranteed, the irony implicit in all such inherently non-self-critical pronouncements—that they themselves enact the very inflation of the subject they pretend to militate against—will also, of course, remain, and remain open and available to critique as well. Indeed, perhaps the single most critical consideration in soliciting the contributions to the exploratory work that became this book, and agreeing, upon the initiative of Haaris Naqvi, our extraordinary Editor at Bloomsbury, to re-examine the subject of the subject by foregrounding its questioning in print, was knowing that the oracular mode would be the resort of none of them. The absence of such unreflective judgments can be judged commensurate with the degree of critical agency exercised by each. And in this each does some measure of justice to its subject.

Claudia Brodsky

PART ONE

SUBJECTS

1 I THINK, THEREFORE I FEEL

Marshall Brown

Descartes scholars debate the meaning of the connective "ergo."[1] Does "ego cogito, ergo sum" mean that thinking is a cause of being and being the result of thinking? Or does it mean that thinking is merely a sign or evidence of being? Does "ergo" designate a result or merely an inference? In the former case, being is conditioned by thought; in the latter, being might be more extensive than thought. How being is to be understood—whether your being (your existence as a being, your identity) depends on your thinking, or whether your thinking is a more focused expression of your vaster and more diffuse being—that question depends on how the formula is read. A Heideggerian coinage provided different verbs for the two possible senses of being, *sein* for merely existing in advance of thought, *wesen* for the being that emerges out of consciousness and is conditioned by it, existing as an entity in a world. (I believe that the Heideggerian usage of the verb "wesen" beginning in the 1930s is entirely consistent with his earlier critique in *Being and Time* of Descartes's notion of being for its abstraction from any world.) But Descartes did not have two different words, neither did the Romantics, and neither does any natural language known to me, not even Spanish, which does have two words for being, but conditioned on temporality rather than on consciousness.

Descartes scholars have not convincingly answered the question of which direction his implication points. What has remained a problem was, surely, always problematic. Without Heidegger to help him, he did not have the words to refine his utterance. Still, as I have argued elsewhere, there is a residue in the murk.[2] Latin usage limits the meaning of "cogito" to judgments, excluding anything that might be considered mere intuitions or reveries. A thinking thing—res cogitans—is a rational animal. Being stands in some sort of relation of implication to judgment. But judgment must stand in some relationship to a judging mind. If thinking could be merely daydreaming, then it might be lodged almost anywhere. Animals might think, or (as some ecocritics now assert) even plants. But Descartes's syllogism presumes a syllogist. That is why—at least in my view—he seems regularly to have preceded the perfectly well-formed Latin formula "cogito ergo sum" with the grammatically superfluous pronoun "ego." The ego must come first. But even if there is a clear sense of how a thinking being thinks, there is no such clear sense of the being of the thinking being. The Cartesian heritage bequeathed to future generations the mystery of an ego—an identity—that preceded thinking syntactically, logically, and metaphysically.

Kant's Copernican revolution put the question of identity front and center. The Kantian world of experience is constituted by transcendental conditioning—by the pure forms of sensible intuition governing perceptions of space and time and by the categories of the understanding that make consciousness possible. It is not clear whether the conception of the transcendental ego defined being or simply displaced it into an indefinite intellectual region. But in any event it turned Descartes upside down by beginning philosophy with beings rather than with thinking. And then what Kant posits as a starting point becomes—or, indeed, had already become—a focal point in imaginative writings. Selfhood is a mysterious, indefinite or even infinite "I am"; it is known before being understood. It dawns; it does not result.

The touchstones of self-feeling are undoubtedly well known to anyone interested in the topic. Perhaps most famous among them are the lapping waves in the fifth of Rousseau's *Reveries of a Solitary Wanderer* that "suffisoient pour me faire sentir avec plaisir mon existence, sans prendre la peine de penser" ("sufficed to cause me to feel my existence with pleasure, without bothering to think") and the echo of Rousseau in Wordsworth's *Prelude*:

> Thus while the days flew by, and years passed on,
> From Nature and her overflowing soul
> I had receiv'd so much that all my thoughts
> Were steep'd in feeling; I was only then

> Contented when with bliss ineffable
> I felt the sentiment of Being spread
> O'er all that moves, and all that seemeth still,
> O'er all, that, lost beyond the reach of thought
> And human knowledge, to the human eye
> Invisible, yet liveth to the heart.
> (*Prelude*, 1850, II: 396–405)³

Both passages postulate a feeling of self oblivious to thought. But of course neither story ends there. As the opening of Hegel's *Phenomenology* convincingly argues, a sentiment pure and immediate in itself has no duration. The sentiment of being is nothing without a sensing self, and for Wordsworth it entails specifically not Rousseau's thoughtlessness but a feeling thought that recovers what, otherwise, might be "lost": the lost cannot be found in knowledge, that is, not in cogitation, but rather in a feeling thought that touches the heart. And while Rousseau denies taking the trouble to think, he opens the *Reveries* by asserting his unique existence—"Me voici donc seul sur la terre" ("here am I, then, alone on earth")—and, a short paragraph later, his existence as a thinker: "et plus je pense à ma situation présente..." ("and the more I think on my present situation").⁴ And do not forget that third word of the entire text, that "donc" that echoes Descartes's "ergo." "On earth," as Rousseau repeatedly situates himself, he is a reasoner; on the waters he no longer troubles himself to think, but even in the boat his feeling remains a kind of thought. Indeed, the fluidity of waters and their thinking does not differ all that greatly from the earth, and he knows it. If the water is "all that moves," the earth merely "*seemeth* still" and amenable to reason, while in fact the "flux and reflux" that Rousseau enjoys on the lake is equally characteristic of the earth: "Tout est dans un flux continuel sur la terre," he writes in the Fifth Promenade, and he repeats it at the opening of the Ninth: "Tout est sur la terre dans un flux continuel" ("everything on earth is continually in flux").⁵ As Michel Serres has reiterated more poetically than anyone else since, everything flows, *panta rhei*, and thought is, by consequence, "steeped," that is, immersed, were it only in being surrounded by "steep and lofty cliffs" that willy-nilly impress "thoughts" on a self that dreams of merely feeling. For Wordsworth there is nothing that does not "feel the touch of earthly years," for even his stones regularly grow "old"; nothing that is not "rolled round" like the "spinning" cliffs when Wordsworth skated on the ice.⁶ The world, in a pun so obvious that Wordsworth seems not to have needed to make it, was by nature whirled, with his name for the whirling often being revolution. What does not move cannot be felt (and hence cannot be thought); the primal feelings that are the ground of thought are, as less often cited lines of *The Prelude* say,

> Those hallowed and pure motions of the sense
> Which seem, in their simplicity, to own
> An intellectual charm; that calm delight
> Which, if I err not, surely must belong
> To those first-born affinities that fit
> Our new existence to existing things,
> And, in our dawn of being, constitute
> The bond of union between life and joy.
> (*Prelude*, 1850, I: 551–58)

Sense, life, and joy mingle to constitute the intellect that links our existence to the world. Feeling is linked to thinking, but thinking remains an anti-Cartesian state that is independent of judging. "An intellectual charm" is not cogitation.

The bond between sensation and sentiment is crucial in this complex. Feelings feel, at least primal feelings do; there are no emotions without a ground, and no ground without an emotion. The contrary situation is communicated in an upside-down (6+8), despairing sonnet written in the mid-nineteenth century by John Clare:

> I feel I am—I only know I am,
> And plod upon the earth, as dull and void:
> Earth's prison chilled my body with its dram
> Of dullness, and my soaring thoughts destroyed,
> I fled to solitudes from passions dream,
> But strife persued—I only know, I am.
> I was a being created in the race
> Of men disdaining bounds of place and time:
> A spirit that could travel o'er the space
> Of earth and heaven—like a thought sublime,
> Tracing creation, like my maker, free—
> A soul unshackled—like eternity,
> Spurning earth's vain and soul debasing thrall
> But now I only know I am—that's all.[7]

Clare's freedom is self-destroying, his eternity a double negative ("unshackled"), his sublimity empty. Spurning the thrall to a material world, acknowledging physical existence only as a plodding chill without form, his self-feeling deteriorates to a destitute self-knowing. The disembodied "thought sublime" is no thought at all, just the refrain to which the poem vainly circles round. If I just think—that is, if I only think and hence only know—then I cannot feel and have no real existence.

Well before Wordsworth, in fact barely a year after the *Reveries* appeared, Kant's *Prolegomena to Any Future Metaphysic* had echoed Rousseau's feeling of self. Kant here restates the Cartesian principle as follows: "Nun scheint es, als ob wir in dem Bewußtsein unserer selbst (dem denkenden Subjekt) dieses Substantiale haben, und zwar in einer unmittlebaren Anschauung" ("Now it seems as if we have this substantial [self] in the consciousness of ourselves [in the thinking subject], and indeed in an immediate intuition"). But then a footnote defining "das absolute Subjekt" ("the absolute subject") turns the tables on Descartes: it says that the absolute subject or the pure apperception of the self, is "ein Gefühl eines Daseins ohne den mindesten Begriff" ("a feeling of an existence without the slightest concept"). This sounds like Rousseau trumping Descartes. However, the note turns back on Rousseau to claim that the feeling of self is, after all, "nur Vorstellung desjenigen, worauf alles Denken in Beziehung (relatione accidentis) steht" ("only a representation of that to which all thinking stands in relation").[8] (*Prolegomona zu einer jeden künftigen Metaphysik, die als Wissenschaft wird auftreten können,* A 136). In Kant's two-step, feeling precedes concept formation and is inferred as the ground of our existence as consciously thinking entities, but then it proves far different from Rousseau's bliss ineffable. As Kant made clear in a crucial essay three years later, "What Does It Mean: To Orient Oneself in Thought," feeling is a fundamental relationship of self to world: orientation is "das Gefühl eines Unterschiedes an meinem eigenen *Subjekt*, nämlich der rechten und linken Hand" ("the feeling of a distinction in my own subject, namely of the right and the left hand").[9] But not just a feeling. For while the *Prolegomena* denies that any concept attaches to the feeling of existence, the orientation essay calls the expanded feeling a concept after all: "Endlich kann ich diesen Begriff noch mehr erweitern, da er denn in dem Vermögen bestände, sich night bloß im Raume, d. i. mathematisch, sondern überhaupt im *Denken, d. i. logisch* zu orientieren" ("Finally, I can extend this concept even further, since it would then consist in the ability to orient oneself not just in space, i.e. mathematically, but generally in *thought*, i.e. *logically*")[10] The ground of thinking both is and is not itself a thought. Thinking and feeling are two sides of one coin. Indeed, an essay a decade later, "On a Recently Emergent Superior Tone in Philosophy," heaps scorn on a "Philosophie aus Gefühlen" ("philosophy made of feelings") and on the demand of "die allerneueste deutsche Weisheit . . ., *durchs Gefühl zu philosophieren*" ("the very latest German wisdom, *to philosophize through feeling*").[11] While I cannot think without being steeped in feeling, feeling is not independent of thought. Hence the implicit new syllogism: I think, therefore I feel.

In one of his frequent Hamlet moods, John Keats, in a famous letter of November 22, 1817, yearned for "a Life of Sensations rather than of Thoughts!"[12] Pure feeling here is a wish-fulfillment for an afterlife from a poet fretting about his health and alluding to a poem about sorrow sent a few weeks earlier to two correspondents. Keats appears here as a man "sicklied o'er with the pale cast of thought" (*Hamlet* 3.1.86). Feelings are the root, for Keats as for so many other Romantics. But thoughts are the branch from which the roots cannot be torn. So Keats wrote in a later and equally famous letter that is stuffed with poems famous and obscure,

> Do you not see how necessary a World of Pains and troubles is to school an Intelligence and make it a soul? A Place where the heart must feel and suffer in a thousand diverse ways! Not merely is the Heart a Hornbook, It is the Minds Bible, it is the Minds experience, it is the teat from which the Mind or intelligence sucks its identity. (April 21, 1819)[13]

I think, therefore I feel; I feel, and in consequence I am plagued with thoughts. Or blessed with them, as he had written a year earlier: "The difference of high Sensations with and without knowledge appears to me this—in the latter case we are falling continually ten thousand fathoms deep . . .—in the former case, our shoulders are fledge<d>, and we go thro' air . . . and space without fear," in what he calls "a parallel of breast and head" (to Reynolds, May 3, 1818).[14] This complex is essential to understanding the force of the word "sense" in the first line of the Ode to a Nightingale and the "drowsy numbness" that he wishes to remove him from the world's fever and fret. In contrast to Rousseau—or at least to Rousseau's wishful pretenses—Keats cannot feel his existence without taking the trouble to think.

"Gefühl ist alles" ("Feeling is everything") is a climactic seduction line from Faust to Gretchen (Goethe, *Faust*, 3456), echoed by the repeated formula, "es muß von Herzen gehn" ("it must come from the heart") (said, in varying versions, by Faust to Wagner, lines 544–45; by Mephisto to Faust, line 3058; by Mephisto dressed as Phorkyas, lines 9685–86). But all of these are suspect. Better than self-absorbed pure feeling is the Rousseauist feeling of existence, understood as an orientation to outwardness that corrects a solipsistic inwardness. Wilhelm Meister finally learns that at the climax of his education, with the pain of renunciation that for Goethe is inseparable from self-knowledge: "Nur der lebhafte Schmerz, der ihn manchmal ergriff, daß er alles das Gefundene und Wiedergefundene . . . so notwendig verlassen müsse, nur seine Tränen gaben ihm das Gefühl seines Daseins wieder"[15] ("Only the vivid pain that sometimes seized him, from the . . . great necessity of having to abandon what had been discovered and rediscovered, only his tears restored the feeling of his existence"). "Existence" here is "Dasein," being-there, and the feeling in Goethe, as in Kant, consists in orientation. While steeped in nostalgia, in renewing his connection to his grandfather's art collection, Wilhelm can relocate himself with respect to his origins. His self-discovery is paired with that of the Harper in the next chapter. Restored to sanity, the Harper recovers a sense of self: "Nun, da mich die gütige Natur durch ihre größten Gaben, durch die Liebe wieder geheilt hat, da ich an dem Busen eines himmlischen Mädchens wieder fühle, daß ich bin, daß sie ist, daß wir eins sind . . ."[16] ("Now that benevolent nature has cured me anew through her greatest gifts, through love, that I feel anew on the bosom of a heavenly maiden that I am, that she is, that we are one . . .") But the Harper's orientation is momentary: grammatically it is confined to a subordinate clause, and in the plot it is foiled by the revelation of his unintentional incest. The recovery of the feeling of self in memory is overthrown by the loss of clear social positioning. And Wilhelm's recovered sense of self also leads not to stability but to further and greater wandering: it does not constitute *Bildung* but merely permits *Bildung* to begin. Here too, then, the feeling of self proves fluid. And the fluidity is emotional as well as experiential. Shortly after the recognition moments that I have cited, Wilhelm concludes this book by echoing in reverse the biblical anecdote portrayed in his grandfather's painting—"Ich kenne den Wert eines Königreichs nicht" ("I do not know the value of a kingdom")—and then by declaring his ineffable bliss: "aber ich weiß, daß ich ein Glück erlangt habe, das ich nicht verdiene und das ich mit nichts in der Welt vertauschen möchte"¹⁷ ("but I know that I have achieved a blessing [fortune, luck] that I do not deserve and that I would not change for anything in the world"). Ignorance is bliss, as they say. Self-feeling, for all these writers, is an aliveness and openness to the world in which flux and uncertainty are masked by a veil of self-satisfaction.

In the Cartesian syllogism, the "I am" and the "I think" are mutually self-confirming. But they are so only under the condition of presupposing an enduring I that is the thing that thinks, and that is. Thinking and being are nothing in themselves; they must inhere in something. But that ego is a mystery. In terms of Descartes's early remark that he ascended the stage of the world masked, the person is a persona. To be a thing, it would have to have a separate existence or nature. But Descartes is clear that the being of the ego is coterminous with its thoughts. The syllogism is true, as he says in the *Meditations*, "quoties a me profertur, vel mente concipitur"¹⁸ ("each time I utter it, or conceive it in my mind"), but only so long as he is uttering or conceiving it. There is no inherent duration, no subsistence, beyond the fits of mental activity—indeed, no world, unless sustained by God's continual creation. As Heidegger points out in *Being and Time*, the cogito is neither an intuition nor a mode of presencing, as "traditional ontology" (meaning, in particular, Husserl) presumed in associating it with the ancient concept of dianoia.¹⁹ For—although Heidegger's reasoning here is not philological—*cogitare* is an iterative verb that happens by moments, whereas *dianoein*, to think through something, is inherently sustained. The Romantic sense of self teases apart the ego from its thoughts, engendering the mixed feelings of inexpressible satisfaction in autonomous existence with inexplicable sadness or even grief at separation. While different texts foreground different elements, reflecting on them together reveals the turbulent mixture of feeling and knowing that all, to some degree, work to resolve.

Or maybe not all. At least one great high Romantic text goes to extremes perhaps without pulling back from the brink. That is Heinrich von Kleist's shattering adaptation of the Amphitryon story. Here, at the exact middle of the play, Alkmene asserts her existence with passionate fervor. She knows her husband at least as infallibly as she knows herself, and she does and will know herself through the most immediate certainty, no matter what happens to the thing in which her selfhood is clothed:

O Charis!—Eh will ich irren in mir selbst!
Eh will ich dieses innerste Gefühl,

Das ich am Mutterbusen eingesogen,
Und das mir sagt, daß ich Alkmene bin,
Für einen Parther oder Perser halten.
Ist diese Hand mein? Diese Brust hier mein?
Gehört das Bild mir, das der Spiegel strahlt?
Er wäre fremder mir, als ich! Nimm mir
Das Aug, so hör ich ihn; das Ohr, ich fühl ihn;
Mir das Gefühl hinweg, ich atm' ihn noch;
Nimm Aug und Ohr, Gefühl mir und Geruch,
Mir alle Sinn und gönne mir das Herz:
So läßt du mir die Glocke die ich brauche,
Aus einer Welt noch find ich ihn heraus.[20]

[O, Charis! Sooner will I err in myself (than in Amphitryon)!
Sooner will I take this inmost feeling
that I absorbed at my mother's breast
and that tells me, that I am Alkmeme,
for a Parthian or a Persian.
Is this hand mine? This breast here mine?
Does the image shining at me from the mirror belong to me?
He would be more alien to me than I am! Take away
My eye, then I hear him; my ear, I feel him;
Take away my touch (*Gefühl*—literally, feeling), I breathe him yet;
Take eye and ear, touch from me and smell,
All senses from me and grant me just my heart;
And you have left to me the bell that I need,
I will discover him from a world.]

Were this true, it would guarantee a stability beyond the flux of all other Romantic assertions of selfhood. And with the certainty of the woman's self-knowledge would come the certainty of knowledge of her partner, of the other, and of the world. But the action of the play destroys this passionate claim that self-feeling is also substantial self-knowledge. For the very next scene brings Jupiter's seduction, couched in words of the utmost ambiguity. Alkmene's fall is inevitable, and the conclusion of the action, in Kleist's version, leaves the divine restoration of order irremediably in doubt.

"Dubito, ergo sum" has long been considered Descartes's alternative version of his syllogism. Thinking and doubting are, at bottom, one.

"I think, therefore I feel" links the intensity of selfhood to its uncertainty. Uncertainty is anxiety, inscrutability, potential, all three in ever-varying ratio. Descartes is unraveled: he is rescued by being overcome. Any change is a transformation, and any transformation a deformation. That is how history moves, and seldom so radically as when the Romantics consumed Descartes, digested him, and transformed him into nourishment for a new spirit.

Notes

1 My thanks to Claudia Brodsky for getting me started on this essay and prodding me along on it.
2 See "Kant's Misreading of Descartes," in my *Turning Points: Essays in the History of Cultural Expressions* (Stanford: Stanford University Press, 1997), 156–71, to which the present essay is a sequel.
3 William Wordsworth, *Selected Poetry*, ed. Mark van Doren with an Introduction by David Bromwich (New York: Modern Library, 2002), 196.
4 Jean-Jacques Rousseau, *Oeuvres Complètes*, 5 vol., ed. Bernard Gagnebin, Robert Osmont, and Marcel Raymond (Paris: Pléiade, 1964), I: 995.
5 Rousseau, *Oeuvres Complètes*, 1: 1045, 1047, 1085.
6 Wordsworth, "A Slumber did my spirit seal," ll. 4-7; *Prelude* I.455, in Wordsworth, *Selected Poetry*, 150, 182. On Wordsworth's stones, see "Wordsworth's Old Gray Stone" in my *Preromanticism* (Stanford: Stanford University Press, 1991), 301–61.
7 John Clare, "I Am," in *I Am: The Selected Poetry of John Clare*, ed. Jonathan Bate (New York: Farrar Straus and Giroux, 2003).
8 Immanuel Kant, *Prolegomona zu einer jeden künftigen Metaphysik, die als Wissenschaft wird auftreten können*, in *Werke*, ed. Wilhelm Weischedel, 22 vols. (Frankfurt: Suhrkamp, 1981), A 136, V: 136.
9 Kant, "Was heisst sich im Denken orientieren," A 308, V: 269.
10 Kant, "Was heisst: sich im Denken orientieren," A307, 309, V: 268, 270.
11 Kant, "Von einem neuerdings erhobenen vornehmen Ton in der Philosophie," A416, VI: 390.
12 *The Letters of John Keats*, 2 vols., ed. Hyder E. Rollins (Cambridge, MA: Harvard University Press, 1971) 1: 185.
13 Keats, *Letters*, II: 102-3.
14 Keats, *Letters*, I: 207.

15 Johann Wolfgang von Goethe, *Wilhelm Meisters Lehrjahre*, in *Neue Gesamtausgabe der Werke und Schriften*, 22 vols. ed. Liselotte Lohrer (Stuttgart: Cotta, 1950–68), VII: 663.

16 Goethe, *Werke*, VII: 677.

17 Ibid., 708.

18 René Descartes, *Meditationes de prima philosophia*, ed. Geneviève Rodis-Lewis (Paris: Vrin, 1978), 25. The contemporary French translation reads "toutes les fois que je la prononce, ou que je la conçois en mon esprit" (ibid.). The point is echoed shortly after: "Ego sum, ego existo; certum est. Quandiu autem? Nempe quandiu cogito" (I am, I exist, that is certain. But for how long. Namely, for as long as I think); *Meditationes*, 27.

19 Martin Heidegger, *Sein und Zeit* (Tübingen: Niemeyer, 1967), 96 (§21). Husserl's concept of a transcendental subjectivity presumes a "Stream of *Cogitationes*" (title of §14), "a streaming life of consciousness" radically at odds with the Cartesian text: Edmund Husserl, *Cartesianische Meditationen*, ed. Elisabeth Ströker (Hamburg: Meiner, 1987), 33.

20 Heinrich von Kleist, *Amphitryon*, lines 155–67; *Sämtliche Werke und Briefe*, 2 vols., ed. Helmut Sembdner (Munich: Hanser, 1964), 1: 282.

Bibliography

Brown, Marshall. *Preromanticism*. Stanford: Stanford University Press, 1991.

Brown, Marshall. *Turning Points: Essays in the History of Cultural Expressions*. Stanford: Stanford University Press, 1997.

Clare, John. *I Am: The Selected Poetry of John Clare*. Edited by Jonathan Bate. New York: Farrar Straus and Giroux, 2003.

Descartes, René. *Meditationes de prima philosophia*. Edited by Geneviève Rodis-Lewis. Paris: Vrin.1978.

Goethe, Johann Wolfgang von. *Neue Gesamtausgabe der Werke und Schriften*, 22 vols. Edited by Liselotte Lohrer. Stuttgart: Cotta: 1950–68.

Heidegger, Martin. *Sein und Zeit*. Tübingen: Niemeyer, 1967.

Kant, Immanuel. *Werkausgabe*. 22 vol. Edited by Wilhelm Weischedel. Frankfurt; Suhrkamp, 1981.

Keats, John. *The Letters of John Keats*, 2 vols. Edited by Hyder E. Rollins. Cambridge, MA: Harvard University Press, 1971.

Kleist, Heinrich von. *Sämtliche Werke und Briefe*, 2 vols. Edited by Helmut Sembdner. Munich: Hanser, 1964.

Rousseau, Jean-Jacques. *Oeuvres complètes*, 5 vols. Vol. 1. Edited by Bernard Gagnebin, Robert Osmont, and Marcel Raymond. Paris: Pléiade, 1964.

Wordsworth, William. *Selected Poetry*, Edited by Mark van Doren with an Introduction by David Bromwich. New York: Modern Library, 2002.

2 SOME DARK INTERIORITY: A BRIEF CONCEPTUAL HISTORY

Eduardo Lerro

At the level of difference, the idea of an interior necessarily denotes that which is not exterior and thus presupposes a location or space somehow away from or other than the supposedly exterior. Yet an interior also needs somehow to be in or within something. In this sense, water might be said to occupy the interior of a glass, or to be held by a glass's interior. Thus, as the preceding sentence already begins to suggest, in order adequately to describe an interior as something other than the merely necessary conceptual opposite of an exterior, some form of genitive assignation will likely need to be employed: one would say that the interior is "of" the object whose interior space or quality it describes. That which its interior holds or names is predicated upon the existence of the object whose interior it denotes: it belongs somehow to that object; or, it "is," in some way, "the glass's."

The same is not true in reverse. To describe the exterior of something, one need not imply or refer to the existence of an interior. Thus one can imagine endlessly metonymic, non-contradictory attributes being assigned to or predicated of any given object—"the short-haired, black, blue-eyed, [etc.] cat," or "the cat is short-haired, black, blue-eyed, [etc.]," for example. And while it remains true of our metonymically composed, hypothetical cat that a description of its exterior can imply the concept of its interior, it is also true that any cat so described need not have one: one can imagine a flat depiction of a cat without an interior more readily than one can imagine a feline interior without a cat.

The concept of an interior, then, appears to depend upon acts of qualitative attribution tied to modes of denoting or predicating an already given object. The more complex concept of "interiority," by contrast, operates at multiple levels of description, in that it adds to the simple noun "interior" a condition or quality of being. Etymologically, the suffix "-ity," from the Middle English, -ite, Old French ité, and Latin -itatem (nominative -itas), denotes the way of being, state, or inherent condition of the substantives it supplements. In rendering independent of specific, describable qualities some thing or space whose existence, as the "interior" of an exterior, appears to depend on those qualities, "interiority" introduces a second, more abstract level of qualitative description or predication to the conception of an interior. It thus implies a potentially generalizable secondary quality of being "interior" that is not limited to this or that object, but rather can be extended to all objects. This is not to say that the notion of an interior cannot also or does not necessarily imply a generalizable concept, since, in order to operate as a noun, it must do both, but rather that the concept of "interiority" allows or compels us to postulate, in addition to the necessarily genitive relationship of an interior to an exterior, a generally qualitative condition of interior-*ity* attributable to any interior.

The *Oxford English Dictionary* defines interiority as follows: "*The* quality or state of being interior or inward"; "Inner character or nature; *an inner element*" (emphases added). Under the second of these definitions, which, because most closely related to conceptions of "interiority" in literature, is central to the present analysis, ten historical examples are given:

1 1701: J. Norris *Ess. Ideal World* i. vi. 391. What St. Augustine ... inculcates concerning both the interiority, and the community of truth.

2 1704: J. Norris *Ess. Ideal World* ii. xiii. 549. Some of his expressions ... relate to the interiority of Truth.

3 1803: *Edinb. Rev.* 1 26. Interiority and exteriority, by which is meant the distinction of the attributes of an object as originally existing in itself or as acquired from without.

4 1818: Bp. Jebb in C. Forster *Life* ii. (1836) 140. Those deep *interiorities* (if I may be allowed the expression), which will ever be the refreshment and delight of the most pious worshippers.

5 1884: H. W. Beecher *Plymouth Pulpit* March 19, 496. He had been a breaker of the law in its essential spirit, in its interiority, all the way through.

6 1890: W. James *Princ. Psychol.* II. xvii. 43. It is surely subjectivity and interiority, which are the notions *latest* acquired by the human mind.

7 1934: E. Bowen *Cat Jumps* 51. Voices came out from some dark interiority.

8 1941: *Theology* XLII. 156. The characteristic of the new period was, as Hegel put it, interiority.

9 1967: *Listener* October 26, 552/1. Alan Bates as Gabriel Oak suffers . . . from Schlesinger's reluctance to suggest, as Hardy might put it, interiority.

10 1973: *Times Lit. Suppl.* November 2, 1348/4. For all its imaginative ambitiousness, the volume lacks a certain human interiority.[1]

In terms of content, the first through fifth, and then the eighth historical entries are either explicitly religious or philosophical in nature. Of the remaining four, one is psychological and three are literary. Viewed chronologically, one can also distinguish a difference between the entries that come before and after 1884. The first five usages are religious,[2] philosophical, or both, and each treats the interior nature or quality of an abstract concept: universal truth (entries one and two); the philosophical concept of an object (entry three)[3]; general religious principles (entry four); and Christian moral law (entry five),[4] respectively. Prior to the 1890 usage, then, the assignation of interiority as a quality is limited to universalized, abstract concepts rather than either human or material objects.

Viewed as a subgroup within the word's full historical range, the five most recent usages might also be said to differ from their predecessors in that they have reached a conceptual stability lacking in the former group: what from 1701 to 1884 had been conceived as a general, alternately metaphysical, religious, or philosophical quality applicable to various sorts of abstractly conceived, nonhuman, and nonmaterial objects, coalesces, after 1890, into a single, qualitative, human trait applicable to the interiors of both particular human beings and humans generally conceived.

Much of this change is already implicit within the context from which the *OED* takes the sixth citation, written originally by William James.

To the sentence from *The Principles of Psychology* excerpted by the *OED*, James has appended the following lengthy footnote:

> For full justification the reader must see the next chapter. He may object, against the summary account given now, that in a babe's immediate field of vision the various things which appear are located *relatively to each other* from the outset. I admit that *if discriminated*, they would appear so located. But they are parts of the content of one sensation, not sensations separately experienced, such as the text is concerned with. The fully developed "world," in which all our sensations ultimately find location, is nothing but an imaginary object framed after the pattern of the field of vision, by the addition and continuation of one sensation upon another in an orderly and systematic way. In corroboration of my text I must refer to pp. 37–60 of Riehl's book quoted above on page 82, and to Uphues: Wahrnehmung und Empfindung (1888), especially the *Einleitung* and pp. 51–61.[5]

In the first sentence of the excerpt just cited, James refers his reader to the book's "next chapter," entitled "Imagination," in order more fully to explain what he means by interiority. In that chapter, James rejects the idea of a monolithically conceived and mechanically functioning faculty of imagination and offers the individual's imagination as an object of study in its place, claiming that the scientific study of the imaginations of particular persons offers the best path for researching something he conceives to be both universal and plastic.[6] He clarifies what he means by interiority when he writes of the imaginative "faculty" of "visualizing" that, "I have myself for many years collected from each and all of my psychology-students descriptions of their own visual imagination."[7] Indebted to Kant and Neo-Kantians like Riehl, James considers "imagination" a universally present but limitlessly unique human faculty, the condition of possibility for which is "interiority," which James describes as "The fully developed" internal "'world,' in which all our sensations ultimately find location . . . nothing but an imaginary object framed after the pattern of the field of vision, by the addition and continuation of one sensation upon another in an orderly and systematic way."[8] The subjectivity to which James links his now spatially conceived "world" of interiority can thus be understood as the individually conceived space within which each research subject finds his or her own self-identification, an internalized mirror image of the world whose capacity for production is universal but whose content is unique to the particular individual.

In the 1890 James citation, then, we find reflected several significant shifts in the meaning of "interiority": the term now applies not to abstract concepts but to the interior lives of human beings, and takes both the general and individual human subject for its referent; it explicitly links self-identification and the definition of individual identity to a world-mirroring internal space; it has gained a spatial and an imaginary identity; and, advancing these concepts under the rubric of a single term, it offers itself as a discrete, "imaginary object" around which a scientifically minded research discipline can be constructed.

James's redefinition of interiority introduces a conceptual transformation in usage from which the subsequent usages cited by the *OED* do not regress. The 1934 reference, taken from a short story by Elizabeth Bowen, also describes interiority as something human, spatial, and plastic, endowed with the power to speak.[9] The 1941 reference, taken from the second half of a two-part article written by Gerald Vann and printed in the journal *Theology*, refers to an overarching historical change in politics, religion, philosophy, and social psychology.[10] The 1967 reference, excerpted from a review of John Schlesinger's film adaptation of Thomas Hardy's *Far From the Madding Crowd*, criticizes the performance of the actor, Alan Bates, for failing to exhibit a sufficient internal motivation for the actions of his character, Gabriel Oak.[11] And the 1973 reference, from the London *Times Literary Supplement*, still echoing James, similarly criticizes a literary text as itself lacking in "human interiority," closing the circle between real and imaginary objects by transferring James's conception to the spatial form of the "volume" itself.[12]

Of these four most recent citations, all from the mid-twentieth century, three are directly related to literature, and the fourth, which openly claims "Christian sociology" and social psychology as its subjects, makes literary-historical "epochs" a part of its theme and argument.[13] This too represents a significant change, in that the conceptual contexts in which the word "interiority" is employed now demonstrate inverted metaphysical priorities: before James's redefinition of the word, "interiority" had been contextually associated with religious and philosophical concepts; after James, this metaphysical and spiritual focus is replaced by a pragmatic, psychological one. What was formerly presented as a more vaguely conceived internal quality or capacity becomes increasingly identified with a discrete interior "world" presented as a spatially objectified place. This increasingly localized objectification of interiority's referents naturally brings with it a necessary change in its imagined content: the personal drama of interiority postulated hypothetically by James becomes both more intense and more confined, a theatrical landscape in which all content is personal and literary "voices" or "personality," equated with the "symptoms of a weird landscape of the mind,"[14] are staged and criticized within the same observer.

That the majority of the more recent usages cited by the *OED* stem from literary works or their consideration indicates that this change in the sense attributed to "interiority" also reflects a coincident change in the sense attributed to literature. Compare these with the similarly marked "psychological change," from "objectivity to subjectivity," attributed to Renaissance thought in the article from which the *OED* takes the 1941 reference. Gerald Vann writes:

> In political life, the danger of an authoritarian regime is that it tends to make men disinclined to think for themselves; the danger of a democratic regime, that it tends to sacrifice unity to individual freedom and responsibility. Now the fundamental psychological change which took place at the time of the Renaissance, a change which is true of the religious as well as of the secular world, was the change from objectivity to subjectivity; the characteristic of the new period was, as Hegel put it, interiority—"it is now the principle universally admitted, to hold fast to interiority as such, rejecting, and regarding as impertinent and lifeless, externality and authority". The new spirit is manifest in Luther and Descartes alike. As in philosophy centrality is given to the ego, so in religion the primary importance is given to the individual. Subjective experience is emphasized at the expense of external authority.[15]

Entitled "The War and Christian Reunion—II," the stated goal of the second part of Vann's article is to encourage the Christian community to transcend denominational divisions in order to build "the post-war world" "according to Christian, as opposed to pagan, principles," by way of an immediate, "immense—and a *united*—effort."[16] Vann's language throughout is impassioned, and the tone of his Christian-centric argument in favor of solidarity represents a polemical and religiously motivated rhetorical plea that calls upon a broad range of disciplinary concepts (literary history, philosophical history, liberation theology, sociology, psychology) to issue a universal appeal to all Christians. The single term uniting the various strands of Vann's own "effort" here is "interiority": "political life," "psychological change," "the Renaissance," otherwise disunited religious and secular "worlds," the philosophical "change from objectivity to subjectivity," and the "new spirit" of the "individual" embodied in the works of Luther and Descartes are all gathered under a conception of "interiority" and identified with a new phase of Christian historiography. The histories of philosophy, religion, art, psychology, theology, and political life have been elided to a single concept—"interiority"—and put in service of Vann's quest to rebuild and unify the postwar world according to Christian principles.

The sentence from Vann's article that the *OED* cites is followed by a quotation from Hegel, which reads as follows:

Das allgemeine Prinzip ist jetzt, die *Innerlichkeit* als solche festzuhalten, die tote Äußerlichkeit, Autorität zurückzusetzen, für ungehörig anzusehen. (emphasis added)[17]

A more literal rendering of it than Vann's (unreferenced) version reads as follows:

The general principle now is to hold fast to inwardness as such, to make the authority of dead externality, itself seen as undue [or improper], recede into the background.

What interests us here is Vann's interpretation and usage of the word *Innerlichkeit*, which he calls "interiority."[18] One could argue, despite the consensus of standard reference sources to the contrary, that "inwardness" and "interiority" are merely two words for the same Hegelian concept. In order for such a claim to hold, however, "inwardness" should be substitutable for "interiority" in the definitive modern usage of the latter term cited by the *OED*; namely, that advanced by James. But it is not. Again, the sentence written by James and cited in the *OED* reads: "It is surely subjectivity and interiority, which are the notions *latest* acquired by the human mind." As the footnote in which he attempts to clarify his novel use of the term demonstrates, "interiority" names, for James, a quasi-physical space within which "imaginary objects" and "sensations" find their "location."[19] The space of James's "interiority," in other words, stores "imaginary objects" that have been metaphorically theorized to possess the physical, spatial aspect of tangible things, each of which has been assigned a unique, locatable place within the human psyche, which functions in James's theory as something like a cognitive storehouse.

Said differently, the conceptual and disciplinary analogies employed rhetorically by Vann to advance his argument in favor of a single and unified Christianity have re-cast their own conflated forms of nonempirical history and "fundamental psychological change" in essentially Jamesian psychological terms. What at first appeared to be a broad and hazy usage of pseudo-Hegelian terminology appears now to be another sort of conceptual restriction, a kind of second act to James's: as James inverts the metaphysical priorities of earlier usages by re-imagining the general, religious, and philosophical conditions of "inwardness" as an objectified and objectifying, internally spatialized "interiority," so Vann converts the nonmaterial, historical forms of philosophical, aesthetic, political, and religious activity and reflection into so many dramas taking place within the "interiority," or "psychological" space, of an individual conceived generally. Thus Vann reduces everything in world history—all of those complex, interdependent, historically mediated phenomena of time, art, literature, politics, nature, and religion that Hegel so exhaustively treats—to an essentially decorative but nonetheless inevitable outcome of a Christian psychology that doubles as a synonym for faith, a kind of religious universalization of historical phenomenology translated into the language of James's psychologically spatialized understanding of human "interiority."

Vann is not alone here, and his position should be understood as part of a much larger phenomenon. Though he does not cite it, the translation Vann used to quote Hegel is taken from a 1930 English translation, by E. I. Watkin, of an article entitled "St. Augustine and the Modern World" that was originally written in German by the influential theologian Erich Przywara.[20] In that markedly dialectical article, Przywara demonstrates that, "The modern world is indeed the advent of Augustine, but an advent to overcome it from within," which Augustine achieves through transcending the "bankruptcy of Protestantism" represented by "Hegel and Kierkegaard."[21] The finer points of Przywara's particular theological argument are not important here, but the general movement of his conceptual thought is. Where Hegel's representation of conceptual change over time generally moves from the objective or dogmatic toward the more subjective and secular, Przywara, following Hegel's method but rejecting his laicization of content, proffers a specific religious figure as an historically transcendent force, effectively translating *Geist* and *Innerlichkeit* into dogmatic religious language and recapitulating their philosophical history as the history of Christian theology. Przywara's conceptual use of interiority differs from the radically psychologized version given by Vann, but the general movement of their thought in regard to religion, history, and interiority remains fundamentally the same.

Perhaps most important to the present analysis, however, is that Vann, following Hegel in *The Lectures on Aesthetics,* enlists literature in order to legitimate his demonstration of history and his characterization of historical periods. Referring to Russian Christian philosopher Nikolai Berdyaev in order to classify the "different stages of man" supposedly represented by Dante, Shakespeare, and Dostoevsky, Vann performs a literary analysis in keeping with his implied view that all thought is essentially Christian and all literature is essentially religious.[22] As was the case with Przywara, the specifics of the position are not important here, but the general mode of thought is, and in three significant ways. The first is simply that Vann's understanding of "interiority" is of a piece with that of the other twentieth-century authors cited by the *OED*, all of whom use the term in James's modernly psychologized fashion and do so in reference to or within a piece of literature: Bowen in her short story; Vann regarding Dante, Shakespeare, and Dostoevsky; Rhode in reference to a film adaptation of *Far From the Madding Crowd*; and Eagleton in a critical essay on poetry. Secondly, in privileging literary criticism as a means of demarcating and defending historical changes in philosophical thought and psychology, then framing that criticism as evidence of a need for direct social action, the objective of Vann's theological argument is similar in aim to the social and political arguments made via literature by Lukács and many other prominent twentieth-century Hegelian and Marxist literary critics and theoreticians. Thirdly, in his identification of Descartes, Luther, and the Protestant Reformation as the causal agents in a primarily psychological transformation for which literary forms present the best evidence, Vann also finds himself at home alongside such influential, if apparently less politicized or openly Hegelian, theoreticians of the novel, such as Ian Watt, whose work plainly demonstrates a deeper than acknowledged debt to Hegel.

On the fifth page of *The Rise of the Novel,* while setting forth its plan, Watt deploys almost verbatim the same conceptualizations of history and modernity, first laid out by Hegel and cited above, which so centrally preoccupy Przywara, Watkin, Vann, and Berdyaev,[23] writing that "the greatness of Descartes was primarily one of method, of the thoroughness of his determination to accept nothing on trust," and that he "did much to bring about the modern assumption whereby the pursuit of truth is conceived of as a wholly individual matter, logically independent of the tradition of past thought, and indeed as more likely to be arrived at by a departure from it."[24] From here, Watt goes on to sketch what is essentially a theoretical history of a literary form that, while still cleaving to Hegel's own, openly strives to depart from him, as when, in reference to the *Aesthetics*, Watt writes that the connections Hegel draws between the novel and the epic are "of such a theoretical and abstract nature that one cannot make much of them without neglecting most of the specific literary characteristics of the two forms."[25]

In the years since Watt published *The Rise of the Novel* (1957), the critical community has learned to be as mistrustful of the plainspoken as Watt shows himself to be of the "theoretical and abstract," and in that sense most critics recognize that rhetorical claims to straightforwardness and good common sense are oftentimes expressive of more abstract theoretical content than they admit. This is certainly true for Watt, who moves from a simplified, implicit restatement of Hegel's theory of philosophical modernity gradually to incorporate into his argument a multitude of other insights gleaned from philosophy, political economy, sociology, and religion. Indeed, among the most striking aspects of Watt's still impressive book is the seemingly purposeful lack of rigor with which it presents its broad, syncretic claims, both latent and expressed. Of the former type, the most significant here are the role and function of psychology, which, as they do for James and Vann, underwrite the whole of Watt's conceptual apparatus. He writes:

> This emotional artificiality is very general in *Tom Jones*.... The fact that Fielding's characters do not have a convincing inner life means that their possibilities of psychological development are very limited. Tom Jones's character, for example, exhibits some development, but it is of a very general kind. Tom's early imprudences, his youthful lack of worldly wisdom, and his healthy animality, for example, lead to his disgrace, his expulsion from the Allworthy household, his subsequent difficulties on the road and in London, and his apparently irrecoverable loss of Sophia's love. At the same time his good qualities, his courage, honour and benevolence, all of which have been glimpsed at the beginning, eventually combine to extricate him from the nadir of his misfortunes,

and restore him to the love and respect of those who surround him. But although different qualities come to the fore at different times they have all been present from the beginning, and we have not been taken close enough to Tom's mind to be able to do anything but take on trust Fielding's implication, which is that his hero will be able to control his weaknesses by the wisdom he has learned of experience.[26]

If what we are advancing here is true—that James inverts the metaphysical meanings and historical ramifications of interiority, effectively spatializing by localizing it in the psychic storeroom of "interiority"; and that Vann identifies forms of nonmaterial history with a similarly conceived psychologized space presented as a narrative, Christian version of that same concept of interiority—then one might further say that Watt synthesizes these changes and pushes them even further in the same conceptual direction by making them fully expressive, presenting them not only as the conceptual grounds for human history and psychology, but also as the externalization of a psychologically regulated interior world. Fielding, the man; the novel, *Tom Jones*; the historical form of the novel; the material facts of English history; and ideal standards of ethics and behavior are all in a constantly inter-reflective, progressive relationship with Tom Jones the character, whose objectified interior, operating as a world-historical benchmark, is as fully real as Watt himself. Interiority, for Watt, both functions as the general conceptual grounds for human history and psychology and represents the externalization of an individual, psychologically regulated, interior world. And although he does dwell at some length on Puritan self-reflection and other forms of inwardness also of great interest to Hegel,[27] Watt does not use the word "interiority" in the internally spatialized sense that James and Vann do, but only because his psychological theodicy does not allow him to do so. For Watt, everything in the world of the novel—imagined as a fact-based, earth-bound, anthropological object nonetheless sufficiently "abstract" and Hegelian that it is still presumed important enough for its contents to bear the weight of world-historical philosophical significance—transparently reflects something about the mind of a character, the mind of an author, the mind of an epoch, and the mind of the critic. The psychological interiority that James localizes and Vann narrativizes Watt turns into an abstract standard by which everything in literature and human history is to be judged, measured, and diagnosed: the intellectual justification for a form of explanation whose logic is fully embodied in the self-revealing facts of a world whose every detail emits psychological significance to the omniscient critic-clinician.

All of which is to say that what had been known as interiority is now functioning as a definition of realism. The standard for the real is now understood to be a psychological one and the localized interiority first posited by James has become the theoretical world of the novel. Central to this view of literature are idealized concepts of plausibility and probability. Viewed and employed as the regulative concepts for universal psychological diagnoses, they underpin Watt's position and method throughout the book.[28] Watt's assessment of *Tom Jones* above has almost entirely to do with an idealized, experiential standard of human psychology against which the possibility for the real is posited and out of which the definition of reality reflexively returns. Clarissa and Pamela are more real than Moll because they have a more "convincing inner life," which determines a more likely "psychological development" and explains, in turn, their behavior, their time, their place, and indeed all of history. Tom is "imprudent" when young but his "animality" is "healthy"; he is brave, courageous, and honorable; and his revealing behavior clearly links his mind to Fielding, whose authorial narrative consists of equally transparent, inter-reflective signs of Tom's psychology, his own psychology, and the psychology of eighteenth-century England as a whole, all of which work together to foreshadow Tom's inevitable victory.

Watt's central premise—that the novel, historical artifacts, or thoughts recorded in philosophy and literature all reveal, upon interpretation, a unified meaning whose various modes of signification can be directly deduced—is shared by Hegel, as Watkin's translation of Przywara's essay and even a passing knowledge of Hegel make clear. The important difference between Watt and Hegel, however, has less to do with the nature of the novel as an object of thought, and much more to do with the nature of the thought through which the novel becomes an object of thought. In the later *Logic*, Hegel writes the following of thought that takes itself as its subject:

> Logic is usually said to be concerned with forms only and to derive the material for them from elsewhere. But this "only," which assumes that the logical thoughts are nothing in comparison with the rest of the contents, is not the word to use about forms which are the absolutely real ground of everything. Everything else rather is an "only" in comparison with these thoughts. To make such abstract

forms a problem presupposes in the inquirer a higher level of culture than ordinary; and to study them in themselves and for their own sake signifies in addition that these thought-types must be deduced out of thought itself, and *their truth or reality examined by the light of their own laws. We do not assume them as data from without, and then define or exhibit their value and authority by comparing them with the shape they take in our minds.* If we thus acted, we should proceed from observation and experience, and should, for instance, say we habitually employ the term "force" in such a case, and such a meaning. *A definition like that would be called correct, if it agreed with the conception of its object present in our ordinary state of mind. The defect of this empirical method is that a notion is not defined as it is in and for itself, but in terms of something assumed, which is then used as a criterion and standard of correctness.* (emphasis added)[29]

When Watt writes of "psychological development" in relation to *Tom Jones* above, or about Calvinism and its relationship to the development of capitalism,[30] or about philosophy and its relationship to history, or about religion and its relationship to sociology,[31] or about any of the other "assumed" historical givens or "data" (in Hegel's words) he considers important to the supposed rise of the novel, he is acting in perfect accord with the definition of empirical method Hegel condemns here. The mistake of empiricism for Hegel lies in the circular method of thought through which it defines objects, not in the type of object thought about and defined. Central to the reasoning behind such a position is that, for Hegel, all thought is always underwritten by the rules of logic, and logic, as Hegel tells us above and elsewhere, does not seek material justification, since its rules are self-governing and inherent.

What Hegel means by this can best be explained in literary-critical, rather than metaphysical terms, by recalling Kenneth Burke's observation,[32] which he makes while presenting the logical basis for his theory of speech as the "entitling" of complex "nonverbal situations,"[33] that "negation" is a purely mental, language-based concept and thus cannot and does not correspond to any kind of natural form.[34] Since all language is underwritten by distinctions that rely on difference, it is the nonnatural form of "negation" that is also most necessary to the formulation of all human thought. This or that statement or state of affairs may be true or false, but "negation," as a concept, a mental and verbal operation, cannot—both by definition and if language is to function in the first place—be verified materially or experientially. For Hegel, as for Burke, "negation" is a logical, not an empirical, given or fact, and it is this notion of logic, operating in independence from but always in reference to empirical "data," that Hegel elucidates above. This is why Hegel can deduce logically from phenomenal objects in the world, or from a work of literature or plastic art, and remain in the realm of what he calls the "spiritual." As things that present themselves to the mind through the senses, all of these, regardless of either their "assumed" cultural status or what we "empirically" learn about them, trigger the logical apparatus that underwrites thought and makes them available as objects of reflection and interpretation to the thinking subject.

This is not so for Watt, for whom the "empirical" "correctness" of objects depicted within an artistic form is determined by what Hegel would call "something assumed," by which he means something derived from the "empirical method." For Hegel, to make general statements based on deductions of this type—which is to say, by extending an observation beyond the individual instance, even (or perhaps especially) if it is presented in the form of scientifically verifiable data—is to arrive at no logical definition of the object at all, since such generalizations merely paper over the profoundly conceptual problem of universality, which they evade with a purely fictive, or false, rhetoric of probability.

Vann's recapitulation of Watkin's translation of Przywara's interpretation of Hegel's *Lectures on the History of Philosophy*, as well as Berdyaev's literary analysis and Watt's conception of psychology, are also contradicted by Hegel's logic, insofar as their respective forms of reasoning substitute various dogma and nonuniversal standards of behavior and cognition for self-governing rules. It follows from this that Hegel's *Innerlichkeit* can never properly be the sort of object that can be explained or theorized by probability, but rather only dialectically through the rules of syllogism. This is self-evident in the fact that, despite the reach of his claims, in reading Hegel, one never statistically measures the likelihood that he is right, or qualifies the historical or philosophical significance of Kant or Boehme against what each may have had for breakfast or worn to the dinner table. By aligning Hegel's dialectical definition of "modern philosophy" (*neuere Philosophie*) with socio-historically determined religious and material definitions of human existence, Przywara, Vann, Berdyaev, and Watt have significantly departed in principle from the thinker whose definition of modernity and method for understanding history underwrite their own.

The transformation of interiority from James to Watt might now be stated more simply as a transformation from a universally logical form of internal justification into an empirical form of universal justification. Indeed, the first five and last five usages of the term cited by the *OED* appear to fall on either side of that divide. What was for Beecher the "essential spirit" of the law, its very "interiority, all the way through," becomes for James a "field of vision" on which "subjectivity and interiority," imagined in individual terms as a set of universal "notions" "acquired by the human mind" play themselves out. This, in turn, becomes the psychological and spatial backdrop for Vann's Christian narrative of "subjective," nonempirical history, which finally terminates in Watt's externalization of a universally conceived, individual psyche's interiority, in which an imagined material "inside" mirrors a given material "outside" and the historical "reality" of character, novel, author, and world positively reflect each other.

These changes in the conceptual foundations of interiority are expressed in entirely different terms, supporting the notion that the conceptual foundation of the human interior, rather than its mere definition, has undergone a number of profound shifts. After James's spatialized conception, each noted usage refers to "interiority" in terms defined in turn by James's particular usage, in whole or in part. Before James, each usage noted, while not directly concerned with literature, is clearly and directly dependent on abstract, nonmaterial and thus only verbally representable conceptions, and so may be considered more literary than those that equate literature (and "interiority") with a positive storehouse of objects in space.

This division suggests a deep historic difference in conceptions of the nature of literature itself, one in which James's pragmatic view of subjectivity supplants Hegel's "inward" one, and acts of identification rather than transformation come to define the idea of the "real." Viewing interiority in James's, and, by extension, Watt's manner would comport well with a number of well-established conceptual frameworks for understanding the pronounced physical dimension of twentieth-century aesthetic movements or styles, such as Modernism or Expressionism. What James's psychology of "imagined objects" and Watt's theory of mimetic "interiority" cannot describe, however, are understandings of the psyche and of realism—as of "inwardness"—that preceded their own, including, most prominently, those of the eighteenth-century authors with whom Watt's account begins. In his excellent article, "How the

Novel Became Middle Class," George Boulukos convincingly argues that it is not until the late nineteenth century that "aspiring students and newly professional professors . . . begin to link the novel to a class that insisted on social, moral, and economic progress and imply that to study the eighteenth-century novel is at once to imbibe and analyze such values."[35] Central to Boulukos's argument is the idea that this moral ideology of the novel came into existence alongside the need and justification for professional university curricula, and that the "rise of the novel," and much of the rest of what has been said to rise along with it, is less organically linked to the eighteenth-century than the nineteenth- and twentieth-century middle classes. Boulukos concludes that the ideology of the "rise" (of the novel in particular) also offers a "'scientific,' historical, and interpretive approach" to literature that works in support of an approved and historically specific pedagogical regime.[36]

Boulukos's argument is incisive and convincing. We would only add to it that Watt's pseudo-Hegelianism, in transforming Hegel's spiritually focused historical argument regarding the significance of Descartes, Protestantism, and *Innerlichkeit* into a culturally focused, positivist one, also converts it into a moral defense for a view of history and the novel that maintains Hegel's bias in support of Christianity as the primary force for moral progress at the same time as it circumvents Hegel's resistance to defining that progress in progressively positivist terms. This particular type of pseudo-Hegelianism, which Vann, Przywara, Watkin, Troeltsch, Weber, Perry Miller,[37] and probably countless other early- and mid-twentieth-century thinkers and critics have made use of in their work, is especially pernicious in relation to theories of formal development. Easily conflated with a positivistic rhetoric of classification, a developmental history of literary form is often mistakenly conceived as describing the "visible" or "sensible" half of an object's content. Form itself is often consequently supposed—as Hegel, the originator of all such histories, was careful not to do—to be purely phenomenal. Watt is not entirely naive to this problem, yet he does not take its consequences seriously, preferring to dismiss as unnecessarily abstract and unhelpful those aspects of Hegel's thought that do not suit his rhetoric. That Watt's influential theory should by evading such complications find itself in league with positivistic materialism at the same time as it advances both an ambitious middle-class pedagogical agenda and conservative Christian ideological preferences may or may not prove surprising, depending on the ideological preferences of Watt's reader.

Moreover, since James's 1890 reframing of the meaning and purview of "interiority," the concept has undergone further semantic transformations reflecting increasingly narrative-based psychological conceptualizations of human life and thought. These developments not only bring Watt's general thesis and method into question, but also cast doubt on more widely held notions of the mind or psyche as an historically stable, universal, and general actor for which the name but not the referent changes. The emphatically objectified meta-awareness of human interiority as a spatial construct reflected in Eagleton's 1973 usage, for example, has already strayed widely from the conceptualization set forth by James, not to mention those of Norris, Forster, or Beecher. This is not to say that, before Vann or Watt, there were no human interiors; nor is it to advance the idea that they have not significantly changed: the former notion would be absurd and the latter is the latent implication in Watt's argument regarding the eighteenth century that we have attempted to disclose here. It is rather to say that realist "interiority," as Watt and, writing in Watt's long shadow, countless literary historians receive it, may have instead first arisen in the late nineteenth and early twentieth centuries, through influential conceptual re-definitions and reversals that twentieth-century literary critics went on to absorb. The relation of these revised conceptions to the portrayal of character in eighteenth-century fiction would remain, then, a matter of investigation, as open to question and reflection as those fictions themselves remain.

Notes

1 I have numbered the entries to make them easier to cite and refer to, but they have not been altered beyond that. *Oxford English Dictionary*, online ed., s.v. "interiority," http://www.oed.com.

2 This includes the fourth example, though the *OED* citation is somewhat deceptive. The original citation refers to the "deep interiorities" of Jebb's religious insight, emphasizing its profundity and depth, not his personality or psyche. Charles Forster, *The Life of John Jebb, D.D., F.R.S: Bishop of Limerick, Ardfert and Aghadoe: With a Selection from his Letters*, 2 vols. (London: J. Duncan, 1836), 1: 140.

3 The source to which the *OED* citation refers is an English translation of an article on Kant written originally by Charles Villers, entitled, *Philosophie de Kant, ou Principes Fondamentaux de la Philosophie Transcentale*, in which Kant's idea of the noumenon is equated to the concept of "interiority"

and then recapitulated as an attribute. Charles Villers, "The Philosophy of Kant, or, the Fundamental Principles of Transcendental Metaphysics," *The Edinburgh Review, or Critical Journal* 1, no. 2 (1802): 254–80.

4 This definition of interiority, by Henry Ward Beecher—son of Lyman Beecher, brother to Harriet Beecher Stowe, and infamous preacher and evangelist—entirely conflates the ideas of essence, object, and interiority in such a way that there remains little meaningful distinction among them.

5 William James, *The Principles of Psychology*, 2 vols. (New York: H. Holt, 1890), 2: 43.

6 James writes:

> Until very recent years it was supposed by all philosophers that there was a typical human mind which all individual minds were like, and that propositions of universal validity could be laid down about such faculties as "the Imagination." Lately, however, a mass of revelations have [*sic*] poured in, which make us see how false a view this is. There are imaginations, not 'the Imagination,' and they must be studied in detail.

Ibid., 49–50.

7 Ibid., 56.

8 The reference to Riehl, which describes the temporal order in which sensations are cognized by the perceiving subject, clarifies the cited words "*latest* acquired" as referring not to a sort of evolutionary or developmental theory of consciousness, but rather to something directly related to the functions of the human mind when conceived universally. Though both volumes of *The Principles of Psychology* use children to exemplify different developmental models, the usage offered here refers only to succession *qua* sequence.

9 The revealing paragraph from which the *OED* excerpts Bowen's extraordinary usage reads as follows:

> Theodora said she had been re-reading Shakespeare—this brought them point-blank up against *Othello*. Harold, with Titanic force, wrenched round the conversation to relativity: about this no one seemed to have anything to say but Edward Cartaret. And Muriel, who by some mischance had again been placed beside him, sat deathly, turning down her dark-rimmed eyes. In fact, on the intelligent sharp-featured faces all round the table something—perhaps simply a clearness—seemed to be lacking, as thought these were wax faces for one fatal instant exposed to a furnace. Voices came out from some dark interiority; in each conversational interchange a mutual vote of no confidence was implicit. You would have said that each personality had been attacked by some kind of decomposition.

Elizabeth Bowen, *The Cat Jumps, and Other Stories* (London: V. Gollancz, 1934), 51. Department of Rare Books and Special Collections, Princeton University Library.

10 Gerald Vann, "The War and Christian Reunion—II," *Theology* 42, no. 249 (March 1, 1941): 157.

11 Erich Rhode, "Films," *The Listener* (October 26, 1967): 551.

12 The full paragraph from which the citation is taken, from a review by Terry Eagleton of a book of poetry by Tom Leonard, reads:

> Not all the poems, however, fail in this way to transcend their own fragments; taken within their own limits, most work effectively as a sort of verbal painting, as linguistic still-life. But they aren't wholly that: if their images have on the one hand the sharp, cleansed lucidity of an attentiveness to the bric-a-brac of an external world, this merely conceals their true status, as symptoms of a weird landscape of the mind. And yet for all its imaginative ambitiousness, the volume lacks a certain human interiority.

Terry Eagleton, "Difficult Perceptions," *The Times Literary Supplement* (November 2, 1973): 1348.

13 Vann, "Christian Reunion," 154–55.

14 See endnote 12.

15 Vann, "Christian Reunion," 156.

16 Ibid., 152.

17 The sentence appears within the subdivision, "Period of the Thinking Understanding," from the section, "Modern Philosophy" ("Neuere Philosophie"), of Hegel's *Lectures on the History of Philosophy*. G. W. F. Hegel, *Werke in zwanzig Bänden*, 20 vols. (Frankfurt: Suhrkamp, 1970), 20: 121.

18 Of the four printed English/German dictionaries consulted, which range in publication date from 1957 to 2004, all list "inwardness" as the primary translation for "Innerlichkeit," and none lists "interiority" anywhere. Of the major, readily available, non-crowd-sourced online dictionary resources, all list inwardness as a primary definition, and only one, leo.org, mentions "interiority," and it only does so as a tertiary definition. Moreover, the two major authoritative German historical dictionaries of the eighteenth and nineteenth centuries covering the time period that corresponds to the first five citations for "interiority" in the *OED* cited above, those of J. C. Adelung and the Grimm brothers, either do not include a reference for the word "Innerlichkeit" (Adelung) or use it exclusively in the non-spatialized sense that I am attributing to those entries in the *OED* that come historically prior to the James citation (Grimm). The latter resource, elaborating the term only in the plural, "im plur. von den innern seiten einer menschennatur" [*sic*] ("in the plural, from the inner sides of a human nature"), lists four supporting citations. The first, corresponding to the singular and attributed to Jean Paul, includes the phrase, "innerlichkeit des Lebens" [*sic*] ("the inwardness of life"), still clearly echoing Morris, Jebb, and Beecher's pre-James usages. The second, third, and fourth citations, the former attributed to Dahlmann and the latter two to Goethe, continue in this course, Dahlmann's including the phrase, "die innerlichkeit der damaligen zustände" [sic] ("the inwardness of the prevailing conditions"), the third including the phrase, "zu so vielen geheimniszvollen, seltsamen innerlichkeiten gesellte er den klarsten menschenverstand" [sic] ("to so many secretive, strange interiorities he joined the clearest intellect"), and the fourth reading as follows: "über die innerlichkeiten des menschen, seine anlagen und entwickelungen fortwährend zu sinnen und zu spinnen" [sic] ("continually to reflect on and concoct stories about the inwardness of man, his arrangements and developments").

As should be clear even from the limited contexts excerpted for our purposes here, none of these usages approximates the post-James usage of the English word "interiority" cited by the *OED*. The usage that comes closest to spatializing the term in James's psychological sense is that employed by Grimm's dictionary itself when, in defining the plural usage, it refers to the "innern seiten einer menschennatur." The use of the word "seiten" (sides) here could seem to extend the concept of "innerlichkeit" in a spatial direction. Yet I would argue that this is not the case, and for three reasons. The first is that, though the phrase "innern seiten" ("inner sides") will in German always contain an implicit spatiality, the word "seiten," like the English word "sides," can and most often does, when employed spatially, refer to a flat surface. This would suggest that the "innern seiten" here refers to something more like an interior facet, aspect, or dimension, as opposed to a volume or empty space. Secondly, in that the word *seite* is also the sole German term for "page," another possible literal, if, in effect, more poetic translation of the phrase, "von den innern seiten einer menschennatur," would read: "from the inner pages of a human nature." Such a metaphorical complement further supports a non-spatialized reading of the word, "inner," here. Thirdly, none of the entries to which Grimm refers in support of its definition sounds anything like the James or post-James usages. Though the German history of the term "Innerlichkeit" is not the primary subject of this paper, and though these findings are far from conclusive, they do indicate that, as compared to their German equivalent, a major shift in meaning occurs in the English usage of "interiority" and "inwardness" as recorded in both the *OED* and the Hegel translation cited earlier in this essay. See *Cassell's New German Dictionary*, 1st. ed., s.v. "Innerlichkeit"; *Cassell's German-English English-German Dictionary*, 1st ed., s.v. "Innerlichkeit"; *Collins German-English English-German Dictionary Unabridged*, 5th ed., "Innerlichkeit"; and the same term at http://en.pons.eu, http://dict.leo.org, and http://www.wordreference.com; Jacob Grimm and Wilhelm Grimm, *Deutsches Wörterbuch*, 16 vols. (Leipzig: S. Hirzel Verlag, 1854–1971), 1: LXXII, LXXV–LXXVI, LXXVIII; 4: 2134.

19 See endnote 5.

20 Watkin's translation of Hegel reads:

> In this new age the leading principle is thought, the thought which originates from itself, that interiority which is a universal feature of Christianity and the distinctively Protestant principle. It is now the

principle universally admitted, to hold fast to interiority as such, rejecting, and regarding as impertinent and lifeless, externality and authority. In accordance with this principle of interiority, thought, thought for its own sake, is now the pure quintessence of inwardness, interiority which posits itself for its own sake.

Martin C. D'Arcy, *A Monument to Saint Augustine: Essays on Some Aspects of His Thought Written in Commemoration of his 15th Centenary* (London: Sheed & Ward, 1930), 251–86.

21 Ibid.

22 Vann's analysis paraphrases and closely follows that of Berdyaev. Hegel's influence on both is undeniable and clear. Vann writes:

> Berdyaev, in his study of Dostoievsky [sic], makes an illuminating comparison between the different conceptions of man in Dante, Shakespeare, and Dostoievsky. For the first, representing the period of theocentric humanism, man is part of an objective world order; he is "one of the grades in the universal hierarchy"; "God and Satan, heaven and hell are not revealed within the human spirit and by human experience: they are given to man from outside." With the period of anthropocentric humanism, of which Shakespeare is the greatest representative, there comes "an absolutely new notion of the world"; there was no longer a single ordered cosmos, but an infinity of worlds, the "infinite empty sky of the astronomers," and man "was lost in these vast solitudes . . . so he turned inward to himself, entering the psychic realm." In so doing, in elaborating a conception of the world directed "towards its psychic and not its spiritual aspect, away from man's ultimate spiritual self," man "renounced the centre of his soul and remained at the periphery." Dostoievsky marks another epoch, another stage. With the denial of God and the spirit, man had become a "flat creature in two dimensions—he had lost that of depth"; but when the "creative and joyous energy that marked the Renaissance" had dried up, "sudden rumblings were heard and the volcanic nature of the underworld was manifested. In man himself and abyss opened and therein God and heaven, the devil and hell were revealed anew"; the humanist "experiment in liberty was carried over to another plane and another dimension, and it is there that man's destiny is now working itself out. Human freedom abandoned the psychic world . . . and plunged into the depths of the spiritual world. It is like a descent into hell. But there man will find again, not only Satan his kingdom, but also God and heaven; and they will not longer be revealed in accordance with an objective order imposed from without but by way of a face-to-face meeting with the ultimate depths of the human spirit, as an inwardly revealed reality." The transcendent order of the theocentric world gave way before the immanent order of the man-made world; history cannot be reversed; it remains to discover anew the transcendent order in the light of our experience of the immanent.

Vann, "Christian Reunion," 154–55.

23 See endnote 20.
24 Ian Watt, *The Rise of the Novel: Studies in Defoe, Richardson, and Fielding* (Berkeley: University of California Press, 1957), 13.
25 Ibid., 239–40.
26 Ibid., 274.
27 Ibid., 75, 177, 205, 209, 225, 234.
28 Employed in conjunction, these concepts form a de facto definition of realism openly embraced by Watt throughout *The Rise of the Novel*. See, for example, his critique of Moll's characterization: "It is this freedom from the probable psychological and social consequences of everything she does which is the central implausibility of her character as Defoe has drawn it." Watt uses probability as a socially inflected historical criterion to justify his conjectures about the rise of the realistic novel form; as a psychological standard for successful (or, "realistic") character portrayal; and as a basis for the nearly interchangeable concept of the plausible. For explicit references to plausibility, see 15, 106, 112–14, 123, 194, 252; for probability, see 35, 40, 48, 60, 107, 114, 128, 198, 263, 296.
29 G. W. F. Hegel, *Hegel's Logic: Being Part One of the Encyclopaedia of the Philosophical Sciences (1830)*, trans. William Wallace (Oxford: Clarendon Press, 1975), 40.
30 Watt, *Rise*, 60–70, 73–76, 90–92.
31 Watt cites and adapts the arguments of Max Weber and Ernst Troeltsch (themselves both highly indebted to Hegel's *Lectures on the History of Philosophy*), most notably Weber's "triple rise" theory of post-Reformation social development. For Watt's discussion of Weber, see 63–90; for Watt's discussion of Troeltsch, see 73–75.
32 Kenneth Burke, *Language as Symbolic Action: Essays on Life, Literature, and Method* (Berkeley: University of California Press, 1966), 359–79.
33 Ibid., 361.
34 Of natural forms, Burke writes, "and recall that we are here using 'natural' in the sense of the nonverbal, to designate that sort of less-than-verbal world that would be left if all word-using creatures and their verbalizings were suddenly obliterated." Ibid., 375.
35 George Boulukos, "How the Novel Became Middle Class: A History of Histories of the Novel," *Novel* 42, no. 2 (Summer 2009): 250.
36 Ibid., 251.
37 I include Miller here because of the timing, influence, and nature of his arguments. Consider, for example, the landmark work *Orthodoxy in Massachusetts*, in which Miller cites Troeltsch's *Protestantism and Progress* when framing the historical significance and social consequences of the American Puritans' break with former doctrines. In *Protestantism*, Troeltsch locates the origins of the "freedom of conscience" and the "rights of man"

doctrines in the Rhode Island Constitution, by way of the English Puritan Revolution. See Perry Miller, *Orthodoxy in Massachusetts* (Boston: Beacon Press, 1959), 59; and, Ernst Troeltsch, *Protestantism and Progress*, trans. W. Montgomery (New York: G. P. Putnam & Sons, 1912), 89–197.

Bibliography

Boulukos, George. "How the Novel Became Middle Class: A History of Histories of the Novel." *Novel* 42, no. 2 (Summer 2009): 245–52.
Bowen, Elizabeth. *The Cat Jumps, and Other Stories*. London: V. Gollancz, 1934.
Burke, Kenneth. *Language as Symbolic Action: Essays on Life, Literature, and Method*. Berkeley: University of California Press, 1957.
D'Arcy, Martin Cyril. *A Monument to Saint Augustine: Essays on Some Aspects of His Thought Written in Commemoration of His 15th Centenary*. London: Sheed & Ward, 1930.
Eagleton, Terry. "Difficult Perceptions." *The Times Literary Supplement*, November 2, 1973.
Forster, Charles. *The life of John Jebb, D.D., F.R.S. : Bishop of Limerick, Ardfert and Aghadoe: with a selection from his letters*. 2 vols. London: J. Duncan, 1836.
Grimm, Jacob, and Wilhelm Grimm. *Deutsches Wörterbuch*. 16 vols. Leipzig: S. Hirzel Verlag, 1854–1971.
Hegel, Georg Wilhelm Friedrich. *Hegel's Logic: Being Part One of the Encyclopaedia of the Philosophical Sciences (1830)*. Translated by William Wallace. Oxford: Clarendon Press, 1975.
Hegel, Georg Wilhelm Friedrich. *Werke in zwanzig Bänden*. 20 vols. Frankfurt: Suhrkamp, 1970.
James, William. *The Principles of Psychology*. 2 vols. New York: H. Holt, 1890.
Miller, Perry. *Orthodoxy in Massachusetts*. Boston: Beacon Press, 1959.
Onions, C. T., G. W. S. Friedrichsen, and R. W. Burchfield. *The Oxford Dictionary of English Etymology*. Oxford: Clarendon Press, 1996.
Rhode, Eric. "Films." *The Listener*, October 26, 1967.
Troeltsch, Ernst. *Protestantism and Progress*. Translated by W. Montgomery. New York: G. P. Putnam & Sons, 1912.
Vann, Gerald. "The War and Christian Reunion—II." *Theology* 42, no. 249 (March 1, 1941): 152–59.
Villers, Charles. "The Philosophe of Kant, or, the Fundamental Principles of Transcendental Metaphysics." *The Edinburgh Review, or Critical Journal* 1, no. 2 (1802): 254–80.
Watt, Ian P. *The Rise of the Novel: Studies in Defoe, Richardson, and Fielding*. Berkeley: University of California Press, 1957.

3 UNSEXING SUBJECTS: MARIE DE GOURNAY'S PHILOSOPHY OF SEX ELIMINATIVISM

Eloy LaBrada

1 Introduction

What do we mean when we say that someone "is" a sex (be it female, male, intersex, or otherwise)? Is sex something we are born with or something we become? Is it crucial or incidental to what it is to be human? And what defines sex (chromosomes, dispositions, social conventions)? In this paper, I offer a social ontological analysis of the early modern French philosopher Marie de Gournay (1565–1645), who makes the provocative and avant la lettre claim that sex is not essential to being human and that, furthermore, sex is not a pregiven, natural fact but socially constituted all the way down. In so doing, she suggests that the sexual subject is a socially contingent production rather than a natural given. While it might seem anachronistic to call an early modern thinker like Gournay one of the first "social constructionists," we can at least plausibly say that she advances some of the first nurture over nature arguments about "sex," which for Gournay means something like the presumed natural differences between men and women. My reading of Gournay brings to light three innovative claims she makes about the non-naturalness of sex which curiously presage twenty-first-century debates about the sexual subject:

i   Sexual difference reflects the contingent social properties we attribute to it rather than natural facts. How we understand sex could have been, and could be, otherwise.

ii Many traits we assume to be indicators of natural sexual differences are in fact the product of socialization and education, which causally brings them about.

iii Metaphysically speaking, there is no such thing as natural sexual difference *as such*, but we mistake various social properties, functions, and roles to be natural "sex." Sex is just the name for enfranchised or subjugated social roles. If this is right, then to achieve social justice and equality we will have to consider un-"sex"-ing ourselves.

As we will see, this innovative proposal is both promising and problematic. Drawing from contemporary analytic social and feminist ontology, I will cash out Gournay's claims about the sexual subject, which shows us how the categories of the human and sex were debated in the early modern era and which compels us to consider what the contemporary legacies of that debate might be. I first sketch the early modern debate over the human subject in which Gournay intervenes (Section 2). I then address Gournay's general thesis, methodology, and some issues surrounding the terms "equality," and "sex" (Section 3) before analyzing Gournay's three innovative claims (Section 4). I conclude with some reflections on the contemporary relevance of Gournay's claims (Section 5).

2 Subjects of debate

Gournay's writing on sex should be situated within the early modern debate called the *Querelle des femmes*, or the "quarrel about women," a debate which exposes the limits of a certain humanist version of the subject. The *Querelle* refers to a series of literary and philosophical debates dating from the Middle Ages through the early modern period in Europe. These debates—some serious, some satirical—usually concern the political and social status of "women" and "men" in European letters and society as well as their natures and behaviors. Literary and philosophical luminaries such as Christine de Pisan, Boccaccio, Agrippa, and Castiglione debated the various virtues and traits of men and women, their political, religious, or civic roles and duties, and their access to education.¹ These debates over sexual difference, I would emphasize, are fundamentally about *what it is to be human* and, furthermore, these debates expose the limits of a certain kind of canonical humanism, one that conceives of a universal human nature without considering social inequality.²

By "canonical humanism" I do not mean the doctrine of "Renaissance humanism" as a whole, which usually just refers to a renewed interest in classical thought and in the human being during the early modern era in Western Europe. Rather, I mean a particular philosophical view about what human beings are. Following Kate Manne, we can think of canonical humanism as consisting of *conceptual-cum-perceptual* and *moral psychological* claims, as Manne calls them.³ The *conceptual-cum-perceptual* claim is that humans can perceive and recognize each other as humans "as such," not just as featherless biped homo sapiens with language, but as *persons* or *subjects* deserving moral consideration; on this view, we recognize humans as enminded like ourselves, as having certain valuable capabilities (like rationality, sympathy, or agency), as engaging in recognizable "human social relations," and as being "intelligible" objects of human affection either actually or "potentially."⁴ The moral psychological claim is that once we "recognize" a fellow human perceptually and conceptually, then we are supposedly heavily "disposed" or "motivated" to treat them in a particularly moral way (with sympathy, pity, agency, fellowship, etc.).⁵ So, for canonical humanism, after we recognize a fellow human, we are then allegedly inspired to treat them in a particular, usually humane, way.⁶ This would be canonical humanism's promise, then, namely, the recognition of universal human capabilities and the humanity of all.

However, these two claims have failed, both historically and presently, to deliver on the promise of canonical humanism: historically, not everyone has been taken to be human, especially with regard to gender, class, race, and social position, among other factors. As an anonymous, semi-satirical, and polemical treatise of 1595, *Disputatio nova contra mulieres,* famously declares: "Women are not human."⁷ The treatise might have been parodic, but its misogynistic content only lent support to those who already took seriously women's fundamental disvalue and subpersonhood. For, historically, those socially positioned as women have not only been denied civic and legal rights, but were themselves considered to be the legal property of men in the West under the doctrine of *couverture*. Likewise, as historians and postcolonial theorists remind us, non-Western populations and cultures have been both treated and depicted as subhuman in the course of Western history. So although canonical humanism assumes that once we recognize the "humanity" of others we are then disposed to treat them well, this has not borne out: some are not recognized as human or, if they are, are seen as lesser humans or "subpersons."[8] It should be emphasized that this is not a problem with every possible kind of humanism but a problem *with a certain kind of humanism*, one that presupposes an exclusionary definition of the human. The real question is why we define the human in the ways we do, which has been subject to change ever since the "human" has been conceived as a category. Why do we ask what distinguishes the human from the animal or nonhuman, pointing to a contrast-class of nonhuman entities, when it is not even certain what the human itself is? Why do we, those who ask the question, even think that we could satisfy the application-conditions of our own concept of the human?[9]

Matters become all the more complex when those treated like subpersons or nonhumans speak back and demand human rights, seizing hold of the very category of the human from which they have been excluded.[10] In an early modern context, philosophers and writers like Gournay, Lucrezia Marinella, and Gabrielle Suchon spoke in the name of the human, demanding a right to humane treatment, even though, as women, they were thought by their sexist opponents to be lesser humans, if not less than human. The crisis over "who" or "what" the human is or could be is thus not a recent product of transhumanism or posthumanism, but has been part of a complicated history that has accompanied Western thought for quite some time. The *Querelle* thus raises questions that, I would suggest, continue to bear on our present thinking about the subject, namely (i) What do we gain or lose by advocating for the category of the human subject (and what is that category? Which one?); (ii) What is the relation between the human and other social categories like race, gender, and sexuality?; (iii) What do we gain or lose by adopting canonical humanism?; (iv) And how do discourses about the roles and features of gender, race, and sexuality conspire with social practices and institutions to differentially humanize or dehumanize certain members of a social body?[11] Focusing on Gournay's intervention in the *Querelle* can usefully shed light on these questions, by moving us to consider the ways in which who counts as a human subject is delineated by political and social concerns just as much as they are by metaphysical ones.

3 Gournay

3.1 Text

Gournay was a philosopher and author working in various genres throughout her fifty years of writing. Gournay is known for being the self-avowed *"fille d'alliance"* or "adopted daughter" of the renowned Renaissance humanist Michel de Montaigne, whom she had met in her early twenties after reading his *Essais* (Gournay would be the editor of the 1595 edition of the *Essais*).[12] Gournay is arguably one of the first skeptical *feminist* philosophers in Western Europe. I want to vivify the uniqueness of this philosophical contribution by focusing on her treatise *Egalité des hommes et des femmes* (Equality of Men and Women), the first version of which was self-published in 1622. As with most of her texts, Gournay revised this one throughout her life.[13]

This brief text, dedicated to the queen, Anne of Austria, is probably a response to Alexis Trousset's sexist pamphlet from 1617: *Alphabet de l'imperfection et malices des femmes* (Alphabet of the imperfection and wickedness of women). Gournay's treatise is usually read as offering skeptical counterarguments to dogmatic arguments made by sexists about why women differ from men.[14] As a Montaigne scholar, Gournay was conversant in the brand of pyrrhonic skepticism Montaigne explores in his *Essays*. According to this brand of skepticism, one can always give equipollent counterarguments to any dogmatic argument, leading to a suspension of judgment about which argument is true.[15] When inquiring into "whether *P*" is the case, the skeptic presents equally persuasive reasons for believing both *P* and not-*P*, thus making matters undecided.[16] Typically, scholars have construed Gournay's purpose in this treatise along these lines: as a skeptical effort to counter every dogmatic argument that women are inherently different from men with an equally valid counterargument that they are not, in order to destabilize our certainty over which argument is true.[17] On this reading, Gournay would be rendering the matter of woman's nature undecided: for every dogmatic sexist argument about natural sexual difference *P*, Gournay would be offering an "undercutting defeater," namely a counterargument meant to undercut our reasons to believe *P* without thereby offering a reason to believe not-*P*.[18]

While such a reading aptly characterizes a part of Gournay's skeptical methodology, it is also incomplete: Following Marguerite Deslauriers,

I will demonstrate that Gournay is not just offering undercutting defeaters to cast aspersions on the belief that women and men are different in order to make matters undecided.[19] Rather, she is also giving us reasons to believe that they *are not* different, that is, Gournay is offering "rebutting defeaters" to her opponents, undercutting the reasons to believe *P* by giving us reasons to believe not-*P*.[20] Although Gournay will employ skeptical techniques, we would be missing something important if we saw her as simply countering any claim about *what sexual difference is* with a counterclaim about *what sexual difference is not* and thus leaving matters suspended. Instead, Gournay undermines reasons to believe what dogmatists say about woman's difference from man by giving us positive reasons to believe that there is no natural difference between them at all: the distinction between the sexes, or sexual difference, she argues, should be equalized to the point of being eliminated. As a humanist, Gournay assumes that we cannot argue for equal treatment of humans while insisting on their sexual difference as a *natural* fact; a part of reaching equal treatment requires, on her view, the equalization or neutralization of natural sexual difference itself. And she does this by making three innovative claims about how sexual difference is socially made rather than naturally given. Gournay's brand of humanism is thus not quite like the canonical humanism I described above, even if, as we shall see, she certainly draws from it.

3.2 *Thesis, method*

Gournay's text begins with a startling assertion: she remarks that typically the debate over the status of women has been framed in terms of women's supposed inferiority or superiority to men when there might be no definite difference between them at all: "The majority of those who take up the cause of women against arrogant privilege [*preference*] that men attribute to themselves [*s'attribuent*], give to them full value for their money, by redirecting the preference to them [*elles*]" (278; 75). The problem, for Gournay, is that the framework within which the debate is being formulated presupposes that we first know what men and women are such that we can then determine their inferiority or superiority. But if one frames the debate in terms of hierarchy, where one sex must necessarily be better or worse than the other, all one is doing is inverting positions within a hierarchical structure that itself remains unquestioned. You can change the position of the players in a game, but if the game remains unchanged, you are still playing the same game.

Notice that Gournay begins by speaking of "preferences" or privileges attributed to men and women, rather than simply defining men and women *as such*. At issue for her is what qualities are attributed to men and women and why. Against the then-popular Aristotelian view that women were naturally less developed versions of men,[21] Gournay proposes that nature is opposed to hierarchy and asymmetry when it comes to "sex": "I who fly all extremes; I am content to *equalize* them [*les esgaler*] to men: nature being opposed in this regard as much as to superiority as to inferiority" (278; 75; emphasis added). Gournay is saying that when it comes to the matter of sex, we cannot simply consult "nature"—be they factic, physical features of the human body or intrinsic mental features—to find an innate asymmetry between men and women. This is a bold claim, insofar as it flies in the face of the then-popular Aristotelian worldview according to which nature is structured in terms of hierarchical fundamentalities and primary asymmetries.

Gournay's concern with *equalizing* ("esgaler") here is usually understood as the political demand that those taken to be women be treated equally to those taken to be men. And that is certainly part of the argument. But I would suggest that, as a pyrrhonic skeptical philosopher, the sense of "equality" for Gournay here also means "equipollence" (*isostheneia*) or the sense in which we equalize or neutralize a dogmatic claim. For the skeptic, if we bring to bear an opposing counterclaim to a given metaphysical claim in order to make uncertain which claim is the true, then we have made them "equal." This will be Gournay's methodology: by philosophically equalizing or neutralizing metaphysical claims about the inherent differences between men and women, she assumes we'll achieve political equality. The political and skeptical senses of "equality" are thus not opposed but complementary.

3.3 "Sex" terminology

Now there is the matter of sex terminology. I have been using Gournay's vocabulary of "man, woman" and "sex," but have also intermixed some contemporary-sounding terms, like "sexual difference." Still, we must be careful in this regard. For Gournay never uses the term "gender"/"genre" but only speaks of "sex," of "men and women," of "difference," and at one point "males and females." Thus, Gournay does not subscribe to the sex/gender distinction that many contemporary feminist theorists endorse, according to which sex indicates anatomical features and biological properties and gender denotes the social meanings and roles imposed upon sex. Gournay muddles such a distinction, speaking instead of "sex" as being masculine and feminine (or sometimes as male and female). The concept of "sex" Gournay probably would have been working with would have been somewhat vague and undefined. Jean Nicot's dictionary, *Le Thresor de la langue francoyse* (1606), for example, defines "femme" or woman as the "the sex of women [*tout le sexe des femmes*]" without, however, offering any definition of "sex" itself. Intriguingly, the dictionary's definition of "man" or "homme"—"*en general tout homme*," in general every man or all mankind—does not relate the concept "man" in any way to a conception of sex, precisely because in French "l'homme" means both "man" and "human."[22] In this sense, we can see that having a sex is something mostly associated with "being a woman," as if to be a man were to have no sex, since man stands in for the human in general.[23] We can see, then, why Gournay will want to denaturalize sex: it is only attributed to women and serves as a sexist justification for women being different from men, who are supposedly just human. What I want to underscore is that when Gournay speaks of "sex" and "women" or "men" we cannot assume that she is using the first as a sex term and the second as a gender term as we now understand this distinction. Instead, Gournay's use of "sex" conflates bodily traits *and* their social meanings. Importantly, for her it is a concept mostly associated with being a woman (*femme*) rather than being human (*homme*). As we will see, not clearly distinguishing between sex and gender is not a problem for Gournay, since her project is not to delineate the proper boundaries of sex and gender, but to equalize and neutralize them. These preliminaries aside, we can now proceed to Gournay's three major claims that seek to do just this.

4 Gournay's major claims

4.1 Discursive construction claim

Recall that earlier, Gournay remarks that those called men "attribute to themselves [*s'attribuent*]" certain features and privileges, becoming what they are by means of conferring certain traits on themselves and on others. Gournay's first claim is that the inferiority ascribed to women is a result of certain dogmatists attributing such features to them, saying that women "lack dignity [*manquent de dignité*]" and "lack intellectual sufficiency [*manquent . . . de suffisance*]" (278; 75). These dogmatists also attribute features of superiority to themselves. But Gournay is skeptical over how it might be that these dogmatists could attribute superior qualities to themselves in a noncircular way. For the dogmatist presupposes the very premise that he is supposed to prove, taking for granted that men are superior in order to explain why men are superior: "Is it credible . . . that those who desire to exalt and empower [*fortifier*] themselves through the weakness of others must claim that they can exalt or empower themselves by means of their own power [*force*]?" (279; 76). As Gournay says, the dogmatists "exalt and empower themselves" by means of their "own power," circularly assuming and appealing to the very strength they are supposed to ascertain.

Gournay then remarks that when the dogmatist is asked to justify his circular reasoning, he just responds with the stipulative assertion that man's superiority is "just how it is," drawing his authority from simply laying *claim to* "the credit of being masculine [*le credit de masculin*]" (278; 75). The dogmatist attributes superiority to himself, either by circularly assuming that this is the case or by stipulatively saying that it is the case: "if they lay claim [*prennent droict*] to being gallant men of intellectual ability, since they declare themselves to be such by edict, why would they not, by another edict that says the opposite, make women stupid [*rendront-ils les femmes bestes*]?" (279; 76). The language here of *taking* and *making* is strong: certain individuals lay claim or seize (*prendre droit*) the right to be intelligent men just by declaring themselves to be such, as if by fiat. And by a similar edict, they *make* (*rendre*) women "bêtes." The French word *bêtes* means both beast and stupid and has a complicated conceptual history in French thought, as Derrida's recently edited seminars *La bête et le souverain* explore in detail.[24] For Gournay, some individuals "take the right" to be men, as if by edict, and, by another edict, make others into foolish beasts. These dogmatists make women into beastly fools by using "whatever false or mistaken criteria there may be [*à quelque tort & fausse mesure que ce soit*]" (279; 76), often stipulating that woman's physique denies her intellectual ability: women do not have the "constitution and physical make up [*temperament & des organs*]" (278; 75) to excel in the way men do, so the dogmatists say. In this way, the dogmatists associate the feminine sex with the body, stupidity, and animality by offering attributions and stipulations that trade on prejudice.

In contemporary terms, we would call these attributions and stipulations *performative acts* whereby dogmatists try to make it the case that women are such-and-such by simply declaring it. In Austinian language, the dogmatist issues forth a *verdictive*—a claim that such and such "is so" that makes x "count" as being the case by purporting to represent the world— and *exercitives*—a claim that such and such "is to be so" that makes x actually become the case by seeking to change the world.[25] Gournay makes this clear when she states that the dogmatists want to define women's nature "by an absolute and obligatory decree [*d'un arrest irrefragable & necessaire*]" (278; 75). The legal language of "decree" indicates that it is by certain (speech) acts that dogmatists performatively enact and institute a demeaning definition of what it is to be a woman. The dogmatist is not only saying that women should "count" as inferior but in saying so he is making a claim that will provide the conditions for the perception, conceptualization, and treatment of women as inferior insofar as the claim is trying to pass itself off as fact.[26] To be sexed is nothing more than the attribution of contingent social properties to individuals and this attribution occurs by means of unfounded stipulations and declarations that this is how things just naturally are. Such sexist performative acts seek to *bring into being*, as if by ordinance or edict, sexual difference as an inevitable or irreducible fact.

Gournay substantially changes the terms of the debate. The disputants in the debate are not portrayed as women and men —as if their sex were already defined and established—, but as persons fighting over the attributes associated with being a man and being a woman: the dogmatists take credit for their naturally masculine traits and *reduce* women to fools by imputing opposing, demeaning traits to them. Gournay's strong claim is that *one is sexed if and only if one has enfranchising or disenfranchising social properties attributed to oneself*. Sex is socially conferred: women and men *are made up,* in the sense that they are made both *by* and *of* social attributions. Being a "man" just is to be declared privileged, being a woman just is to be declared subordinate.[27]

Following Sally Haslanger and Ásta Sveinsdóttir, we can call Gournay's first major claim a *discursive construction claim* according to which,[28]

> to a considerable extent men and women are such as they are, and how they are, because of what properties are conferred on them and the ways they are categorized based on context-dependent perceptions and practices.

Men and women are what they are based on the properties we assign to them and what we say about them (and what they ascribe to or say about themselves). It is for this reason that Gournay finds an ally in Socrates and Plato who, in the *Republic,* she observes, "attribute to women the same rights, faculties, and functions [*leur assignent mesmes droicts, facultez & fonctions*]" (279; 76-7). If sex is no more than its attributions, the normative goal should be, as Gournay says, to attribute the *same* ones equally to everyone, just as Socrates and Plato did.

According to Gournay's first claim, the property of being sexed is conferred just in case those in power arrogate authority to themselves and make prejudiced claims about sex, using whatever false criteria they can to "ground" that conferral.[29] Hence, for Gournay, being sexed is mind-dependent: we confer sexed properties on individuals depending on how "we apply our concepts" of what we think sex is.[30] This general framework needs to be filled in, however: for if these conferred properties are socially contingent prejudices rather than natural facts, why have they gained so much traction?

4.2 *Causal construction claim*

Gournay's second claim in her treatise will try to answer this question, by attacking the dogmatists' assertion that women are by nature more ignorant than men:

> Why would the education of women in public matters and in letters, of a kind equal to men's, not bridge the gap that commonly appears between their minds and those of men, when we see that such training is of such importance that, when only one part of it—namely, dealing with the world—is common among French and English women and lacking among Italian women, the latter are by and large exceeded by the former? I say "by and large" because in particular the ladies of Italy sometimes excel; and we have drawn from them queens and princesses who did not lack intellectual ability. Why indeed might not the right sort of upbringing [*nourriture*] succeed in filling the gap between the intellectual powers of men and women . . . simply by dint of one part of that upbringing [*nourriture*] of ladies, namely conversation and commerce with the world? (282; 81–2)

In this passage, Gournay points out that the relative differences among individuals might be related to education, and so women are not always ignorant and men intelligent. Education, she claims, is causally responsible for one's abilities. The historian of philosophy Eileen O'Neill reconstructs Gournay's argument thus: Italian women are deprived of the intellectual and social privileges granted to English and French women, and so for the most part they do not showcase a similar intellectual ability when compared to English and French women. And yet, there are in fact Italian women whose intellect has far exceeded that of English and French women, namely those Italian women (like queens) who were educated and exposed to social contact. Hence Italian women, who are presumed to show limited intellect, at times come to excel more than those presumed to show greater intellect, namely English and French women.[31] And this is because of a certain kind of nurture/"nourishment" (*nourriture*) they receive, namely education and social experience.

Gournay uses this example to adduce the argument that certain properties we take to be natural sex facts, like inherent differences in intellect between the sexes, are brought about by socialization and education. For it may seem that men excel in intellectual ability compared to women, which might lead us to presume that sex establishes intellectual ability. But it is also the case that men are exposed to "conversation and commerce" in the world in a way women are not; men are given educative and social advantages. Given the same advantages, women would be intellectually equal to men. Gournay is thus making the claim that education and engagement with the world can "bridge the gap" that seems to exist in levels of ignorance between the sexes.[32]

Note the language of "nurture" in this passage: in French the word is *nourriture* or rearing/upbringing, which implies that men and women are literally *nourished* by social institutions. Gournay's point is that while we think women's intellectual inferiority is natural, original, or perennial, it is in fact contingent upon social education, namely, the "ignorance and inexperience in which they [*elles*] are nurtured [*nourries*]" (281; 80). Education creates the properties we take to be natural sex facts. Paralleling Ron Mallon's definition of causal social construction, we can call Gournay's second claim a *causal construction claim*, according to which,[33]

> The supposed intellectual inferiority of women is the effect of how they are educated or nurtured. Socialization through education to some meaningful extent causes the traits we mistakenly assume to be inborn sex-typical facts, like intellect, to exist and persist.

Gournay's point is to show that claims about women's intellectual nature are not absolute, intrinsic, or universal but must be relativized to the cultural practices that bring them about; claims about women's nature are not mind-independent truths. We must modify our criteria for specifying the sexed nature of individuals by relativizing them to the social conventions and customs that bring them about.

4.3 Eliminativist claim

Lastly, Gournay advances what I take to be the strongest premise of her argument. Using Platonic and Aristotelian concepts of form/species and selectively borrowing from the Genesis narrative of creation, Gournay asserts that the "human animal" is properly speaking neither man nor woman:

> The human animal, understood correctly, is neither man nor woman [*l'animal humain n'est homme ny femme*], the sexes having been made [*estans faicts*], not so as to constitute a difference in species, but only for the sake of propagation. The unique form and distinction of that animal consists only in the human rational soul [*l'âme humaine*].... Nothing is more similar to a cat on a window sill than a female cat. Man and woman are so thoroughly one that if man is more than woman, then woman is more than man. Man was created male and female [*L'homme fut creé masle & femelle*]—so says Scripture.... Now, in those whose nature is one and the same, it must be concluded that their actions are so as well. (285; 86–7)

Drawing from Marguerite Deslauriers' and Eileen O'Neill's reconstructions of Gournay's argument, we can summarize Gournay's final claim thus. Gournay adduces the Aristotelian argument that the form of a given entity constitutes the essential properties it must have to belong to a species: its essence makes it what it is. Recall that, for Aristotle, an essential predication specifies what an entity is, or its essence (e.g., "Hypatia is human").[34] An accidental predication specifies how the entity is, or a property that qualifies it but that it does not need in order to be the entity that it is (e.g., "Hypatia is tanned").[35] Accidental predications of properties—like being tanned or untanned—are contingent, whereas essential predications of properties—like being human—are not. Being tanned is accidental since Hypatia could have been fair skinned but still be human, inasmuch as the necessary or essential feature of what makes her human lies elsewhere (not in skin phenotype).[36] For Gournay, if the essential form for being human is the rational soul, then sex is accidental: one could remove or discard sex, and the human would remain.

Gournay then makes the neoplatonic point that sex is not an essential property for defining the human but only used for propagation. Sex qualifies *how one is* accidentally, but not *what one is* essentially, for one could perfectly well be human without being sexed.[37] Male and female might seem to be bodily contraries when it comes to sexual reproduction but they are not contradictories when it comes to being human.[38] For to be sexed is not *what it is to be human*, precisely because being sexed is not what defines membership within the human species. Just as it would be ridiculous to conclude that a male or female cat constitute two different species (when they are both cats), so too would it be ridiculous to conclude that man and woman constitute two different species (when they are both humans).[39] I would wager that Gournay's point is even stronger: just as it would be ridiculous to see a cat and *sex* it as a man or a woman, so too is it ridiculous to see a human and sex it as a man or a woman. The then-popular claim that "women are not human" thus becomes incoherent on Gournay's view, for if the sexes do not constitute two difference species, but *one*, then men and women are not alike but equal: one is no more a man than one is a woman if one has a human soul, since that is the essential property for membership in the human species.[40] Gournay was not alone in advocating this view. As the historian Thomas Laqueur contends, up until the late eighteenth century, there was no entrenched dual sex model in Western medicine, but a one-sex model, drawn from the Greeks, according to which male and female sex organs were the inversions of one and the same organ.[41]

Gournay finds further support for her claim in *Genesis*. If God made "man" in his own image, and if God also made "man male and female" then, by that logic, male and female were both made in God's image, meaning they have an identical "Form/soul" insofar as they come from the same creation.[42] And if males and females possess the same soul/form, then they are one and the same. As Gournay adds, it would be "foolish . . . to imagine that God is masculine or feminine [*fade d'imaginer masculin ou feminin en Dieu*]" (290; 94). So if God has no sex, and mankind was made in God's image, then mankind is not sexed in its essence. Even if Jesus Christ was seemingly "born" a man, Gournay remarks, this was only for pragmatic social reasons or "demands of social propriety" [*necessaire bien-seance*] for "if he had been of the sex of women [*s'il eust esté du sexe des femmes*]" Jesus "would have been unable without scandal" to move about in public (290; 94). Gournay thus closes her argument with a startling counterfactual claim here: Jesus *could* just as well have been born a woman, but he was embodied as a man in anticipation of human social norms and practices, which would have forbidden a woman to proselytize in public.

Gournay's unique philosophical point, then, is that whenever we reduce someone to being male or female, man or woman, masculine or feminine, we are mistaken: there is a human there, first and foremost. Sexual difference is an incorrect way to distinguish humans if they are of the same species. In saying that the human animal is fundamentally neither man nor woman, Gournay asserts that *what it is to be a human* is *not to be sexed*, with the consequence that one is not a man or a woman because one has a male or female body. This supports Gournay's earlier discursive and causal constructionist claims that one is sexed as a woman or man solely by virtue of being socially privileged or subjugated. Drawing from Haslanger and Mari Mikkola, we can reformulate Gournay's third claim as an eliminativist proposal about sex:

i   The sexes of women and men ontologically depend on how we think, "what we do," and the social positions in which we find ourselves.[43] To be a sex is to sufficiently satisfy or meet certain social conditions (rather than biological ones).[44]

ii One is sexed as woman or man if and only if one is socially disenfranchised or enfranchised—that is, subject to particular forms of social subjugation or privilege—based on whether one is assumed to play a female or male role in biological propagation.[45]

iii Hence, there is no such thing as "natural sex" as such, since to be sexed is by definition to hold a social position of inequality, not just to have a male or female body, insofar as both bodies are human.[46]

To take stock: Gournay's first claim was that men and women are what they are because we confer features on them and stipulate the properties they have through social practices; her second claim was that some of these features are causally constructed or "nurtured" through social education.

Her third claim is stronger still: defining what it is to be a man or a woman itself requires, by definition, "reference to social factors" and actors, as Haslanger puts it, since, strictly speaking, the human is neither man nor woman. In this sense, social subjugation and/or privilege is *constitutive* of what it is to be sexed since, strictly speaking, the human animal, as Gournay says, is neither a man nor a woman. One can only be a man and a woman relative to the properties that are conferred onto one by social practices and institutions. Sex thus refers to no more than the state of being subjugated if one is "sex-marked" a woman, or the state of being enfranchised, if one is "sex-marked" a man, as Mikkola phrases it. In this sense, the status, signification, and function of sex do not represent natural facts. Rather, sex is a social category that, in defining certain sexes as inferior, is both constructed and false, and the normative task that lies before us is to *eliminate* sex insofar as it is constitutively and oppositionally unequalizing.

One might initially find Gournay's social constructionist and sex eliminativist claims to be incompatible, a charge frequently brought against social construction theorists: if Gournay claims that sex is socially constructed then how can she also claim that, strictly speaking, there is no such thing as sex, only social constructions we take to be sex? For would it not seem that a social construction of sex has effectively and successfully constituted sex: if it is the case that sex *is* something, namely a construction, how could it be false?[47] We can see from the way social prejudices are baked into the definition of sex why Gournay can argue that sex is both *constructed* and *false* without being incoherent. Consider, as Katharine Jenkins argues, that if sex is socially constructed, this means that sex depends on collective social attitudes and practices: a sufficient number of people (or substantial subset of those people) have accorded a certain social status and signification to the category of "sex" which functions to organize the population into sexes accorded different rights and privileges and making them count as different kinds of subjects (or non-subjects, as the case may be) based on who is marked as a given sex (where to be a sex is to count as the subject or object of enfranchising or subjugating treatment).[48] It is constructed because the category of sex is laced with prejudices that operate according to a circular, self-confirming logic. For as soon as one is categorized as a woman, one is constructed to count as a lesser being, and as vulnerable to particular mistreatments and subordinating acts. And if one is taken to be lesser and vulnerable to particular mistreatments then one is subjugated (in a sense, it is not just that one "counts as" a subjugated class but, equally, that one can causally become subjugated insofar as being considered inferior can lead to one being handled so).[49] Therefore, the category of sex subjugates because it is itself founded on unequal social status and relations.[50] And if sex tracks subjugation rather than natural facts, then sex is socially constructed all the way down.

But this construction is also false because, as Jenkins points out, it tries to disguise its subjugating function as a natural, brute fact, attempting to pass itself off as a natural state of affairs.[51] This construction of sex as a brute or pregiven fact is not representing some natural fact about the inherent difference between men and women since there is none. Following Kate McGowan, we can say that what is constructed is not so much an object ("sex") or a proposition about "sex" but the fact that sex has come to be considered a natural fact—and what is false is that we have taken a non-fact to be a natural fact. The socially constructed fact is one that takes a non-fact to *be* a natural fact, in this case about sex.[52] Therefore, sex is both constructed and false. Note that it is perfectly coherent for Gournay to be skeptical about whether sexual difference is a natural fact and to, nonetheless, talk about sex as a social fact. She can talk about sex as a social fact because it is the case that people live as if or as though sex were a natural, self-evident given and this has led to certain persons being treated unequally: it is this social inequality that is the real, undeniable fact.

5 Conclusion

Gournay's understanding of sex significantly differs from other seventeenth-century women writers, like Madeleine de Scudéry, who insist that women and men have different personalities and practice virtue differently. Gournay does not want "different but equal" sexes since for the sexes are not inherently different but only differently socialized. Indeed, one controversial consequence of Gournay's humanist view is that we ought to consider *unsexing* ourselves if we are to achieve social justice. That is, Gournay implies that if we are to enact social justice, we ought to *eliminate* sex as way of organizing society since sex is constitutively oppressive. In the terms of twentieth-century and contemporary French feminist theory, we can say that Gournay's humanism and sex eliminativism would align with Monique Wittig, who also argues that sexual difference is a constitutively oppressive category that should be eliminated.⁵³ For Wittig, gender/sex are constitutively oppressive political classes: it is not just that some genders are subject to oppression, but the demand to be a gender is itself oppressive.⁵⁴ The conventionalist claim is that sex/gender categories are the products of social practices and conventions; the abolitionist claim is that these conventions are inherently oppressive ones, with the result that gender needs to be debunked as the social fabrication it is and dispensed with altogether.⁵⁵ While one might object that gender is not oppressive in and of itself, only how one is mistreated based on false beliefs about one's gender, Wittig asserts that having to be a gender/sex is oppressive *as such*. Thus, gender/sex concepts and categories should be eradicated.⁵⁶

Gournay's views would conflict with differentialist feminists like Luce Irigaray, who claims that sexual difference is an insurmountable condition of subjectivity and society. But differentialist feminists run into a methodological problem: how can those like Irigaray who claim that Western culture and thought have excluded the possibility of sexual difference find (and know) this so-called sexual difference which would be both before and beyond what we know and say within our contemporary discourse? How does Irigaray gain epistemological and methodological access to the excluded possibility of sexual difference? It is one thing to point out that there are gaps, silences, and exclusions in our sex concepts (there are). But it's another to conclude that these gaps, silences, and exclusions are the symptoms of an excluded sexual difference. Differentialists simply stipulate that there is an ontological sexual difference (or at the very least the possibility of sexual differentiation within being) that our contemporary discourse excludes, but in stipulatively asserting this they circularly presume that *there just is* sexual difference, that is, an unsurpassable ontological condition of both subjectivity and society. It is question-begging to assume that sexual difference is fundamental and foundational to culture since that assumption presumes there already is something like a fundamental or foundational sexual difference "out there."

Unlike Irigaray, Gournay's work implies that, were we to abolish certain versions of sexual difference and the oppressive social practices that undergird it, there would be no more men or women, only humans. Gournay's strongly humanist position requires that social justice do away with sexual difference when it is the product of social prejudices, customs, and relations that make sexual difference a category useful only for purposes of subordination. In this lies, too, Gournay's strong contribution to a different kind of "humanism"—one that takes into account how the human is socially sexed—an argument with increasing importance to our reading and rereading of early modern thought.

There are detriments, of course, to Gournay's humanist views for contemporary gender politics. Gournay would probably say that what we now call gender is inherently oppressive, so we ought to eliminate it. However, one might respond that this view does not properly differentiate *gender classes* (how one is classed) from *gender identity* (how one responds to being classed or not classed). Katharine Jenkins, for example, suggests that *gender classes* might by definition be oppressive (insofar as they present themselves as binary and cisnormative) but *gender identities* need not be. For how one negotiates gender/sex can be pleasurable, positive, and alliance-building.[57] Gender identity would be the "map" or "guide" according to how one is categorized (or not) as a gender class:

> S has a gender identity of X iff S's internal "map" is formed to guide someone classed as a member of X gender through the social and/or material realities that are, in that context, characteristic of Xs as a class.[58]

Even if gender classes are constitutively oppressive, our "internal map" formed in response to those classes is arguably not, for gender norms can lose their constraining purchase as they are adopted.[59] Hence, the humanist call to abolish sex and gender and just be human would probably be misunderstood and resisted by everyday social agents.[60] Likewise, if we want "public toleration"[61] for gender nonconformity, one might contend that we should promote diverse gender expressions and respect non-mainstream gender identifications as "presumptively valid"[62] rather than just do away with gender tout court. On this view, the acknowledgment of multiple forms of gender expression is prone to engender a more inclusive social life rather than obliterating gender expression altogether. So Gournay's robust humanism remains problematic, insofar as it is unclear whether we can just shed deeply embedded social categories like gender or sex.

However, why are we so sure that gender identities are positive responses to gender classes (rather than, say, deformed desires or adaptive preferences)? Does one even need to identify *as* a gender to fight *against* gender oppression, cissexism, or heteropatriarchy? One would defend eliminativism and abolitionism regarding sex/gender by noting that gender/sexual identities only follow from there being gender/sex categories in the first place (with which one can identify or disidentify)—and thus the elimination of gender categories would require the formation of alliances based on something other than identity.[63] I tend to agree with Gournay, Wittig, and Haslanger that, metaphysically speaking, oppression is constitutive of gender and that, normatively speaking, it ought eventually be abolished (even if, for pragmatic purposes, gender remains useful as a category or heuristic for tracking oppressive relations because many believe and behave as if there were such a thing as gender). It falls to the eliminativist however, to explain precisely what we are eliminating (and in which contexts). Are we abolishing gender concepts, terms, beliefs, or behaviors? Likewise, in what sense is gender being understood here (as an identity, a relation, a category, a concept, an experience, etc.)? Similarly, will not any such analysis need to take scale into account, i.e., whether it regards individuals or groups? Finally, could the argument not be made that, rather than do away with gender, our task now is to develop new, non-oppressive gender categories given that implementing gender eliminitivism is both counterintuitive and pragmatically infeasible (since a multitude of social agents not only believe in but also *enjoy* gender)? Is the question, then, not just what we "should" do, but what we "can" and "want" to do?

It is doubtful that the maintenance of gender categories can be justified by the pleasure some subjects take in them. Indeed, many things that may feel good are not for that reason good for one. While some might argue that nonnormative gender expression is crucial to expanding our sense of how life can be lived, it is still worth asking what we gain by continuing to subscribe to gender categories like "man" or "woman" (including their manifestations as cis or trans) and what we lose when we do. Indeed, even if one argues that we should proliferate and diversify nonbinary gender identities rather than eliminate gender tout court, I would argue that if gender is by definition a constitutively disequalizing way of organizing and conceiving bodies normatively,[64] then a proliferation of multiple, nonbinary genders—which we may wish to encourage—would lead not to multiple genders but to the eventual elimination of gender itself. For if folk conceptions of gender are by definition binaric, insofar as ordinary speakers assume gender terms distinguish female and male bodies, then a diversification of gender beyond this binary division, to the point at which it no longer makes descriptive sense, would be to no longer "have" gender as an intelligible category (and that is a good thing!). The various traits and properties that were before clustered around specific genders would instead become dispersed and distributed among a wide range of bodies and persons, without a unifying gendered "substance" or "subject" to undergird them as one's gender proper. The property-clusters we have hitherto associated with "genders" would be diffused and co-opted by various bodies such that gender would become incoherent. Indeed, if there are many nonbinary "genders," it makes no sense to call them genders, since to label them as a gender, albeit a nonbinary one, is still to make reference to the binary system of gender against which these nonbinary genders are being defined. The fact that we have nonbinary *genders*, defined in relation to the binary gender system they reject, only confirms the fact that gender concepts are inescapably embedded in a binary frame (because enmeshed in hetero- and cis-normative assumptions about biological sex). If we reduce sex to the organs people have, or if we define gender by genitalia—as if the bodies people had determined the kind of sexual identity they are or can be—then we fall into cissexism and biological reductionism. If gender/sex distinctions remain "strongly pragmatically constructed,"[65] rather than merely reflective of real-world differences, the point should be to eradicate gender/sex as classificatory schemas for organizing bodies.

Perhaps, for the present, "gender" and "sex" are best employed as heuristic tools for tracking inequality; for political mobilization; and for progressive social movements devoted to combatting gender-based injustice in that false beliefs in qualitative gender/sex differences result in qualitatively different treatments of individuals and groups. But ultimately, it is doubtful that "gender"—and the kinds of weighty ontological commitments that belief in gender entails—can serve a useful purpose as an entity or identity that should be maintained in the long term.[66] Still, irrespective of whether, strictly speaking, sex or gender "as such" exist—like Gournay, I suspect they do not—as social constructions they continue to have consequential effects as they did, even if to a different degree, for those in Gournay's time. Unlike many of her fellow philosophical contributors to the *Querelle*, Gournay provides one of the first philosophical accounts of how sexual difference is bound up with social inequality and the profound injustices that are its result. Her analysis leaves us with a political suggestion both promising and daunting: if sex is socially constituted—grounded in our social perceptions and practices—then we can either insist on inventing a new construction of sex, one that is not normatively unequal and, thus, oppressive, or, as

I would argue, we can insist on eventually eliminating the construction of "sex" altogether.[67] In rereading Gournay in light of our era, we come to find that this early modern controversy over the nature of the human subject and sex is far from over—if anything, what we come to find is that this controversy is now our own.

Notes

1. See Joan Kelly "Early Feminist Theory and the 'Querelle des Femmes,' 1400-1789," *Signs* 8, no. 1 (1982): 4–28 and Eileen O'Neill, "Justifying the Inclusion of Women in Our Histories of Philosophy: The Case of Marie de Gournay," in *Guide to Feminist Philosophy*, ed. Linda Alcoff and Eva Kittay (Oxford and Cambridge, MA: Blackwell, 2006), 17–42.
2. See my "Unlivable Loves: Hélisenne, Nietzsche and the Metaphysics of Love," *JNT: Journal of Narrative Theory* 46, no.1 (2016): 1–38 for a philosophical exploration of the metaphysics of the subject in early modern thought.
3. These distinctions come from Kate Manne, "Humanism: A Critique," *Social Theory and Practice* 42, no. 2 (2016): 389–415. See also Susan Moller Okin, "Feminism, Women's Human Rights, and Cultural Differences." *Hypatia* 13, no. 2 (1998): 32–52.
4. Manne, "Humanism," 395–96.
5. Ibid., 396.
6. Ibid.
7. For further contextualization of the *Disputatio nova contra mulieres, qua probatur eas homines non esse*, see Manfred P. Fleischer, "'Are Women Human?'—The Debate of 1595 between Valens Acidalius and Simon Gediccus," *The Sixteenth Century Journal* 12, no. 2 (1981): 107–20 and Marianne Alenius, "Women Are Not Human Beings: Nordic Women's Literature": http://nordicwomensliterature.net/article/women-are-not-human-beings.
8. See Charles W. Mills, *The Racial Contract* (Ithaca and New York: Cornell University Press, 1997).
9. These are some of the questions Jacques Derrida raises in *L'Animal que donc je suis* (Paris: Galilée, 2006).
10. See Judith Butler, *Undoing Gender* (New York: Routledge, 2004), 2–3.
11. Ibid., 2.
12. Gournay's edition was vehemently criticized for its critical preface. See Gournay, *Preface to the Essays of Montaigne*, ed. and trans. Richard Hillman and Colette Quesnel (Tempe, AZ: Medieval and Renaissance Texts and Studies, 1998).
13. I will be translating from the 1641 French version published in *Les avis, ou les Présens de la Demoiselle de Gournay* (Paris: s.n., 1641). Hereafter I will

cite page numbers in the text starting with the French edition pagination and then following with the English translation pagination from *Apology for the Woman Writing and Other Works*, ed and trans. Richard Hillman and Colette Quesnel (Chicago: University of Chicago Press, 2002).

14 See O'Neill, "Justifying."

15 Sextus Empiricus was a Pyrrhonic skeptic from the second or third century, whose surviving work, *Outlines of Pyrrhonism,* sketches the skills, views, and trade-offs of this mode of skepticism. See Richard Popkin, *The History of Scepticism: From Savonarola to Bayle* (Oxford: Oxford University Press, 2003); Robert Pasnau, "Snatching Hope from the Jaws of Epistemic Defeat," *Journal of the American Philosophical Association* 1, no. 2 (2015): 257–75; Isabelle Krier, "Souvenirs sceptiques de Marie de Gournay dans 'Égalité des hommes et des femmes'," *Clio* 29 (2009): 243–57; and O'Neill, "Justifying."

16 This characterization is drawn from Benjamin Morison, "Sextus Empiricus," *The Stanford Encyclopedia of Philosophy* (Spring 2014 Edition), Edward N. Zalta (ed.), URL = http://plato.stanford.edu/archives/spr2014/entries/sextus-empiricus/.

17 See O'Neill, "Justifying," and Krier, "Souvenirs."

18 See Sarah McGrath, "Relax! Don't Do It! Why Moral Realism Won't Come Cheap," in *Oxford Studies in Metaethics,* ed. Russ Shafer-Landau (Oxford: Oxford University Press, 2014), 210.

19 See Marguerite Deslauriers, "Marie de Gournay and Aristotle on the Unity of the Sexes," in *Feminist History of Philosophy: The Recovery and Evaluation of Women's Philosophical Thought*, ed. Eileen O'Neill and Marcy P. Lascano (Dordrecht: Springer, forthcoming), for the claim that Gournay is not just making skeptical arguments.

20 McGrath, "Relax! Don't Do It!," 210.

21 See *Generation of Animals* IV 6 775a15-16.

22 These are both sourced from *ARTFL: Dictionnaires d'autrefois*: http://artflsrv02.uchicago.edu/cgi-bin/dicos/pubdico1look.pl?strippedhw=femme and http://artflsrv02.uchicago.edu/cgi-bin/dicos/pubdico1look.pl?strippedhw=homme.

23 Simone de Beauvoir would make the same remark in *le Le deuxième sexe* (Paris: Éditions Gallimard, 1976 [1949]): "The relation between the two sexes is not that of two electricities, of two poles: man represents at once the positive and the neutral to the point that one says in French 'les hommes' to designate human beings, the singular meaning of the word 'vir' having been assimilated to the general meaning of the word 'man'" (16).

24 *Séminaire la bête et le souverain. Volume II (2002-2003)* (Paris: Galilée, 2010).

25 See Rae Langton, *Sexual Solipsism: Philosophical Essays on Pornography and Objectification* (Oxford: Oxford University Press, 2009), 93–5. Langton usefully glosses the illuctionary-perlocutionary distinction in J. L. Austin,

How to Do Things with Words (Oxford: Clarendon Press, 1962), as a difference between "the action performed simply *in* saying something" (illocution) and "the action performed simply *by* saying something" (perlocution) (32) or the difference between "legitimating something" (illocution) and "making people believe that something is legitimate" (perlocution) (35).

26 Langton, *Sexual Solipsism,* writes that illuctionary verdictives make it the case that x counts as y (constitutively) but that this can lead to causal perlocutionary effects: "Suppose a child is authoritatively ranked as having a lower than average intelligence, and is believed by her teachers to have a lower than average intelligence. The child can, to a certain degree, really come to have a lower than average intelligence…When you are ranked as worse, you are treated as worse, and then really become worse" (95).

27 Here I'm already referencing Sally Haslanger's definition of gender and Ásta Sveinsdóttir's conferralism, which I discuss below.

28 This definition is calqued on Ásta Sveinsdóttir's conferralism in "The Social Construction of Human Kinds," *Hypatia* 28, no. 4 (2013): 716–32, and borrows from the language of Sally Haslanger's definition of "discursive construction" in *Resisting Reality: Social Construction and Social Critique* (Oxford: Oxford University Press, 2012), 88. See also Mari Mikkola's entry, "Feminist Perspectives on Sex and Gender," *The Stanford Encyclopedia of Philosophy* (Spring 2016 Edition), Edward N. Zalta (ed.), forthcoming URL = http://plato.stanford.edu/archives/spr2016/entries/feminism-gender/.

29 I am drawing from Ásta Sveinsdóttir, "Social Construction as Social Significance," presented at the "Feminist Ontology Workshop," at MIT, October 2015.

30 Rebecca Mason, "Are Social Kinds Mind-Dependent?" unpublished manuscript, 9.

31 O'Neill reconstructs this skeptical argument in "Justifying," from which I'm drawing.

32 See once again O'Neill for a deft reconstruction of this argument.

33 I'm drawing from Ron Mallon, "Naturalistic Approaches to Social Construction," *The Stanford Encyclopedia of Philosophy* (Winter 2014 Edition), Edward N. Zalta (ed.), URL = http://plato.stanford.edu/archives/win2014/entries/social-construction-naturalistic/.

34 For an extensive reading of Gournay and Aristotle, see Deslauriers, "Gournay and Aristotle," from which I'm drawing in this discussion.

35 I thank Phil Corkum for discussing the *what is/how is* distinction with me.

36 Deslauriers, "Gournay and Aristotle," 13. Deslauriers discusses Gournay's use of Aristotle's *Metaphysics* VII 4.

37 I thank Phil Corkum once again for the formulation of this incisive distinction between *how something is* versus *what something is.*

38 See Deslauriers, 16 for extended discussion.

39 Deslauriers points out that the passage from Aristotle that Gournay might have been familiar with is *Metaphysics X* 9 1058b21-4: "And male and female are indeed modifications peculiar to [the] animal, however in virtue of its substance but in the matter, i.e. the body" (Cited in ibid., 15).

40 As Deslauriers notes in "Gournay and Aristotle," Gournay's claim that men and women are not "similar" but the same differs from Montaigne who, in Book III chapter 5 of the *Essais*, "Sur des vers de Virgile," sees men and women cut from the same mold, Gournay sees them *as the same*; whereas Montaigne sees the difference not so great, Gournay sees no difference at all (11).

41 Thomas Laqueur, *Making Sex: Body and Gender from the Greeks to Freud* (Cambridge, MA: Harvard University Press, 1992). See also Michel Foucault, *Histoire de la sexualité* (Paris: Gallimard, 1976).

42 See O'Neill, "Justifying" for an excellent exegesis and gloss of Gournay's "Form/soul" argument from which I'm drawing here.

43 Rebecca Mason, "Social Ontology Naturalized," Unpublished Manuscript.

44 Here I am relying on Mari Mikkola, "Ontological Commitments, Sex and Gender," in *Feminist Metaphysics*, ed. Charlotte Witt (Dordrecht: Springer, 2011), 68.

45 Here I am relying on Haslanger, *Resisting*, 230.

46 I am drawing from Haslanger, *Resisting* 230 and Mikkola, "Ontological," 67.

47 For this discussion of how an entity can be both "constructed" and "wrong/false" I am drawing from Katharine Jenkins, "What Women Are For: Pornography and Social Ontology," in *Beyond Speech*, ed. Mari Mikkola (Oxford: Oxford University Press, forthcoming), 10–13. I am also drawing from Mary Kate McGowan, "On Pornography: MacKinnon, Speech Acts, and "False" Construction." *Hypatia* 20, no. 3 (2005): 22–49.

48 Jenkins, "What," 10; Haslanger, *Resisting*, 230.

49 See McGowan, "On Pornography," 45.

50 Jenkins, "What," 10.

51 Ibid., 12. See also Haslanger, *Resisting*.

52 As McGowan, "On Pornography," puts it: "The fact that [a claim] is constructed in such cases, however, is not the 'fact' that came to be viewed as a fact. It is the fact that that fact came to be viewed as a fact. . . . The fact that [it] is regarded as a fact is a constructed fact. This fact is a fact because of things we do" (37).

53 Monique Wittig, *The Straight Mind* (Boston: Beacon Press, 1992).

54 Mikkola, "Ontological," 74.

55 Ibid., 68 for the relation between conventionalism and abolitionism.

56 Ibid., 69.

57 See Mikkola, "Feminist," for the "positive value" argument.

58 Katharine Jenkins, "Amelioration and Inclusion: Gender Identity and the Concept of *Woman*," *Ethics* 126, no. 2 (2016): 410.

59 Judith, Butler. *Gender Trouble: Feminism and the Subversion of Identity* (New York: Routledge, 1990).

60 See Mikkola, "Feminist."

61 Stephanie Julia Kapusta, "Contesting Gender Concepts, Language and Norms: Three Critical Articles on Ethical and Political Aspects of Gender Non-conformity" (PhD Diss. University of Western Ontario, 2015).

62 See Talia Bettcher, "Trans Identities and First-person Authority," in *You've Changed: Sex Reassignment and Personal Identity*, ed. Laurie Shrage (Oxford: Oxford University Press, 2009): 98–120.

63 Thanks to Stephanie Dover for this insight.

64 Following Kate Bornstein, Miqqi Alicia Gilbert in "Defeating Bigenderism: Changing Gender Assumptions in the Twenty-first Century," *Hypatia* 24, no. 3 (2009): 93–112, describes the folk gender system as the assumption that gender is binaric, immovable, genital-based, exclusive, and natural. Theodore Bach in "Gender Is a Natural Kind with a Historical Essence," *Ethics* 122, no. 2 (2012): 231–72, describes this gender system as based on biological reductionist assumptions that genitals make the gender, on "conceptual gender dualisms" (based on "stereotypes," "correspondence biases," and "injunctive gender norms"), "binary socialization practices," social and legal institutional segregation, and binary gender artifacts and social roles (247–48). While it is true that gender systems need not be binary, I would wager that any system organized around gender (be it binary, ternary, quaternary etc.) is constitutively oppressive.

65 On "strong pragmatic construction" see Haslanger, *Resisting*, 90.

66 See my "Categories We Die For: Ameliorating Gender in Analytic Feminist Philosophy," *PMLA* 131, no. 2 (2016): 449–59, where I explore error-theoretic and eliminativist views of gender.

67 See Jenkins, "What," 10.

Bibliography

Alenius, Marianne. "Women are Not Human Beings: Nordic Women's Literature": http://nordicwomensliterature.net/article/women-are-not-human-beings.

Ásta Sveinsdóttir. "The Social Construction of Human Kinds." *Hypatia* 28, no. 4 (2013): 716–32.

Ásta Sveinsdóttir. "Social Construction as Social Significance." Unpublished manuscript.

Austin, J. L. *How to Do Things with Words*. Oxford: Clarendon Press, 1962.

Bach, Theodore. "Gender Is a Natural Kind with a Historical Essence," *Ethics* 122, no. 2 (2012): 231–72.

Balibar, Etienne. "Citizen Subject." In *Who Comes After the Subject?*, edited by Eduardo Cadava, Peter Connor, and Jean-Luc Nancy, 13–57. New York: Routledge, 1991.
Beauvoir, Simone de. *Le deuxième sexe*. Paris: Éditions Gallimard, 1976.
Bettcher, Talia. "Trans Identities and First-person Authority." In *You've Changed: Sex Reassignment and Personal Identity*, edited by Laurie Shrage, 98–120. Oxford: Oxford University Press, 2009.
Butler, Judith. *Gender Trouble: Feminism and the Subversion of Identity*. New York: Routledge, 1990.
Butler, Judith. *Undoing Gender*. New York: Routledge, 2004.
Cohen, Marc. "Aristotle's Metaphysics." *The Stanford Encyclopedia of Philosophy* (Fall 2015 Edition), Edward N. Zalta (ed.), URL = http://plato.stanford.edu/archives/fall2015/entries/aristotle-metaphysics/.
Critchley, Simon. "Prolegomena to Any Post-Deconstructive Subjectivity." In *Deconstructive Subjectivities*, edited by Simon Critchley and Peter Dews, 13–45. New York: State University of New York Press, 1996.
Critchley, Simon. *Ethics, Politics, Subjectivity: Essays on Derrida, Levinas and Contemporary French Thought*. New York: Verso, 1999.
Derrida, Jacques. *L'Animal que donc je suis*. Paris: Galilée, 2006.
Derrida, Jacques. *Séminaire la bête et le souverain. Volume II (2002-2003)*. Paris: Galilée, 2010.
Deslauriers, Marguerite. "Marie de Gournay and Aristotle on the Unity of the Sexes." In *Feminist History of Philosophy: The Recovery and Evaluation of Women's Philosophical Thought*, edited by Eileen O'Neill and Macy P. Laseano. Dordrecht: Springer, forthcoming.
Fleischer, Manfred P. "'Are Women Human?'—The Debate of 1595 between Valens Acidalius and Simon Gediccus." *The Sixteenth Century Journal* 12, no. 2 (1981): 107–20.
Foucault, Michel. *Histoire de la sexualité. vol I: La Volonté de savoir*. Paris: Éditions Gallimard, 1976.
Gertler, Brie. "Can Feminists be Cartesians?" in *Dialogue* 41, no.1 (2002): 91–112.
Gilbert, Miqqi Alicia. "Defeating Bigenderism: Changing Gender Assumptions in the Twenty-first Century." *Hypatia* 24, no. 3 (2009): 95–111.
Gournay, Marie de. *Les avis, ou les Présens de la Demoiselle de Gournay*. Paris: s.n., 1641.
Gournay, Marie de. *Preface to the Essays of Montaigne*. Edited and Translated by Richard Hillman and Colette Quesnel. Tempe, AZ: Medieval and Renaissance Texts and Studies, 1998.
Gournay, Marie de. *Apology for the Woman Writing and Other Works*. Edited and Translated by Richard Hill and Colette Quesnel. Chicago: University of Chicago Press, 2002.
Haslanger, Sally. *Resisting Reality: Social Construction and Social Critique*. Oxford: Oxford University Press, 2012.
Hoffman, Joshua. "Neo-Aristotelianism and Substance." In *Contemporary Aristotelian Metaphysics*, edited by Tuomas E. Tahko, 140–55. Cambridge, UK: Cambridge University Press, 2009.

Jenkins, Katharine. "What Women Are For: Pornography and Social Ontology." In *Beyond Speech,* edited by Mari Mikkola. Oxford: Oxford University Press, forthcoming.

Jenkins, Katharine."Amelioration and Inclusion: Gender Identity and the Concept of *Woman*." *Ethics* 126, no. 2 (2016): 394–421.

Kapusta, Stephanie Julia. "Contesting Gender Concepts, Language and Norms: Three Critical Articles on Ethical and Political Aspects of Gender Non-conformity." PhD diss., University of Western Ontario, 2015.

Kelly, Joan. "Early Feminist Theory and the 'Querelle des Femmes,' 1400-1789." *Signs* 8, no. 1 (1982): 4–28.

Krier, Isabelle. "Souvenirs sceptiques de Marie de Gournay dans 'Égalité des hommes et des femmes.'" *Clio* 29 (2009): 243–57.

LaBrada, Eloy. "Categories We Die For: Ameliorating Gender in Analytic Feminist Philosophy." *PMLA* 131, no. 2 (2016): 449–59.

LaBrada, Eloy. "Unlivable Loves: Hélisenne, Nietzsche, and the Metaphysics of Love." *JNT: Journal of Narrative Theory* 46, no. 1 (2016): 1–38.

Langton, Rae. *Sexual Solipsism: Philosophical Essays on Pornography and Objectification.* Oxford: Oxford University Press, 2009.

Laqueur, Thomas. *Making Sex: Body and Gender from the Greeks to Freud.* Cambridge, MA: Harvard University Press, 1992.

Le Doeuff, Michèle. *Le sexe du savoir.* Paris: Éditions Aubier, 1998.

Mallon Ron. "Naturalistic Approaches to Social Construction." *The Stanford Encyclopedia of Philosophy* (Winter 2014 Edition), Edward N. Zalta (ed.), URL = http://plato.stanford.edu/archives/win2014/entries/social-construction-naturalistic/.

Manne, Kate. "Humanism: A Critique." *Social Theory and Practice* 42, no. 2 (2016): 389–415.

Mason, Rebecca. "Are Social Kinds Mind-Dependent?" Unpublished manuscript.

McGowan, Mary Kate. "On Pornography: MacKinnon, Speech Acts, and False' Construction." *Hypatia* 20, no. 3 (2005): 22–24.

McGrath, Sarah. "Relax! Don't Do It! Why Moral Realism Won't Come Cheap." In *Oxford Studies in Metaethics,* edited by Russ Shafer-Landau, 186–215. Oxford: Oxford University Press, 2014.

Mikkola, Mari. "Ontological Commitments, Sex and Gender." In *Feminist Metaphysics: Explorations in the Ontology of Sex, Gender and the Self,* edited by Charlotte Witt, 67–83. New York: Springer Verlag, 2011.

Mikkola, Mari. "Feminist Perspectives on Sex and Gender." *The Stanford Encyclopedia of Philosophy* (Spring 2016 Edition), Edward N. Zalta (ed.), forthcoming URL = http://plato.stanford.edu/archives/spr2016/entries/feminism-gender/.

Mills, Charles W. *The Racial Contract.* Ithaca and New York: Cornell University Press, 1997.

Montaigne, Michel de. *The Complete Essays.* Translated by M. A. Screech. New York: Penguin Classics.

Morison, Benjamin. "Sextus Empiricus." *The Stanford Encyclopedia of Philosophy* (Spring 2014 Edition), Edward N. Zalta (ed.), URL = http://plato.stanford.edu/archives/spr2014/entries/sextus-empiricus/.

Okin, Susan Moller. "Feminism, Women's Human Rights, and Cultural Differences." *Hypatia* 13, no. 2 (1998): 32–52.

O'Neill, Eileen. "Justifying the Inclusion of Women in Our Histories of Philosophy: The Case of Marie de Gournay." In *Guide to Feminist Philosophy*, edited by Linda Alcoff and Eva Kittay, 17–42. Oxford and Cambridge, MA: Blackweel: 2006.

Pasnau, Robert. "Snatching Hope from the Jaws of Epistemic Defeat." *Journal of the American Philosophical Association* 1, no. 2 (2015): 257–75.

Popkin, Richard. *The History of Scepticism: From Savonarola to Bayle*. Oxford: Oxford University Press, 2003.

Robinson, Howard. "Substance." *The Stanford Encyclopedia of Philosophy* (Spring 2014 Edition), Edward N. Zalta (ed.), URL = http://plato.stanford.edu/archives/spr2014/entries/substance/.

Wittig, Monique. *The Straight Mind and Other Essays*. Boston: Beacon Press, 1992.

PART TWO

CAUSALITIES

4 SHADOWS ON THE WALL OF REASON: DIDEROT BEFORE FRAGONARD

David Ferris

To claim agency is to claim reason or at least the possibility of reason in order to explain why an act has taken place. In this sense, agency is also a rationalization that permits the exercise of judgment by establishing and identifying a subject whose actions can be judged. The last of these categories does however pose an added dimension since the act of an author or artist is judged through works that do not themselves exist as actions but rather as objects even when as in the theater or film the work is performed through the portrayal of a group of agents and their actions. For the latter, action is the form in which these works are presented and, accordingly, both theater and film could be judged as more closely embodying the classical model of agency through which real actions and events are brought within the sphere that makes them susceptible to those rational categories in which the significance of the modern world is now invested (moral, ethical, political, and cultural or aesthetic).

Human agency as the decisive element shaping the modern world is a clear consequence of the turn within the Enlightenment to "the individual use of reason."[1] It is such an individual use that makes an act available for judgments about its meaning. Consequently, what is at stake in the formation of agency and its unquestioned acceptance is the ground on which the modern world validates its critical practices and the areas of knowledge that rely upon those practices. This narrative about agency is, however, not entirely consistent with its own time nor with the critical practice of one of the key exponents of the Enlightenment project and its reliance on critique. In 1765, Diderot published a review of the Salon of that year and included in this publication a short text that stands apart from the descriptive style or the quick judgments that characterizes many of the entries in the *Salon de 1765*.[2] This short text concerns a painting by Fragonard, *Corésus Sacrificing himself to save Callirhoé*, which earned the painter admission to the Académie des Beaux-Arts that year. The subject of this painting, as told by Pausanias, concerns a priest of Dionysus in the city of Calydon, Corésus, who falls in love with a maiden, Callirhoé, who has only hatred for him. Seeking to overcome her hatred, Corésus appeals to Dionysus. At the time of his appeal, Calydon is afflicted by plague and the oracle of Dionysus in response declares that Callirhoé or someone willing to take her place must die in order to bring the plague to an end. Since no one will take her place the scene is set for her sacrifice but at the decisive moment Corésus sacrifices himself with the dagger meant for Callirhoé.[3] This subject tells a story of agency: first, the priest acts as an agent of Dionysus as the one who fulfills the command of the oracle; second, Corésus refuses this instrumental act of agency and performs an individual act of agency by sacrificing himself. It is this individual act that Fragonard's painting focuses on exclusively. This focus points to the extent that this painting portrays an act that parallels the Enlightenment recourse to reason as the basis of establishing an individual as the agent responsible for shaping history and its narratives. At least this much can be said when the narrative that provides the events defining this painting is considered. But, there remains the painting as an object which means that the question of whether this medium and the demands it makes upon its observer confirms the model of agency that the intersection of Pausanias's narrative and its historical and intellectual context seems to permit so easily.

The painting itself is a rather singular work. Its style places it somewhere between the rococo style and the dominance of historical painting as the model of serious art in the eighteenth century. But more significantly its submission to the 1765 Salon at the Louvre secured Fragonard's admission to the academy as an historical painter even if he was never to paint in this genre again. *Corésus* is thus a unique work in Fragonard's oeuvre but it also has a uniqueness within its genre. Despite fulfilling the expectation of this genre—the portrayal of a decisive act, in this case, the sacrifice with which the narrative of Corésus and Callirhoé culminates—this painting also employs an overwrought theatricality which, as some critics have claimed, threatens to reduce the composition to the kind of amusing ingenuity that characterizes the rococo.[4] As a result, the manner of presentation of this painting appears to be at odds with its subject—hence the sense of a fault which easily leads to seeing this painting in the light of the less serious subjects and compositions that characterize Fragonard's subsequent work after 1765. But what is here seen as a fault resulting from an overly theatrical painting may be less a failure to fulfill the genre of historical painting than a realization that the subject depicted and the presentation of that subject, indicate a resistance to the "individual use of reason" as the decisive focus of Fragonard's painting.

Evidence of such a resistance emerges if due attention is given to an effect in Fragonard's painting that so dominates it that it threatens the historicity of the sacrificial moment in which the claim of this genre to define the seriousness of art has been so absorbingly concentrated. This effect emerges from the obscuring shadowy light, part smoke, part shadow, that rises from a brazier and which obscures most of the background while, in a forward billowing movement, threatening to envelop the sacrificial moment on which the light of day is alone allowed to fall. While it is tempting to read the encroachment of the obscuring shadow and smoke as one more theatrical effect in this painting, to do so, runs the risk of taking such theatricality at its face value (that it has no other function than to be theatrical) with the result that it is either a pole against which the enlightened historical moment stands in objective contrast (the theatrical in the service of the historical) or else its excessiveness infects that moment and exposes the historical in art as always having been a performative effect. Once the theatrical is confined to either one of these readings, it is effectively bracketed as if it were simply a failing on the part of the artist or else it is framed as a general condition arising from a conflict between a subject (historical) and a means (painting), namely, that the historical is undermined by its dependence on nonhistorical effects.

The significance of this theatricality is taken up by Diderot in the piece he wrote on Fragonard's *Corésus* for his review of the Salon of 1765. However, it is not addressed directly as if it were solely an aspect of Fragonard's composition in this painting. In fact, Diderot begins by claiming that he cannot address the painting at all—an immediate obscuring of agency. In a remark to Melchior Grimm, his editor, Diderot declares in the opening paragraph of his text: "My friend, it is impossible for me to discuss this painting with you; you know that it was no longer at the Salon when the general sensation it caused called me there" (*Salon 1765*, 141). The first consequence of this absence takes the form of an over-theatricalization of the act of beholding. Yet, this separation of the act of beholding from what is to be beheld does not prevent Diderot from writing about Fragonard's painting. As a result, the line of least resistance in dealing with this text is to go along with Diderot's editor, Melchior Grimm, who, in a remark included in Seznec's and Adhémar's edition of the *Salons*, suggests that such theatricalization is simply a deception.[5] The editors of the Hermann edition of Diderot's works, also eager to set the record straight, go along with Grimm's suggestion and announce that "Diderot feigns to regret not having seen this canvas."[6] Both remarks state the obvious, there can be no doubt that Diderot saw Fragonard's painting. In this context, Diderot's deception seems nothing more than a way of setting up a playful and theatricalized diversion, a variation from the general descriptive pattern of his remarks in the Salon reviews. Is this entry then simply an exception?[7]

Neither of the editorial remarks just cited addresses the question of why Diderot should make the claim that he has not seen Fragonard's painting in the first place, especially in a text intended to address this artist's work. Some sense that another intention than the merely playful is at work begins to emerge when Diderot adds a second layer of "feigning" to this piece on Fragonard. Addressing Grimm, Diderot writes: "It will be up to you to give an account of it; we'll discuss it together; and so much the better for perhaps we'll discover why, after a first round of tributes paid to the artist, after the first expressions of praise, the public seemed to cool towards it" (*Salon 1765*, 141). Like Diderot's failure to see the painting, this actual dialogue, and its displacement of responsibility for seeing the painting on to Grimm ("up to you to give an account of it") is also feigned. As Grimm confirms in a later remark, his words are not his own: "Until now, my dear philosopher, I have allowed you to speak and I have spoken as it pleased you."[8] From this it emerges that Diderot's feigning is not to be restricted to the occasion of his text on Fragonard but now extends to the dialogue that organizes the text he writes on Fragonard. This extension indicates a sustained intention according to which the presence of Fragonard's painting is twice made absent as if to underline that the claim that paintings are made to be beheld is not locatable or dependent on the beholder standing in front of a painting. As a result, the possibility of being beheld is not the condition that determines the beginning *and* end of the significance of a painting as art. By removing the painting as an object whose significance resides in its direct beholding, Diderot indicates that a painting's significance as art is not even the function of an implied beholder or indeed of an act of beholding. In this case, if Diderot's fiction is taken seriously (and his introduction of the founding scene of philosophy's account of visual images, Plato's allegory of the cave, indicates that it should be taken seriously) then, what Michael Fried claims to be "the one primitive condition of the art of painting—that its objects necessarily imply the presence before them of a beholder"[9] would then need to be re-read through this text and the scene of its opening dream.

While Fried has been resourceful in resisting Diderot's text and its narrativization of the question of agency (while insisting that Diderot's account clearly implies that the beholder is the fundamental problematic that defines the consequent development of modern art) it is by no means clear that this resourcefulness can fully account for the overdetermined theatrical strategies Diderot employs. These strategies already indicate that the purpose is less to give an account of Fragonard's painting in terms of a "primitive condition" than as an object separated from the act of an individual agent (or its inversion in a beholder). In this context, it should also be noted that it is precisely this kind of inversion that Diderot resists from the very beginning by invoking Plato's allegory of the cave in his dream. The kind of inversion at stake here is the one that Diderot's ventriloquization of his editor as interlocutor is fond of insisting on, namely that Diderot's not having seen the painting seems to allow him to describe it with the utmost accuracy—an inversion that strains the distancing and difference that Diderot establishes as the condition of addressing painting. When Grimm remarks that the scene Diderot has dreamed is exactly what Fragonard has painted, Diderot merely responds, "that may be [cela se peut]" (*Salon 1765*, 14: 238). Along the same lines, at the end of dialogue between Diderot and Grimm, it is the latter who, speaking in the words Diderot has given him, expresses a preference for Diderot's "painting" over that of Fragonard. These two moments imply that the equivalence between two fictions or theatricalizations (a resource emphasized by Fried in his account of agency of the beholder in defining the problematic of art) may be the crucial fiction against which Diderot's text on Fragonard is directed rather than the affirmation of that equivalence.[10]

As noted above, accepting Diderot's claim as a deception has the direct effect of making this painting readable—as if what can be read is the same as what can be seen when we or Diderot stand before this or another canvas. But can we really accept this easy relation between seeing and reading when such a relation is explicitly cited in this text as producing the dream that takes the place of Fragonard's painting? Not only does the displacement of the observer into a cave reenact the scene of its most enduring and foundational example, Plato's allegory of the cave, but in Diderot's case the possibility of "seeing" Fragonard's painting arises from a scene of reading within his dream. The relation of seeing to reading in which this text originates is described by Diderot as follows:

> Mais pour remplir cet article Fragonard, je vais vous faire part d'une vision assez étrange dont je fus tourmenté la nuit qui suivit un jour dont j'avais passé la matinée à voir des tableaux et la soirée à lire quelques *Dialogues de Platon*.
>
> (*Salon 1765*, 14: 253)
>
> [But to fill out this article on Fragonard, I'm going to tell you about a quite strange vision which tormented me the night after I had spent a morning looking at some paintings and an evening reading some *Dialogues of Plato*.]

The vision is offered as a means of filling up, *remplir*, the empty place left by the failure to see Fragonard's painting but also for an emptiness that recalls the public's coolness to this painting after its initial enthusiasm. But, in Diderot's own words, the vision that will take the place of this painting was a source of torment arising from the combination of two activities: looking and reading. But, why should this combination of looking and reading be such a torment? And why should such a torment take precedence over beholding and the critical agency it enables?

The generalized source of this torment—it arises from looking at paintings in general ("*des tableaux*"), not a particular canvas—indicates the presence of a more general issue in painting than the merit or judgment of a single canvas and all that implies as a judgment of agency represented in such work. But this is only half of the story of this dream. Another cause is called upon to explain its occurrence: Plato's allegory of the cave. Thus, what leads to this dream as a source of torment arises from the intertwining of two causes: the condition of beholding in general and a particular account of beholding. But, also behind these two causes, there lies a third, the failure to have seen Fragonard's painting, a failure that creates the place for this dream in which looking and reading are merged. The dream, in this case, is what comes before Fragonard, an aspect that Diderot underlines when he refers to how, together, they fill out "cet article Fragonard." With this word, *article*, Diderot indicates that what fills up this space is both a writing, "un article" in the sense of "un écrit" but also a writing that also precedes what it names, "un article" in the sense of what precedes a noun.[11] This latter sense also indicates that what is referred to as Fragonard—the title of Diderot's review—may also have to be understood as such an article, so that Fragonard (the name) comes to precede what it names, becomes the word in which the presence of something not yet seen is reflected. The question this displacement of Fragonard poses is the central question of a text whose subject is unavoidably art: the question of how not seeing painting belongs to the experience of a painting. What this text presents as a result of not seeing Fragonard's painting is a dream that takes over the entry on Fragonard and to such an extent that Diderot names everything written from this point on under the title of "The Cave of Plato." The visibility by which painting is identified would itself recede with this result if it did not return in the shadow emphasized by the setting of the dream.

This emphasis recalls not just Plato's allegory of knowledge and understanding but also the story of the origin of art in shadow, the story of the Corinthian Maid told by Pliny.[12] In both cases, Pliny's and Plato's, the story of the shadow is located in a place of darkness. Diderot's own story of the events leading to his dream repeats this setting. Diderot moves from the daylight of the morning when paintings are seen, to the light of evening when Plato is read, and, finally, to the darkness of night when seeing and reading become a torment in the form of a dream. The movement enacted by Diderot is toward a time which denies natural light its role as the source of visual art as well as the source of any reflection on and by this art—quite the opposite of the movement enacted by Plato's allegory which makes a journey to the natural light of the sun the basis for understanding all reflection. What Diderot's movement indicates is that Plato's allegory is less the frame for Diderot's dream than a frame that also has to be read as something reflected upon within this text. Moreover, Diderot's choice that this reflection should occur at night confirms that what is under consideration in this text is not art as a reflection of natural light—that is the task of nature. Rather, as the related story of the Corinthian Maid points out, what is under consideration in

Diderot's text is art as the reflection of a shadow but a shadow confined by a scene that refuses external, natural light, in effect, a scene akin to the time of night. This is precisely the story told by Pliny as the origin of painting, a story that still had currency in the late eighteenth century and was the subject of at least two paintings: David Allan's *Origin of Painting (The Maid of Corinth)* of 1775 and Joseph Wright's *Corinthian Maid* of 1783–84] (in Pliny's account, it is not natural light that gives rise to art but the projection of a shadow cast by a candle against the wall of an interior room). It is also precisely the location in which Diderot places the sequence of scenes that provide the history of Fragonard's painting, in effect, the origin of Fragonard's painting.

The setting of the Platonic allegory of the cave thus has a role to play in Diderot's text other than a mere backdrop suggested by the evening's reading. Diderot makes it clear that what is intended is not a simple return to Plato's cave—as if we should expect a repetition of Plato's allegory whereby Diderot will lead us, like Plato, out of the darkness of the cave and toward an art reflected in the enlightenment of reason. Instead of returning to Plato's cave we remain in its semblance. Diderot writes, "Il me sembla que j'étais renfermé dans le lieu qu'on appelle l'antre de ce philosophe" [It seemed to me that I was confined in the place called the cave of this philosopher] (*Salon 1765*, 14: 253). Plato's cave returns as a shadow of itself, it returns in its semblance. To what purpose is this semblance and why should it torment if it is only a semblance?

What Diderot presents in the semblance of Plato's cave only reenacts the beginning of Plato's allegory: the initial display of shadow figures to those chained in their places. We are presented with the kind of puppet show Plato also presents, except in this case, it leads into a series of scenes which Diderot describes as "des scènes si naturelles, si vraies, que nous les prenions pour réelles" [scenes so natural, so true, that we took them to be real] (*Salon 1765*, 14: 254). As in Plato, the spectators in chains have no sense that what they see is anything other than what is truly there. Only with hindsight, and from the position of writing this review of Fragonard, that is, from afterward rather than before can Diderot reveal that what was seen is a performance of shadows: "Ces charlatans, comme je le vis ensuite, placés entre nous et l'entrée de la caverne, avaient par derrière eux une grande lampe suspendue, à la lumière de laquelle ils exposaient leurs petites figures dont les ombres portées par-dessus nos têtes et s'agrandissant en chemin allaient s'arrêter sur la toile tendue au fond de la caverne" [These charlatans, as I saw afterward, placed between us and the entrance to the cave, had suspended behind them a large lamp in whose light they exposed their small figures whose shadows carried over our heads and, enlarged along the way, came to a halt on the canvas stretched at the back of the cave] (*Salon 1765*, 14: 254). "Comme je le vis ensuite." To know that what is projected is no more than a shadow does not require a journey to the outside of this cave. It is simply a matter of seeing, of seeing afterward "comme je le vis ensuite" what could not be seen before, namely, the means by which a scene, taken to be "so natural, so real," is presented. This is not at all the case in Plato; it is not enough to see the fire that provides the light to cast the shadows in the cave. This fire must also be understood as an image for the natural source of light, the sun. This sun, in its naturalness, that is, in its refusal to be anything else than the sun, then stands as the source of every means by which the world is seen, both literally in the case of light, but also metaphorically, in the sense of understanding and enlightenment. Such, at least, is the allegorical reading of Plato's cave.

In contrast to Plato, Diderot does not entertain an allegory that constantly reveals something "truer" (*alêthestera*) by progressing toward an increasingly brighter outside. What is revealed is that the scenes taken to be natural and so true are not simply a deception. They can only be a deception if a comparison to something truer and more real is made. Within the confines of this cave that knows no natural light—and which occupies the place of art in Diderot's text—no such comparison is made. The natural plays no part, what is seen is the means by which art is revealed as art. And, it is not a question of an art that appears as something else—as if we are meant to judge what Diderot says by leaving the cave of his recalled vision and comparing this vision to the actual painting (that, as we shall see, is already enacted within this text and within Diderot's narrative of his dream).

Despite the fact no journey to a source of light takes place in Diderot's dream, this does not mean that Diderot avoids a journey within his account of such a cave. In Diderot's case, the journey is enacted completely through the shadows projected onto the canvas at the back of the cave. These shadows, and Diderot is explicit here, belong to the realm of art. What is seen as shadow is also painting. Diderot writes: "Aujourd'hui qu'il s'agit de tableaux, j'aime meiux vous en décrire quelques-un de ceux que je vis sur la grande toile; je vous jure qu'ils valaient bien les meilleurs du Salon" (*Salon 1765*, 14: 255) [Today since it is a question of paintings, I prefer to describe several of those I saw in the large canvas;

I swear to you they were worth as much as the best in the Salon]. To see painting as shadow is unavoidable here since what is in the Salon is strictly comparable to what Diderot sees in his dream.

To speak of the shadows in the cave is, then, for Diderot, to speak of not only the Salon, but, in the narrative that follows, it is also to present one of the Salon's most highly acclaimed paintings as a painting that exists as such a shadow. This shadowy aspect is taken up in the scenes subsequently played on the canvas in Diderot's cave, scenes that begin to tell the story of Corésus and Callirhoé. After recounting the first of these scenes (in which a young priest of Dionysus drinks with a group of women and then runs through the streets) Diderot turns to Grimm, whose fictional presence as interlocutor allows Diderot to recount his vision. Diderot asks Grimm for his opinion of what has been projected on to the canvas in the cave. Grimm's response emphasizes the position and perspective of a painter when he declares that what Diderot has described are really "deux assez beaux tableaux, à peu près du même genre" [two rather beautiful pictures, more or less of the same genre] (*Salon* 1765, 14: 256). Grimm's reply betrays the position of historical painting while pointing to the temporal problem posed by Diderot's narrative. This problem of representing what Diderot has seen escalates as Grimm responds to Diderot's subsequent description of a scene in which a young woman refuses the entreaties of the young priest presented in the first scenes. Grimm comments: "Celui-ci pour n'avoir que deux figures, n'en serait pas plus facile à faire" [Though this one has only two figures, that wouldn't be any easier to execute] (*Salon* 1765, 14: 256). Diderot then responds: "Surtout s'il s'agissait de leur donner l'expression forte et le caractère peu commun qu'elles avaient sur la toile de la caverne" [Especially if it is a matter of giving them the strong expression and the unusual character they had on the canvas in the cave] (*Salon* 1765, 14: 256). In this response to Grimm's remark, Diderot calls attention to the difficulty of realizing his vision as a painting. This vision, so often read as it were a reflection of Fragonard's painting, becomes at this moment a vision whose difficulty is precisely the difficulty of realizing it in the medium that it is supposed to be derived from. Clearly, to reconstitute Fragonard's painting is not Diderot's point here as his final words on the scene just described make clear. He concludes this scene by referring to it as "un spectacle de joie extravagante, de licence effrénée, d'une ivresse et d'une fureur inconcevable" [a spectacle of extravagant joy, of unbridled license, of a fury and intoxication that were inconceivable] (*Salon 1765*, 14: 256–57), before breaking off with the word "inconcevable" and uttering the exclamation: "Ah! si j'étais peintre!"

Si j'étais peintre. With these words, Diderot insists that what he has seen in the cave will not become a painting, at least not in his hands. Grimm's responses confirm this. First, when he comments on the spectacle Diderot has just described: "Je connais un peu nos artistes, et je vous jure qu'il n'y en a pas un seul en état d'ébaucher" [I know our artists a little, and I swear to you there isn't a single artist who would be capable of sketching such a picture] (*Salon 1765*, 14: 257). The second occurs immediately after Diderot relates the event that leads to the crucial moment in the story of Corésus and Callirhoé, the voice that announces an imperative from behind the canvas: "Qu'elle meure, ou qu'un autre meure pour elle" [Let her die or let another die for her]. After hearing the chain of events leading up to this moment, Grimm announces that "du train dont vous rêvez, savez-vous qu'un seul de vos rêves suffirait pour une galerie entière?" [the sequence you are dreaming of, do you know that a single one of your dreams would fill an entire gallery?] (*Salon 1765*, 14: 257).

Diderot's account of his vision, in which the narrative history of Corésus and Callirhoé is given, does not yield a painting, but, if it did, and Grimm is the only who conceives of it in this way, an entire gallery of paintings would be needed. The inappropriateness of Grimm's remark is emphasized by Diderot's reply, which again insists on the importance of the temporal while indicating that Grimm has not understood. Diderot replies: "Attendez, attendez, vous n'y êtes pas" [Wait, wait, you don't get it] (*Salon 1765*, 14: 257). Grimm's translation of Diderot's narrative has missed the point by curtailing it in such a summary fashion. What Diderot has to say takes time and Grimm must wait for this time— "Attendez, attendez." But this is not Grimm's only mistake. He translates Diderot's narrative into an entire gallery of paintings as if the question of transforming Diderot's dream into a painting had not only been solved but could be solved in its entirety by a gallery. The conflict between the temporality of history and narrative on the one hand, and, on the other, the spatial world of painting could not be presented more graphically. History, as this conflict shows, does not take place in painting. To expose this conflict hardly seems to be Diderot's sole intention here. Indeed, if Diderot's sole intention in writing about Fragonard in the form of a dream were to underline an incompatibility between the temporality of narrative and the spatiality of painting, there would be no need to set this account of Fragonard's painting in Plato's cave or even for Diderot to claim that he has never seen Fragonard's painting. Reference to Pausanias's account of the history of Corésus and Callirhoé from the *Descriptions of Greece* would have been all that was necessary to have underlined this difference. The question is rather, why does Diderot introduce the question of representing a narrative in painting in a text that turns the source of Fragonard's painting into the effect of shadows that resist their embodiment in painting? A question that goes to the source of historical painting: the question of how to reflect the past in its shadow, the question posed by this genre, and a question that a recourse to agency, critical or painterly, does not entertain.

As we already know from the introduction to this entry on Fragonard, the narrative Diderot describes in his vision takes the place of the unseen canvas of Fragonard. Plato's cave, in this sense, becomes the setting for the narrative that provides the origin as well as the meaning of the event depicted in Fragonard's painting: the event of sacrifice required by the imperative that Callirhoé must die or else someone must die in her place if the epidemic afflicting the town is to be lifted. Diderot recalls us to this setting in the scene he describes immediately after telling Grimm that he does not get it and must wait. The scene is the temple where the sacrifice is to take place, yet, Diderot, after describing this scene, will not call it a temple. Diderot writes: "Voilà le théâtre d'une des plus terribles et des plus touchantes représentations qui se soient exécutées sur la toile de la caverne pendant ma vision" [There you have the theater of one of the most terrible and most touching representations which were executed on the canvas of the cave during my vision] (*Salon 1765*, 14: 258). The place of sacrifice becomes comparable to a theater as Diderot displaces the setting into the scene presented within the cave, thereby confirming the extent to which this whole dream and its setting cannot be distinguished from the images seen on the screen in the cave. Grimm, again, does not understand what Diderot has just done. Grimm understands Diderot's words as referring only to a temple and, above all, to the temple of Fragonard's painting: "le temple que vous veniez de décrire est exactement le lieu de la scène du tableau de Fragonard" [the temple you have just described is exactly the place of the scene in Fragonard's picture] (*Salon 1765*, 14: 258). Grimm, at this point, ignores Diderot's displacement and, in its place, preserves an exact correspondence between the two temples. For Grimm, the understanding at stake in this correspondence is mimetic. For Diderot, if his mimetic relation is to be sustained, it is because of Grimm's misreading of his theater as a temple, a misreading that asserts the primacy of Fragonard's painting in deciding between what a temple is and what a theater is. For Diderot this correspondence is the result of a theatrical effect, the effect of a cave in which shadows have taken on the aspect of "a terrible and touching representation." But where Grimm sees a mimetic correspondence, Diderot simply comments: "Cela se peut" [That could be] (*Salon 1765*, 14: 258). After all, how could Diderot know if he never saw the painting that Grimm proclaims to be identical to the scenes presented in the cave of Diderot's vision? Any deliberate similarity is refused. Diderot even goes so far as to explain it away by remarking that the coincidence may have resulted from him having heard so much talk about this painting. And, as he adds, since his dream obliged him to make up a temple, he has made up Fragonard's.

Diderot's refusal to allow his vision to be derived from Fragonard's painting produces two effects here. First, his own writing on Fragonard, and therefore on art, resists mimeticism as a basis for judging what is produced in the name of art: what Diderot writes about Fragonard is explicitly presented as not being derived from his painting—both in the claim that he has not seen the painting and in his refusal to give any priority to either his vision or Fragonard's painting. Second, the relation between Diderot's dream and what is produced as historical art, in this case Fragonard's painting, can only occur in the form of a theatrical effect, the effect of a representation.

Grimm's two subsequent interventions confirm the operation of this effect as well as the lengths to which representation will go in order to protect itself. The first occurs after Diderot describes the attitude and the positioning of the people within the temple of his vision and then remarks that from his position in the cave he was unable to see anything more. Diderot ascribes this inability to the position he occupied. Grimm explains, in response, that Diderot could see nothing more because there was nothing more to see. For Grimm, what Diderot sees in his vision is all there is to see ("C'est qu'il n'y avait rien de plus à voir, que ce sont là tous les personnages du tableau de Fragonard et qu'ils se sont trouvés dans votre rêve placés juste comme sur sa toile" [That's because there was nothing more to see, because these are all the figures in Fragonard's picture and because they can be found in your dream positioned exactly as on his canvas] (*Salon 1765*, 14: 260). Here the coincidence between Diderot's visions and Fragonard's painting is made by reference to the point at which nothing more can be seen. For one or the other to see more is to see a difference that would destroy the coincidence this text turns upon and insists on maintaining even to the point where sight fails, to the point where nothing can be seen, to the end of a painting if not to the end of painting itself. Lacking a difference to distinguish the vision of the cave from Fragonard's painting, the similarity of one to the other is only confirmed by the congruence of what Diderot cannot see and what is not present in the painting. These two are, however, only equivalent in their effects not in their causes. Diderot cannot see if there is anything more to see. Grimm states categorically that he can see that there is nothing more to see. The similarity of the painting to Diderot's vision becomes in this case a matter of giving interpretive priority to the painting by claiming that the effect of what cannot be seen is the same as an inability to see. Here, Grimm is made to judge the vision in terms of the painting. Diderot, however, immediately reverses this judgment when, in his reply to Grimm's claim that his vision and the painting contain the exact same figures in the exact same positions, he proclaims: "Si cela est, ô le beau tableau que Fragonard a fait!" [If that is the case, what a beautiful painting Fragonard has made!] (*Salon 1765*, 14: 260). If the forced assonance of this apostrophe is not enough of a clue, then a judgment of beauty derived from a vision of shadows, not to mention a hypothetical analogy, indicates more forcefully that Diderot's interest in this text is not at all the interest of his interlocutor, who only attempts to see what the shadows are shadows of. Within the terms of their exchange, it is only if the analogy, which is based on a negative point of reference (where there is nothing to see) is taken to be true, that Fragonard's painting can be judged beautiful, and only then because of Diderot's dream. In this case, the shadow theater of Diderot's dream becomes the source of a judgment. But all this depends on Diderot's "if," on the "if" that arises precisely because there is a difference between what Diderot cannot see and what Grimm says is not there. Grimm, by asserting an equivalence between the painting and Diderot's dream, attempts to dissolve this questionable analogy that the painting of Fragonard becomes an interpretation of Diderot's dream—interpretation in the sense that the exact resemblance explains why Diderot could ever have had such a dream: for Grimm, the dream is only understandable as the imitation of Fragonard. By resisting this interpretation, through an emphasis on the "if" (*Si cela est*) and through the structuring of this text around a dream that takes the place of Fragonard's painting, Diderot underlines that the reference point for this text is not at all Fragonard's painting—that is merely the form in which the subject of this text has been given.

This point emerges with greater clarity as Diderot gives the last of his descriptions of what he saw in the cave of Plato. Again, as Grimm informs us, this last scene reinforces his sense that Diderot's dream and Fragonard's picture are one and the same except, in this case, the emphasis of the comparison shifts from what is presented in the painting to the way in which this presentation occurs. The last scene described by Diderot recounts the moment in which Corésus turns the dagger away from its intended victim, Callirhoé, and turns it upon himself. Diderot's remarks focus on the reactions to this act. One of these is singled out: the response of a gray-haired old man. Diderot writes:

> rien n'égale la consternation et la douleur du veillard aux cheveux gris, ses cheveux se sont dressés sur son front, je crois le voir encore, la lumière du brasier ardent l'éclairant, et ses bras étendus au-dessus de l'autel: je vois ses yeux, je vois sa bouche, je le vois s'élancer, j'entends ses cris, ils me réveillent, la toile se replie et la caverne disparaît
>
> (*Salon 1765*, 14: 261)
>
> [nothing equals the astonishment and pain of an old man with gray hair, his hair standing on end, I think I see him still, the light from a blazing brazier illuminated him, his arms stretched out over the altar: I see his eyes, I see his mouth, I see him lurch forward, I hear his cries, they awaken me, the canvas withdraws and the cave disappears].

The dream ends with a figure that knows no equal in a text, on whose behalf Grimm has not ceased to assert an equal. Moreover, the dream comes to an end by turning to a reflection of its crucial event rather than the occurrence of that event: the sacrifice of Corésus. Why, we might ask, does Diderot do this? Why does Diderot end the dream with a reflection that knows no equal? And, why does Diderot choose to mark its end with the cry of this old man rather than a recovery of equivalence between the act depicted in the painting and the act of its painting by Fragonard?

The cry of the old man precipitates two events: the withdrawal or folding into itself of the screen on which the shadows of his vision are seen, and the disappearance of the cave. The word used for screen here—and this is consistent throughout this text—is *toile*, the same word used to denote the canvas of a painting. It is thus with the disappearance of the very thing on which painting presents its scenes that Diderot's dream and its vision come to end. Grimm, always on the lookout for appropriate analogies, equates this disappearance with the effect of Fragonard's painting. He proclaims: "Voilà le tableau de Fragonard, le voilà avec tout son effet" [That's Fragonard's painting, that's it with all its effect] (*Salon 1765*, 14: 262). In the words Diderot gives to Grimm the defining pronouncement occurs in the form of an inversion: the opening "Voilà le . . ." becomes "le voilà . . .," an inversion that tries one more time to confirm the presence of Fragonard's painting in Diderot's dream. That Diderot should make Grimm respond in this way, at this point, signals the device that has already been at work in Grimm's understanding. This now surfaces as the organizing figure for their dialogue. Its most obvious first appearance occurs in the reversal of their roles. Where Diderot had previously described his dream and Grimm had compared it to Fragonard's painting, Grimm now describes this painting and Diderot compares it to his dream. That Diderot recognizes the force of this inversion without acceding to it can be read in his abrupt two-word response to Grimm's last assertion of the exactness of the match between the dream and Fragonard's painting. Diderot, unable to judge what Grimm proclaims, can only ask, "En vérité?" Grimm's answer to Diderot's question about the truth of this correspondence, that is, Grimm's attempt to tell the truth, to tell the truth of what transpired in Plato's cave and thereby know a truth behind its shadows can only offer in the place of this truth the play of light he had perceived within Fragonard's painting. As in the cave of Diderot's dream it is play put on by light, the play of the shadow that will go before not just Fragonard but also the truth of Diderot's dream. This is why Diderot makes Grimm reveal the light that is to establish that what Diderot's shadows represent is an effect of these same shadows, a revelation that occurs at the moment Grimm is set to confirm the definitive force of his words: "Voilà le tableau de Fragonard, le voilà avec tout son effet." In the following passage, Grimm's words reflect this effect:

> Dans la caverne, vous n'avez vu que les simulacres des êtres, et Fragonard sur sa toile ne vous en aurait montré non plus que les simulacres. C'est un beau rêve que vous avez fait, c'est un beau rêve qu'il a peint. Quand on perd son tableau de vue pour un moment, on craint toujours que sa toile ne se replie comme la vôtre, et que ces fantômes intéressants et sublimes ne se soient évanouis comme ceux de la nuit. Si vous aviez vu son tableau, vous auriez été frappé de la même magie de lumière et de

la manière dont les ténèbres se fondaient avec elle, du lugubre que ce mélange portait dans tous les points de sa composition.

(*Salon 1765*, 14: 262)

[In the cave you saw only the simulacra of what exists, and Fragonard, on his canvas too, would have shown you nothing more than simulacra. You had a beautiful dream, and a beautiful dream is what he has painted. When one momentarily loses sight of his picture, one fears his canvas might withdraw into itself (*se replie*) like yours and that these sublime and fascinating phantoms might vanish like those of the night. If you had seen his painting you would have been struck by the same magical light and the manner in which the darkness blended with it, by the gloominess that this mixture brought to every point of its composition.]

What Diderot makes Grimm reflect is that, in order to sustain the analogy at the heart of his understanding he is forced to compare simulacra. Their positions can be reversed because both have only produced appearances. Only as simulacra do they lack comparisons to anything else. And so emphatic is Grimm that this is the basis of their analogy that we are left to wonder if Fragonard must not also have dreamed Diderot's dream in order to have painted what he painted. After all, Diderot does make Grimm say: "C'est un beau rêve que vous avez fait, c'est un beau rêve qu'il a peint." In Grimm's eyes, Diderot has dreamed art, and Fragonard's art has produced a dream. Their inversion demands this equality. But, the moment that sets the scene for this inversion does not belong to the visual aspect Grimm has emphasized, rather it belongs to a moment Diderot describes as having no equal. It is not Diderot, however, who will guide us this moment but rather a Grimm who has exchanged positions with Diderot.

In order to convey Fragonard's painting in terms of simulacra, Grimm characterizes the play of light on this canvas as "échos se jouant supérieurement entre les figures" [echoes playing superlatively among the figures] (*Salon 1765*, 14: 262). By referring to light as an echo, by seeing the visible in terms of the audible, Grimm incorporates sound as a figure of interrelation into the scene Diderot has just described. In Diderot's description of this same scene, however, sound intrudes upon the dream causing both the medium (light and the canvas screen) and the setting of this visual display (the cave) to disappear (and thereby establishing the inversion of their positions). In contrast, Grimm's figuration of light as an echo regards sound as a medium for understanding the visual, as a medium in which light can be reflected.[13] What is at stake in Grimm's figuration is not just a description of the painting but description itself, the ability to figure painting in sound, in short, the ability to speak about painting, to speak on behalf of painting, and therefore on behalf of light when one is, spatially speaking, before a painting. In short, an equality of the pictorial and the medium of the verbal—nothing less than the possibility of *ekphrasis*.

Even before Grimm can embark on this echoing of mediums, the end of Diderot's dream questions this figuration of sight as sound, not just in the cry that brings his vision to an end but already in the entirety of the final scene he describes. For the cry Diderot singles out as awakening him from his dream belongs in fact to a more general cry, the cry that arises after Corésus turns the imperative of the oracle against himself. Diderot refers to this cry as follows: "un cri général perce et déchire l'air" [a general cry pierces and rents the air] (*Salon 1765*, 14: 261). In the sound of this cry Diderot reflects the sacrifice of Corésus and, with this sound, every figure in Diderot's vision responds to what has just been seen. Diderot also tells us that this sound pierces and tears or rents the air. In effect, this sound pierces and tears the very medium through which sight and painting is given. And this is also the same cry that brings the visual display within the cave to an end.

In Diderot's account, our attention is no longer fixed on the dagger planted in the breast of Corésus but on the reflection of this event in and on those who see it. This reflection is given in a sequence that twice repeats a movement from the look to the attitude of the bodies of the figures present, then comes to rest in the cry of the old man. The movement occurs as follows: Diderot, after recording the cry and the onset of death in Corésus, points to two acolytes who each "regarde avec effroi" [look on with terror] (*Salon 1765*, 14: 261). It is not what they see but the way in which they see that is important here as our attention is directed to see in their eyes what they have seen. The reflection of this terror then passes to the face and arms of another; then back to the equally frightened look (*regard*) of two aged priests; then to a woman who turns away quickly, averting her gaze from the event at the center of this scene, an act that denies to sight the reason for her response; then to a woman who as she leans backward, "une de ses mains s'est portée sur ses yeux, et son autre bras semble repousser d'elle le spectacle effrayant" [one of her hands is placed over her eyes, and her other arm seems to push away from her the terrifying spectacle] (*Salon 1765*, 14: 261). In these descriptions, there is a twice-repeated movement from the eye to the body as a means of reflection. In the second occurrence of this movement, the body becomes a means of reflection to which sight is explicitly denied—precisely the situation that Diderot established for his own reflection on Fragonard. What the reflection present in this movement makes explicit is what has been denied to sight from the beginning of Diderot's description of these figures. We are not meant to see what the acolytes and the two aged priests have seen, rather, we are to see in their look the effect we would have felt if we had seen the moment in which Corésus turns the imperative of the oracle against himself, in effect, inverts his role as sacrificer into sacrifice. Diderot's narrative account makes this effect unavoidable. What there is to see or rather what there was to see, has already disappeared from sight in the moment of its reflection—just like the canvas in the Salon disappears in the reflection of Diderot. The emphasis given to the last two figures who avert or hide their eyes makes this relation to Corésus's act of inversion impossible to ignore. Consequently, in order to see the meaning of this event, the sacrifice, to see its meaning as sacrifice, we look to the reflection that no longer sees the event (that caused this reflection) but rather, only registers it in the transformation of an echo.

As the order in which Diderot presents these figures indicates, sight and reflection are not one and the same even when the eye is the means of reflection. Here, the general cry that pierces and rents the air reveals the destructive aspect that Diderot will figure in the folding of the canvas and the disappearance of the cave. In its reflection, the event that is the source of both this general cry as well as the look of the acolytes, the two aged priests and the two women who no longer look on this event—in this reflection the event of an inversion has already disappeared. Diderot's description reinforces this. Barely six words are given to the event itself: "il s'en frappe lui-même" [he strikes in striking himself]. It is the inevitable role of such reflection in establishing the event that is at the center of this history that is most under scrutiny in a text that has already refused to admit any sight of the event that provides it with a subject: the event embodied in the act of looking at Fragonard's painting of Corésus and Callirhoé, the event from which Diderot's eye is averted from the very beginning.

In Diderot's dream, the effect of this reflection is to cause the disappearance of what is being reflected: the story of Corésus and Callirhoé. This conclusion occurs when sound and eyes come together in the old man with gray hair who precipitates the withdrawal of the *toile*, the surface on which the art of painting has been set in this text. What sound does at this moment is not opposed to what the eye does. This one moment, which Diderot tells us is equaled by nothing else, inverts the sequence Diderot has already presented, the sequence that moves from the general cry to the eye and then to the body: "je vois ses yeux, je vois sa bouche, je le vois s'élancer, j'entends ses cris, ils me réveillent, la toile se replie et la caverne disparaît" [I see his eyes, I see his mouth, I see him throw himself forward, I hear the cries, they awaken me, the curtain pulls back and the cave disappears] (*Salon 1765*, 14: 261). The moment that nothing else equals is the moment in which we are led back to the sound of the cry in which the self-immolation of Corésus is recorded, the same sound that takes away the canvas that Grimm proclaims to be an exact resemblance of Fragonard's painting. Grimm's ability to maintain this resemblance, as we have seen reflected in Diderot's text, depends on re-establishing sound as a medium for sight over and against sound as what causes the loss of sight. But, for Diderot, this transfer of sight to sound produces the loss of sight, a loss that takes the form of confirming the phantasmal appearances seen in the cave. It is to this phantasm that Grimm insists on giving existence by his continual assertion that what Diderot is describing is the painting by Fragonard. Diderot at no point confirms this actually exists. This assertion also makes the shadows in Diderot's Platonic cave understandable by reference to something that is more real—precisely what Plato's own allegory sets out to achieve. The price Grimm pays for this insistence is the price Diderot enacts in the final scene of his dream: the disappearance of the canvas immediately prior to Grimm's pronouncement "Voilà le tableau de Fragonard"—the pronouncement in which we were to see the dream of Diderot reflected in the painting exhibited by Fragonard. The moment this reflection attains such a definite and unambiguous form in Diderot's text is the moment that there is nothing more to reflect. In their disappearance, the apparitions, the shadows are preserved as exactly that. They withdraw with the canvas. Here, the reflexive verb used by Diderot, *se replier*, is important. The canvas does not fold something else into itself as it withdraws, something more real to which it would always point and against which it would always be known as its reflection. Diderot's canvas simply folds or withdraws into itself. It is this withdrawal that Grimm fears. His response to the disappearance that marks the end of Diderot's dream, already cited above, makes this clear. Recall how Grimm describes the effect of Fragonard's actual painting: "quand on perd son tableau de vue pour un moment, on craint toujours que sa toile ne se replie comme la vôtre" [when one momentarily loses sight of his painting, one is always afraid that his canvas might withdraw into itself like yours] (*Salon 1765*, 14: 262). To counter this fear, Grimm will try to fix the place of what Diderot saw. Thus, the old man whose cry precipitates the disappearance of the cave and the folding of the canvas in Diderot's dream takes on a different role in Grimm's account of Fragonard's painting. Grimm states: "Ce veillard dont les cris perçants vous ont réveillée, il y était au même endroit et tel que vous l'avez vu" [This old man whose piercing cries awakened you, he was there in the same place and just as you saw him] (*Salon 1765*, 14: 262). Grimm's remark establishes the painting as the reference of what Diderot dreamed so that this dream will no longer simply disappear but will always be recoverable as a reflection of the painting. The effect of this recovery will be to return Diderot's dream to a simple but playful commentary on Fragonard's canvas, a dream that could only have been dreamed because of Fragonard's painting, a dream that could only have come after Fragonard. But, despite the overwhelming evidence of Grimm's description of the figures, their position, their coloring, and the effect of light in Fragonard's painting, Diderot's response still resists this recovery even at the most climactic moment of correspondence:

> Ce que vous me dites me ferait presque croire que moi qui n'y crois pas pendant le jour, je suis en commerce avec lui pendant la nuit. Mais l'instant effroyable de mon rêve, celui où le sacrificateur s'enfonce le poignard dans le sein, est donc celui que Fragonard a choisi?
> (*Salon 1765*, 14: 263)

> [What you tell me would almost make me believe that I, who does not believe this during the day, am in communication with him during the night. But, the terrifying instant of my dream, the instant when the sacrificer plunges the dagger into his breast, is this therefore the one that Fragonard chose?]

Only during the night would Diderot almost believe that he and Fragonard are in contact with one another. It is only then, in the time of Plato's cave, the time of the dream-vision that takes the place of Fragonard's painting, only then could Diderot entertain the correspondence, Grimm repeatedly claims, but still without quite believing it. This is why he must pose the question about the climactic moment in Fragonard's painting while refusing even to the night, to the time of his dream of shadows, the "commerce" that makes one the image of the other. On this level, Diderot's account of Fragonard is less the account of a particular canvas than an account of a visual world that resists its recovery in language. It is in this context that the final dialogue between Diderot and Grimm takes on its significance.

In this final exchange, Grimm points out several faults in Fragonard's painting. On each occasion Diderot replies that what Grimm describes is exactly as it was in his dream. Diderot performs this inversion four times: "c'est comme dans mon rêve"; "c'est encore comme dans mon rêve"; "je l'ai aussi remarqué dans mon rêve"; "je l'ai rêvé avec ces défauts." The issue at this point of Diderot's text is not to confirm whether or not the painting has these faults. The issue is rather the inversion of judgment that now makes Fragonard's painting refer to Diderot's. This inversion puts the shadow in the place of history so that what is crucial is not the event at the center of this narrative but the reflection of that event—and Diderot's account makes this clear by its concentration on the look and disposition of the figures who see Corésus's self-sacrifice. In this case, the setting, out of which Diderot develops this sense, comes into view as what has been at stake all along since it is above all else a setting of reflection and a paradigmatic setting at that. By removing Fragonard's painting from view, Plato's cave is set up in a most literal way to produce art in terms of the shadow. Removing the painting also enables Diderot to refuse continually a source of light that would act as powerfully as the sun does in Plato's allegory. You will recall the role played by this sun in Plato, for the person freed from his chains and brought to the outside of the cave. Plato writes: "Lastly, I believe, he would be able to look directly at the sun itself, and gaze at it as it is in itself, without using reflections in water or any other mediums" (*Republic*, 516b). Plato's word for mediums here is *phantasmata*. At the point where understanding is to be achieved for Plato, there can of course be no appearance, the shadow will always be the shadow of what is real, the real sun. It is to this understanding that the former captive of the cave subsequently arrives, but by what means, Plato does not explain. He simply says it will be afterward: "Later on he would come to the conclusion that it is the sun which produces the changing seasons and years and controls everything in the visible world, and that it is also at bottom responsible for what he and his fellow prisoners used to see in the cave" (*Republic*, 516b-c). By refusing sight to Fragonard's painting, Diderot also refuses the journey of Plato's allegory to the sun. This is why Diderot's narrative of the story of Corésus and Callirhoé is only given in the cave. To exit this cave, as well as to exit his dream, is to return to a Salon in which Fragonard's painting can still be seen. This is why Grimm, who has seen the painting, takes over the narrative once Diderot describes his awakening by the cry of the gray-haired old man. Grimm in this role provides the reference for the shadows of Diderot's dream but, in accordance to the movement of Diderot's text and the inversion worked by his moment of awakening, the descriptions provided by Grimm are not allowed to take over Diderot's dream. You will recall, everything, Grimm says, is as it is in Diderot's dream and everything Diderot says is as it is in Fragonard's painting, according to Grimm. The point of this comparison is not that one is more real than the other, that one is the shadow of the other, but that the canvas that would be real is equally that of Diderot's dream and that of Fragonard. Truly, or as Diderot says, "en verité" nothing can equal this and the moment that nothing can equal in either account, Diderot's or Fragonard's, is the moment of sacrifice, the moment in which the direction of the history leading to this moment is turned against itself. It is to this inversion that the figures in the canvas, both in the cave and the Salon, are turned as if toward the sun. But what the sun is in this case, as it is within Diderot's cave, is a shadow, a reflection of a moment, an agent seen but not known.

A remark from the "Essais sur la peinture," with which Diderot finishes the Salon, "so that one can judge the grounds that can be made for my criticism or praise," addresses the nature of this moment in a section entitled, "A paragraph on composition in which I hope I will talk about it": "le peintre n'a qu'un instant, et il ne lui est pas permis d'embrasser deux instants que deux actions" [the painter has but one instant at his disposal and he is no more permitted to embrace two instants than two actions] (*Salon 1765*, 14: 386). And, later in the same section: "chaque action a plusieurs instants; mais je l'ai dit et je le répète, l'artiste n'en a qu'un dont la durée est celle d'un coup d'oeil" [every action has several instants; but I have said it and I repeat it, the artist has only one of them and its duration is that of the glance of an eye] (*Salon 1765*, 14: 389). What we see, quite literally, in Diderot's account of Fragonard is the event as we see it in the look or glance of another eye, the event as it occurs is what is seen in its reflection. For Diderot, this is as it is: the event, here the sacrifice, takes place in its reflection. If this is the story of Diderot's text on Fragonard, then the torment of this dream is nothing less than the shadow cast by painting, a shadow that is nothing less than the history of painting itself—as the story of the Corinthian Maid already foretold. It is in the realm of this shadow that Diderot detains Plato's allegory before it can gaze on the sun that knows no shadow and before it exerts its control over the visible world. It is such a shadow that Diderot detains on the wall of reason in the cave of his dream as well as on the canvas of painting. To place oneself *before* Fragonard is to be held by this shadow, not the agent of its creation, and not its mirror image, the beholder.

Notes

1 See Kant, "What is Enlightenment?" for the individual use of reason as the basis for enlightenment. *Philosophical Writings*, ed. Ernst Behler (New York: Continuum, 1986), 263–69.

2 Diderot's text on Fragonard will be subsequently referred to in the edition of the *Salon de 1765* published in the *Oeuvres Complètes*, vol. 14 (Paris: Hermann, 1975), 253–64. All subsequent references to the Fragonard entry will be to this edition and noted parenthetically as "*Salon 1765*."

3 Pausanias, *Description of Greece* (Cambridge, MA: Harvard University Press, 1918).

4 This latter phrase is coined by H. W. Fowler and is cited by Vernon Hyde Minor in his study *Baroque and Rococo* (New York: Harry N. Abrams, 1999), 14. The overwrought or theatrical in Diderot's text has been interpreted by Michael Fried as the index to the emergence of the beholder as a distinctive issue for modern art. See his *Absorption and Theatricality: Painting and Beholder in the Age of Diderot* (Berkeley: University of California Press, 1980).

5 Grimm addresses Diderot and states "you did well to halt before this painting by Fragonard" (*Diderot: Salons*, 2: 197).

6 The editors of the Hermann edition of Diderot's works imply that since, at the end of this piece, Diderot reveals that what he writes is a presentation of Fragonard's painting, the whole question of this feigning can be ignored as a diversion. The claim that Diderot does this rests on Grimm's revelation that he had no part in the dialogue that makes up Diderot's entry on Fragonard. As Grimm states: "j'ai parlé comme il vous a plu" [I spoke as it pleased you]. Consequently, whatever Grimm says can be regarded as if Diderot had spoken. There is a failure here to account for the deliberate fictionality of this entry, a failure to account for Diderot's presentation of this whole dialogue. Once this presentation is read as only a dissembling, Diderot's text is forced back into the simpler form of a representation. Ironically, in the same note used to claim that Diderot in the person of

Grimm reveals his subterfuge, Grimm goes on to draw attention to this fictionality, expressed in terms that reinforce Diderot's relation to this painting: "Vous avez relevé d'une manière très ingénieuse ce qui donne à toutes ces figures un air de fantômes et de spectres que de personnages reels." In *Diderot: Salons*, ed. Jean Seznec and Jean Adhémar (Oxford: Clarendon, 1960), 2: 197–98.

7 The two other paintings are not of the same genre as the *Corésus* canvas. It could be argued that one exception to the dissimilarity between the Corésus piece and these two entries is when Diderot describes himself as actually being in the scene of a painting: "I find myself truly there [je me trouve bien là]" (see "Le Prince" [*Salon 1765*, 14: 226]). This displacement prefigures the Vernet entry for the Salon of 1767, an entry that is as exceptional in that volume of reviews as the Fragonard is in this one.

8 "Jusqu'à présent, mon cher Philosophe, je vous ai laissé dire et j'ai parlé comme il vous a plu." In *Diderot: Salons*, 2: 197].

9 Fried, *Absorption and Theatricality*, 4.

10 On the equivalence of fictions a means of reading Diderot's Fragonard text in order to establish an act of beholding and a beholder, see Fried, *Absorption and Theatricality*, 132.

11 Both senses are recorded in the *Dictionnaire de L'Académie française*, 4th Edition [1762], 590.

12 Pliny, *Natural History*, Book 35, Chap. 5.

13 "Un écho est un son réfléchi: un écho de lumière est une lumière réfléchie. Ainsi une lumière, qui tombe fortement sur un corps, d'où elle est renvoyé sur un autre, lequel en est assez vivement éclairé pour la réfléchir sur un troisième, et de ce troisième sur un quatrième, etc, forme sur ces différents objets des échos, comme un son que va se répétant de montagne de montagne [an echo is a reflected sound: an echo of light is light reflected. Thus a light, which falls strongly upon a body, from which it is sent onto another, which is so clearly illuminated by it to reflect on a third, and from this third onto a fourth, etc., form echoes on these different objects like a sound that repeats itself from mountain to mountain." From Grimm's remark appended to Diderot's text, in *Diderot: Salons*, 2: 198.

Bibliography

Dictionnaire de L'Académie française, 4th Edition, 2 vol. Paris: La Veuve de Bernard Brunet, 1762.
Diderot, Denis. *Oeuvres Complètes*. Edited by Herbert Dieckmann, Jean Fabre, Jacques Proust, with Jean Varloot, 25 vol. Paris: Hermann, 1975–.
Diderot, Denis. *Salons*. Edited by Jean Seznec and Jean Adhémar. Oxford: Clarendon, 1960.

Fried, Michael. *Absorption and Theatricality: Painting and Beholder in the Age of Diderot*. Chicago: University of Chicago Press, 1988.
Kant, Immanuel. "What is Enlightenment?" In *Philosophical Writings*, edited by Ernst Behler, 263–69. New York: Continuum, 1986.
Minor, Vernon Hyde. *Baroque and Rococo*. New York: Harry N. Abrams, 1999.
Pausanias. *Description of Greece*. Cambridge, MA: Harvard University Press, 1918.
Pliny the Elder. *Natural History*. Loeb Classical Library Edition. Cambridge, MA: Harvard University Press, 2014.

5 TIMELY PLOT AND UNPLOTTED TIME: ACTION AND EXPERIENCE BEFORE AND AFTER HEGEL

John Park

This essay explores the radically different senses of causality and narrative emplotment determined by the use of distinct verbal tenses in landmark works of "realist" fiction, specifically, the "lively *present-tense*,"[1] "instantaneous descriptions and reflections,"[2] or "writing to the moment,"[3] described and employed by Samuel Richardson in *Clarissa, or, The History of a Young Lady,* and the unprecedented predominance of the imperfect tense in the narratives of Flaubert. While opposed to each other both formally and representationally, these equally unorthodox narrative modes share a common, negative feature: both reject conventional—preterite and perfect—tenses of causal, narrative sequencing. In so doing, their innovative narrative styles also engage the agency of the subject in new ways, at once calling the efficacy of the subjects of narrative action and causation into question and engaging the reading subject in unavoidable acts of intellectual mediation. In this, both authors' pathbreaking literary styles of narration recall Hegel's specifically *diachronic* philosophy of mediation. For, in undermining our normative sense of causality, these sharply divergent modes of narration converge in their profound interrogation of how the *significance* of immediate sense perception is constructed over time. Whether by indicating the insufficient or misleading content of a purely "present," epistolarily recorded perception, or the inability of the present to present, in itself, meaningful difference or change from the past when recounted in the preterite tense via third-person, "omniscient" narration, the contrasting narrative modes of these two great "realists" indicate that any narrative representation of the real must entail the ongoing, mediating work of a subject.

1 Deixis and allegory in *Clarissa*

This living hand, now warm and capable
Of earnest grasping, would, if it were cold
And in the icy silence of the tomb,
So haunt thy days and chill thy dreaming nights
That thou would wish thine own heart dry of blood
So in my veins red life might stream again,
And thou be conscience-calm'd–see here it is–
I hold it towards you

—John Keats[4]

And NOW is that time, and THIS the occasion. Now, at reading this, will you pity your late unhappy sister!"

—Clarissa Harlowe, to James Harlowe[5]

At first glance, the epistolary form of Richardson's novel appears to delineate a series of events chronologically such that one has simply to read the characters' dated accounts of events in order to acquire a causal understanding of what has happened. In presenting a nexus of plot and knowledge from several individual viewpoints, its episodic, first-person style creates the expectation that the novel as a whole describes real events as these happen in real time. Still, despite the importance of plot to any novel, and to this narrative *of* plotting in particular, Richardson instead emphasizes the way in which each event in *Clarissa* is experienced, apprehended and interpreted, and, in pivotal instances, staged. When, in his "Author's Preface," Richardson describes the (fictitious) authors of the epistles he has gathered as writing "in the height of a present distress . . . the[ir] hearts . . . wholly engaged in their subjects," he indicates, directly thereafter, the necessarily impressionistic or partial understanding resulting from such immediacy of experience, adding cursorily, even cryptically: "The events at the time generally dubious."[6] Indeed, the composition of *Clarissa* out of diverse discursive styles and states of mind, rather than in function of a single, causally entailed plot, may reflect the larger narrative aim Richardson sets for himself. For the purpose of his novel, Richardson writes, is not only to "divert and amuse" those who "look upon (the) Story in it," but to convey a "history" of actual lived experience.[7] Stating he has "addressed [*Clarissa*] to the public as a history of life and manners,"[8] Richardson indicates that he is interested to represent more than any specific "Story" as such. And, indeed, while the "story" proper of this longest of all English novels may be resumed in a few sentences, the motivations, manipulations, expressions, and descriptions—of ignorance, confusion, suspicions, and duplicity—that Clarissa and her correspondents (and they and their correspondents) all experience and enact are as extensive and vivid as those of any subjects "wholly engaged" in the "present" tense of "life"[9] or of their reflections upon it. At the same time, that very vividness underscores the "dubious" appearance of narrated events, as underlying temporal discrepancies of action, reception, and understanding, and the apparently innumerable ways in which these affect the shape, duration, and outcome of its "Story," undermine our own sense of the "here-and-now" as sufficient marker of the "real" the novel represents. For internal and external readers of its kaleidoscope-like letters alike, the immediate reveals itself as an unreliable basis both for constructing and comprehending events causally in *Clarissa*—for attempting, in short, either to contrive or survive a plot. In keeping with the thus nearly entirely internalized progress or "history of life and manners"[10] the novel consequently presents, the focus of its "descriptions and reflections"[11] shifts accordingly from represented objects and events to the language of representation itself.

Already at the beginning of the novel, the letters exchanged between Clarissa and Anna Howe dramatize a certain pressure to write to the moment as if the primary purpose of their letters were to constitute narrations in "real-time." A simple record of a single present moment, such as, "Mr. Solmes is here (April 8th, Saturday, Ten O'clock),"[12] joins a specific temporal marker inseparably to a spatial deictic. Given the intense familial pressures to marry the "despicable Solmes"[13] under which she labors, Clarissa's writing naturally reflects the immediate urgency of her plight. Yet, at the same time, it indicates the limits of perceptions defined by actuality alone. The discrepancy between how things appear in the present and their, as yet, imperceptible process of development or purpose is heightened dramatically in the major turning point of the novel, when Lovelace abducts Clarissa by, on the one hand, persuading her that, at that moment, she herself is being pursued, and, on the other, making it appear to her family, "the implacables,"[14] that she has willingly left her "father's house."[15] First narrated in the novel from the point of view of the very subject whom we later learn it was staged to impress, the circumstances surrounding the event of her departure are recounted by Clarissa in a series of clauses prefaced by the temporal marker, "now:" "Now behind me, now before me, now on this side, now on that, turned I my affrighted face in the same moment; expecting a furious brother here, armed servants there, an enraged sister screaming, and a father armed with terror in his countenance more dreadful than even the drawn sword which I saw."[16] Just as the immediacy of a feigned danger—that of capture and imprisonment by her family—overtakes her longstanding distrust of Lovelace, so the temporal distance between experience and representation, and immediacy and understanding, is the condition ensuring the eventual success of Clarissa's use of allegory in her letter to Lovelace, in which her duplicitous use of the phrase, "my father's house,"[17] secures her the time to die as she designs. When, as part of this design, Clarissa writes to Belford from the grave, "Sir, let me beg of you, for my sake, who am, or as now you will best read it, have been, driven to the necessity of applying to you to be the executor of my will,"[18] her posthumous use of the word, "now," "now" (so to speak) signifies whenever her letter will be read. Here, "now" functions not as a marker of immediacy but of temporal difference—the inalienable difference between life and death, as between the past writing of the word "now" and the present moment of its reception. The turn in the novel from plot to allegory—from immediate causation to bifurcating signification—is, in essence, the turn from a historically delimited, apparently past "now" to any "present" moment of reading.

Toward the end of the novel, Clarissa's posthumous letters begin to make explicit the novel's turn to the actual event of their reading when, rather than narrating events, they address their reader directly:

> There was but one time, but one occasion, after the rash step I was precipitated upon, that I could hope to be excused looking up to you in the character of a brother and a friend. And NOW is that time, and THIS the occasion. Now, at reading this, will you pity your late unhappy sister! NOW will you forgive her faults, both supposed and

real. And NOW will you afford to her memory that kind concern which you refused to her before![19]

Looking forward to Keats's great deictic lyric, "This living hand," that directly exhorts its reader to, "See here it is," Clarissa's "And NOW is that time, and THIS the occasion" addresses the reader in the undefined aftermath of an anticipated death. Like a "hand" that, imagined "cold/ And in the icy silence of the tomb," even as it is described as "living" "now," is brought back to life, or brought into an ever-present afterlife, by its identification with the present of the poem's final deictic address ("Here ... I hold it towards you"), Clarissa also comes to identify "herself" with present acts of self-writing:

> Thus already, even while she writes, in imagination, purified and exalted, she the more fearlessly writes to her sister; and NOW is assured of pardon for all those little occasions of displeasure. . . . And how NOW, made perfect (as she hopes) through sufferings, styles herself,
> —The happy Clarissa Harlow.[20]

Whereas both Lovelace's and his author's identification[21] of their style of writing with the present "moment" is revealed as shortsighted by the most glaring lacuna of the novel—the unrepresented scene of rape laconically reported by its agent as a past event (Lovelace to Belford, "And now, Belford, I can go no farther. The affair is over. Clarissa lives."[22]), Clarissa "styles herself" "happy" in this posthumous letter in a permanent sense. The happiness with which she identifies objectively, in the third-person, in being "made perfect (as she hopes) through sufferings," may be seen to refer to the formal wholeness of the novel, whose content—the sufferings Clarissa has undergone –has now become "perfect[ed]" in a posthumous act of "self-" "styl[ing]" "NOW." If, as Clarissa suggests, one could rest content with a "happy" cohesion of narrative form and content, the novel as a whole would appear to have been "perfect[ed]" *as* a "History," not only "of" but *by* Clarissa.

However, unlike the open-ended address of Keats's poem, Richardson's novel includes diegetic readers to whom the letters are addressed. Through the series of addresses at its end, this epistolary novel maintains the formal tension between the "History" it tells and the imperfect contents of the present-tense accounts by which it tells its story.[23] That tension is brought to its anticlimactic or inconclusive end in the final letter of the novel, which, written by Lovelace's valet, F. J. de la Tour, is additionally labeled a "(Translation)."²⁴ In it, Lovelace's dying apostrophe—"Oh my beloved Clarissa!—Now art thou"—is reported, via internal quotation, as incomplete:

> My chevalier swore by G-d, he was not hurt: 'twas a pin's point: and so made another pass at his antagonist; which he, with a surprising dexterity, received under his arm, and run my dear chevalier into the body: who immediately fell; saying, The luck is yours, sir—Oh my beloved Clarissa!—Now art thou—Inwardly he spoke three or four words more. His sword dropped from his hand. Mr Morden threw his down, and ran to him, saying in French—Ah monsieur, you are a dead man!—Call to God for mercy!²⁵

The peripheral de la Tour's report of Lovelace's final—truncated—verbal act and demise reminds the readers of the novel that this collection of letters has always constructed its story by the indirect means of verbal address. Even the final "expiat[ion]" of his deeds²⁶ that Lovelace would achieve in dying proves doubly mediated by this "Translation" of his final words as reported by an entirely ancillary figure, one who concludes his report with additionally anticlimactic details concerning the costs, now left to him, of managing Lovelace's body.²⁷

Such tension between fulfillment or "perfect[ion]" and open-ended processes of indirection and mediation makes it difficult to claim that, as its titular heroine ultimately intends and plots for "herself," the novel, too, effects a decisive turn from causal emplotment to allegory. This analysis has attempted to trace the movement by which the repeated temporal marker, "now," becomes effectively detached from the moment it indicates and comes to function instead as a marker of the temporal differences and resulting hermeneutic distances the novel's epistolary form brings to the fore. The novel's very use of deictics of presentness across a (fictional) assemblage of letters displays, in other words, experiences of immediacy in the process of being disassembled. Indeed, the landmark literary "realism" of *Clarissa*, it can be argued, inheres not in any representational content but in the distance between immediacy and mediation of content represented at all times by its epistolary form. It is this temporal difference, manifested not in narrative accounts of past events but in ongoing references to the present, that creates the tension in the novel between "plot" and "allegory" to which the novel itself refers.²⁸ At once part and parcel of the novel's "Story" and product of its differential, epistolary form, the distance between every "now" its characters name, as between the "present" these acts of deixis attempt to frame and the open-ended present of their reception as writing, ultimately represents the structural, or non-plot-dependent tension between plot and allegory present everywhere in Richardson's great novel.

2 Consciousness as Phenomenology of Spirit: Allegories of the "here" and "now"

To help illuminate the tension, or negative relation, between plot and allegory that structures Richardson's novel, this analysis turns next to Hegel's philosophy. In its discussion of the fundamental temporal difference separating signification from perception, Hegel's inaugural *Phenomenology of Spirit*, much like Richardson's *Clarissa*, openly employs the deictic markers of presence, "here" and "now." Addressing the age-old problem of achieving "Sense-Certainty" in the first chapter of the *Phenomenology*, Hegel states squarely the two basic deictic criteria any present moment of perception must meet:

> It is, then, sense-certainty itself that must be asked: "What is the This?" If we take the "This" in the twofold shape of its being, as "Now" and as "Here," the dialectic it has in it will receive a form as intelligible as the "This" itself is. To the question: "What is Now?," let us answer, e.g. "Now is Night." In order to test the truth of this sense-certainty a simple experiment will suffice. We write down this truth; a truth cannot lose anything by being written down, any more than it can lose anything through our preserving it. If now, this noon, we look again at the written truth we shall have to say that it has become stale.[29]

Analogous to the changing senses of "here and now" repeatedly demonstrated by their epistolary inclusion in *Clarissa*, Hegel indicates the temporal differentiation at work in the identity of "the Now" by way of "writ[ing]" "Now" "down," referring to the explicit change in the meaning of "Now" that its enduring written notation "pointed out": "The Now, as it is pointed out to us, is Now that has been."[30] Thus, Hegel concludes, "What is pointed out, held fast, and abides is" no longer a particular "now" but "a negative."[31] One could say that the literary realism which Richardson presents in *Clarissa* is, in Hegel's terms, this negative, or what Hegel will later call, when discussing not the construction of "sense-certainty" but the aesthetic: "The freedom of intellectual reflection which rescues itself from the here and now, called sensuous reality and finitude."[32] Rather than such particular descriptions of sensuous reality as "now is noon" or "night," Richardson presents in his "History" of "life and manners" the "genuine reality [*Realität*] . . . beyond the immediacy of feeling and external objects"[33] that Hegel defines as the vocation of art.

Like Clarissa's distinction between "who now is" and "has been," or the turn from forward-moving "plot" to "allegory," the Hegelian negative involves a turn from the "Now . . . as it is pointed out" to the "Now that has been." In a discussion to which this analysis will return below, Paul de Man has similarly defined "allegory" as "the rhetorical process by which the literary text moves from a phenomenal, world-oriented to a grammatical, language-oriented direction."[34] It is this "rhetorical process" that renders Clarissa's particular "Story" *also* "the History of a Young Lady" to which Richardson's title alternatively refers (*Clarissa, or, The History* . . .)[35] Indeed, the two-part, alternating structure of Richardson's title finds its echo in the title of Hegel's opening Chapter: "Sense-Certainty or the 'This' and 'Meaning'" ("Die sinnliche Gewißheit oder das Diese und das Meinen").[36] If we take this "or" as a passage to the reflected artifice of deictic markers, we find that the first posited phenomenal experience of the "here and now" that appears to guarantee the "sense-certainty" of our immediate experience of nature, that is, "Now is night" or "Here is the tree," has been negated by the intervention of a linguistic awareness mediated by the very verbal markers employed to achieve unequivocal "meaning" ("Meinen"). It is thus that, in carrying the process of deixis across the "negative" of perception, that is, in preserving its sense, Hegel redefines the very identity of sense-certainty itself: "It is not just we who make this distinction between essence and instance, between immediacy and mediation; on the contrary, we find it within sense-certainty itself."[37] On Hegel's temporal dialectical view, then, sense-certainty is found to be both first and to have been always already available when articulated in verbal, signified form.

The specifically linguistic condition by which Clarissa's singular story can be understood at the same time as the history of any young lady is posited as a given by Hegel, who freely turns his thought experiments into a collective or individually nonspecific, noncontigent act of inscription, "We write down this truth" ("Wir schreiben diese Wahrheit auf").[38] The inevitable detachment of the written "here and now" from any specific temporal moment by the end of the Chapter reveals not only the different "meaning[s]" of "here and now" that any single subject may indicate at different moments in time but also the different experiences of "here and now" that any number of different subjects may undergo. Hegel's "we," in short, combines the particularity and universal accessibility of the "I" whom we may in turn define as the human subject, that is, whoever it is who marks experience "here and now."

This general movement from the singular to the plural can be seen to define the structure of the *Phenomenology of Spirit* as a whole. Consciousness of the indication and negation of the certainty of particular sensory experience leads in turn to *self*-consciousness, and the social context in which self-consciousness enacts its own actualization. The movement from "Reason" to "Spirit" is a case in point: in it, the experience of nature finds its reflection in the social realm in the actualization of ethical experience, as the temporal composition and consciousness of the "ethical world" parallels that of sense perception: "*Just as* the consciousness of abstract sensuous being passes over into perception, so also does the immediate certainty of a real ethical situation; and *just as* for sense-perception simple being becomes a Thing of so many properties, so for ethical perception a given action is an actual situation with many ethical connections."[39] In "Observing Reason," the most explicitly nature-based section of the *Phenomenology*, Hegel furthermore emphasizes not "Nature's own system" but, rather, "our artificial system" of differentiating between genus and species in nature.[40] While its outcome accords with the process of self-differentiation inherent in nature itself, our artificial differentiation and identification of the forms of nature remains first and last the act of a human subject, Hegel observes, and it is in just such acts, through which human subjects themselves are identified, that Hegel is most interested.

The complexity of the structure of the *Phenomenology* is such that while Hegel appears to bring about a direct comparison between nature and the social (and here, the "social" is the commonly artificial or linguistic), he is clearly aware of the problems inhering in linguistic articulation to begin with. The various "eternal differences," as Hegel would call them, between subject and predicate or, in his philosophical terms, between being-in-itself and being-for-itself, bring to the fore the difficulties involved in identifying the difference between substance and action causally.[41] Similarly, it is because of our inability to explain the relationship between substance and action in causal terms that a negative relation between plot and allegory must effectively obtain.

In commenting on essays by Hans Robert Jauss, Paul de Man points out a difference between Jauss's and Benjamin's notions of allegory in order to reveal a false assumption upon which Jauss's notion of the "horizon of expectation," in part, is based:

> The "anorganic" quality of allegory is, however, not equivalent, as Jauss's commentary seems to suggest, to the negation of the natural world; the opposition between organic and anorganic, in Benjamin, is . . . not between nature and consciousness (or subject) but between what exists as language and what does not.[42]

The critique of hermeneutics that de Man then develops differentiates hermeneutics from poetics by aligning it with a mimetic tradition privileging the object imitated over the aesthetic poetic act itself. Hermeneutics, de Man argues in addition, belongs to a theological interpretive tradition according to which "a hermeneutically successful reading is to do away with reading altogether," whereas the "specifically aesthetic" focus of poetics is "on the process of signification rather than on significance."[43] Such an opposition between a theological and poetic approach to interpretation parallels that between plotted causality and the differential, temporal structure of signification in allegory, as well as that between pre-plotted or religiously encoded and open-ended allegory.

3 Flaubert and narrative time

In his critique of Jauss, de Man defines this distinctively modern problem of interpretation as having mainly to do with the attribution of significance, or "reading," just as Hegel problematizes the making of meaning when, "in modern times," one is confronted by finished products of negation: "In modern times . . . the individual finds the abstract form ready-made."[44] Flaubert seems to eliminate this problem of reading by utilizing language emptied of immediacy and historical particularity, or "this-ness." Whereas *Clarissa* ends with a reported wish for "expiat[ion]" that does not differentiate between action and speech, such an absence of referential differentiation is where Flaubert's style begins.[45] In stark contrast to Richardson's innovative use of an always partial, while "lively present-tense"[46] perspective on events, Flaubert's unprecedented use of tenses, famously compared with the "revolution" in "our vision of things" effected in Kant's critical philosophy by Proust,[47] undermines plotted time and evacuates temporal difference in general in its narration of action and experience. Flaubert's verbal mitigation of the distinction between past and present effects the negation of any attribution of causal, historical sense to narrated events. In this sense, Flaubert, one could say, narrates negatively.

"Un Cœur simple," on which the remainder of this analysis will focus, offers a powerful realization of this narrative mode of negation. From its opening words, "Pendant un demi-siècle" ("during a half-century"), the novella displaces distinct historical inference by leaving the identity of the century in question undefined.[48] In emptying a temporal reference of its referent by signifying fifty years from now or any moment at all, the denotation, "pendant un demi-siècle," signifies pure duration, or difference without signification.[49] Significance as such becomes untenable because the means of signification require the creation of relations between identity and difference. An expression of difference without a point of reference, a point from which the difference proceeds, is difference without identity, in other words, difference qua difference and thus without differential significance.

In accordance with its introductory indication of temporal difference without semantic significance, Flaubert refers repeatedly to significant historical events even while leveling out their narratival value.[50] Throughout the novella, Flaubert refers repeatedly to historical periods defined only by generic denotations of duration (days, months, years) as well as individually denoted historical events in such a way as to write away their significance. The year of the death of Mme. Aubain's husband[51] is treated no differently than the news of the July revolution itself glossed in the text as the date in which a new subprefect is appointed.[52] As such, these historical markers become indices lacking deictic functions. The fact of their inclusion within the text expresses that they are meant to be read as just that, chronological markers emptied of historical sense. In other words, their textual significance rests on their narrative insignificance.[53]

When all that remains of the narration of temporal events is a formal relationship between their beginning and end, events themselves seem to take on a mechanical relationship shorn of dialectical development. The reasons that might mediate between events, connecting one to another in a meaningful way, are conspicuously absent from Flaubert's text, and from that absence the sense of events as a series of immediacies emerges. Even when narrated in the preterite, events that would take on pivotal significance in a more conventional narrative appear instead inconsequential, lacking in connective thread. When, for example, Félicité learns of Théodore's death, the recounting of that event in the preterite, even as it fosters the expectation of a forward movement in time, fails to relate one event to another internally, thereby leaving the reader with an impression of discrete moments materialized externally in the text:

> Ce fut un chagrin désordonné. Elle se jeta par terre, poussa des cris, appela le bon Dieu, et gémit toute seule dans la campagne jusqu'au soleil levant. Puis elle revint à la ferme, déclara son intention d'en partir; et, au bout du mois, ayant reçu ses comptes, elle enferma tout son petit bagage dans un mouchoir, et se rendit à Pont-l'Évêque. Devant l'auberge, elle questionna une bourgeoise en capeline de veuve, et qui précisément cherchait une cuisinière. La jeune fille ne savait pas grand-chose, mais paraissait avoir tant de bonne volonté et si peu d'exigences, que Mme Aubain finit par dire:
> "Soit, je vous accepte!"
> Félicité, un quart d'heure après, était installée chez elle.[54]
>
> [It was an unbounded sorrow. She fell on the ground, shouted out cries, called on to the good God, and wandered around alone in the field until the sun rose. Then she went back to the farm, declared her intent to leave, and at the end of the month, having received her wages, she packed all her small belongings in a handkerchief and went to Pont-l'Évêque. In front of the inn, she asked a bourgeois woman in widow's cap who was looking precisely for a cook. The young girl did not know much but appeared to have so much good will and so little exigencies that Madame Aubain finished by saying, "Very well, I accept you!" Félicité, a quarter of an hour later, was employed in her home.]

Even though each in this narrated series of events occupies a different length of time, each is accorded the same value in the text. The single night Félicité spends in mourning, the final month at the farm, and the fifteen minutes preceding her move into her house are granted equivalent textual significance. As one event follows another consecutively, none influences the other in significance, and the amount of time described loses its dramatic narrative effect. Considered individually, the "end of the month" spent at the farm, for example, could express the gravity of

Félicité's sadness, just as the fortuitousness of her chance encounter with Mme. Aubain, who was searching "précisément" for a cook, might appear reflected by the brevity of time that elapses until Félicité moves into Mme. Aubain's house. However, by virtue of their apparently arbitrary placement within the narrative, both a longer, if unspecified duration, "at the end of the month," and rapid turn of events owing to chance fail equally to induce in the reader the emotions that usually accompany such temporally and causally distinct events. At the same time, the insignificance that each event assumes is understood only *after* the reader has moved on sequentially to the next. The accumulation of this effect, as the novella adds one event to another, desensitizes the reader to the possible dramatic function of each, making the narrative appear less like the narration of a story than a stringing together of facts of no causal consequence, a series of temporal entities as distinct as discrete things non-constitutive of a whole.

This lack of hierarchy of significance undermines the reader's sense of narrative emplotment even as it increases the narrative's aesthetic effect. For without the senses of urgency and causality—of a verbally constructed tension between past and present—the sense of a narrative movement in time never comes to fruition. Similarly, the impression of a present "now" responsible for the dramatization of an event must be constituted by the verbal representation, in hierarchical temporal terms, of actual change taking place. In "Un Cœur simple," by contrast, duration and immediacy exist alongside each other, and the consequence of that temporal paradox, in which the "here and now" as such never occur, is the replacement of the sense of temporal significance with that of time itself.[55] No longer produced by the narrative significance of events, to which the text itself appears indifferent, the reader's sense of time in the novella is derived instead from its only "present" proper, that of the verbal extension of its descriptions.[56] The reader's sense of the time transpiring "in" the narrative is, in other words, the time spent "outside" it, reading its descriptive language. Rather than employing language as a vehicle for indicating the temporal significance of objects, description in the novella inverts that relationship by employing objects for the sake of a temporal experience of language.

This narrative reduction of significance to objects of description allows for a kind of readerly experience but prohibits the comparative attribution of that experience to specific events. Even the potentially sublime sense connoted by Félicité's subjection to a "chagrin désordonné" ("unbounded sorrow") is defeated, as is every subsequent event, by the express immeasurability of its emotional content. Conversely, the immeasurability or boundlessness of the meaning of each event opens the possibility that any one of them, no matter how apparently trivial, may be climactic—or not. That every element in the novella can be substituted for another of equal value across narrative (rather than narrated) time is the structural element that provides the novella with its irreducibly poetic character.[57]

Just as the poetic sense communicated by the language of the novella rests heavily on the absence of a meaningful narrative opposition between past and present, time itself comes to be represented in the narrative as repetition, or what Lukács calls "a one-sidedly negative view of time."[58] While the specificity of Flaubert's descriptions may cause a sequence of events to appear to constitute discrete moments in time, that appearance of individuality is disrupted by the repetitive sense that frames the sense of time in such passages as this one:

> Malgré ses efforts pour paraître gentilhomme jusqu'à soulever son chapeau chaque fois qu'il disait: "Feu mon père," l'habitude l'entraînant, il se versait à boire coup sur coup, et lâchait des gaillardises. Félicité le poussait dehors poliment: "Vous en avez assez, M. de Gremanville! À une autre fois!" Et elle refermait la porte.[59]
>
> [In spite of his efforts to appear as a gentleman to such degree as to raise his hat every time he said: "My deceased father," according to his habit, he would pour himself a drink little by little, and let loose with bawdy remarks. Félicité would show him out politely, "You've had enough, Monsieur de Gremanville! Another time!" And she would close the door.]

The temporal markers of repetition, such as, "chaque fois" ("each time") and "l'habitude" ("habit"), situate each moment in the above sequence of actions within a temporal frame of repetition. The placement of a direct quotation, "Vous en avez assez, M. de Gremanville! À une autre fois!" ("You've had enough, Monsieur de Gremanville! Another time!"), within a temporal environment of repetition eliminates the sense of presence. Furthermore, through the narrative use of the imperfect, "Félicité le poussait dehors poliment" ("Félicité would show him out politely"), the sense of a single instance generally attributed to a direct quotation is lost and turned instead into a part of an ongoing, scenic description.

Such representations of time as repetition have the effect of demarcating time purely in terms of space. The novella's summary description of Félicité's history amounts to an account of her daily schedule that parallels the description of Mme. Aubain's house. The repetition of waking up early at daybreak so as to not miss mass, working "sans interruption,"[60] and, when dinner is over, clearing the dishes, resembles the uninterrupted continuity with which Flaubert's descriptions of the interior of Mme. Aubain's house pass in space from one room to another:

> Au premier étage, il y avait d'abord la chamber de "Madame," très grande, tendue d'un papier à fleurs pâles, et contenant le portrait de "Monsieur" en costume de muscadin. Elle communiquait avec une chambre plus petite, où l'on voyait deux couchettes d'enfants, sans matelas. Puis venait le salon, toujours fermé, et rempli de meubles recouverts d'un drap. Ensuite un corridor menait à un cabinet d'études; des livres et des paperasses garnissaient les rayons d'une bibliothèque entourant de ses trois côtés un large bureau de bois noir.[61]
>
> [On the first floor, there was first Madam's bedroom, very big, with a wall paper of pale flowers extended, and containing the portrait of Monsieur dressed as a dandy. It communed with a smaller room, where one saw two children's cribs without mattresses. Then came the lounge, always closed, and full of furniture covered with sheets. Then a hall led to the study; books and pages filled the shelves of a bookcase that surrounded a large black wooden desk on three sides.]

When we consider that meaning severed from time makes the representation of time dependent upon spatial description, all we can know about time in the novella—the fact of its passing—appears represented in the figure of ruins holding no significance other than that of time that has passed. From the description of Mme. Aubain's house, the sole value that is ascribed to such remains is their signification of a visible past: "Les deux panneaux en retour disparaissaient sous des dessins à la plume, des paysages à la gouache et des gravures d'Audran, souvenirs d'un temps meilleur et d'un luxe évanoui"[62] ("The two panels in return disappeared under ink pen sketches, landscape paintings, and engravings by Audran, mementos of a better time and vanished luxury"). Similar to the opening of the novella, the past "temps meilleur" ("better time") named here holds no significance for other elements of the narrative, except for that of its temporality. Represented by means of objects indicative of the past whose discrete spatial descriptions accumulate in the writing, time appears here in the materiality of enduring objects, and thereby, in a sense, in its own objectivity. The representation of time strictly by means of objects and *as* object without meaning requires the negation of subjectivity. The objects and entire architectural description of Mme. Aubain's house, as well as the "mementos of a better time" associated with it, represent the past as both present to mind and inert, historicized without history.

Flaubert treats subjective thought in an even more radical manner, purging subjective agency from its indirect narration. After Félicité is reported to listen to "un abrégé de l'Histoire sainte"[63] ("an abridged sacred history"), the following, unattributed question arises, one which undermines, through its conspicuous naiveté, or innocence of religious knowledge, the foundation of Christian canonization itself:

> Pourquoi l'avaient-ils crucifié, lui qui chérissait les enfants, nourrissait les foules, guérissait les aveugles, et avait voulu, par douceur, naître au milieu des pauvres, sur le fumier d'une étable?[64]
>
> [Why had they crucified him, he who cherished children, fed the people, cured the blind, and in humility, had wanted to be born among the poor, on the manure of a stable?]

While these reported thoughts may have originated with Félicité, their presentation makes it equally plausible that they merely relate what others have told her; something she has overheard; or words employed rhetorically by a priest in the service of a homily (this last possibility strengthened by the further narrative observation that, "in as far as dogma was concerned, [Félicité] understood nothing" ("Quant aux dogmes, elle n'y comprenait rien."[65]). Unable "to imagine"[66] in theological terms the holy spirit she will later associate with a stuffed parrot, Félicité is in any event unable to *understand* what she hears. Instead, this central "subject" of the novella instead appears subject to sensory impressions alone: her "belief" in viewing images that she is "seeing paradise" itself ("Elle croyait voir le paradis"[67]); the alternation of sadness and rapture she undergoes in the act of listening—"she cried as she listened . . . she remained in a state of adoration" ("elle pleura en écoutant[68] . . . elle demeurait dans une adoration"[69])—and finally, her literal, serial visualization of the discrete subjects of the biblical text she hears: "paradise, the flood, the tower of Babel, cities on fire, dying people, idols smashed . . ." ("le paradis, le déluge, la tour de Babel, des villes tout en flammes, des peuples qui mouraient, des idoles renversées...."[70]).

Described as a container of unconnected objects, the mind or "interior" of Félicité corresponds to the interior space of Mme. Aubain's house. As that "interior" allots individual rooms or, in French, "pieces" (*pièces*) of "space" to diverse sensory impressions, so the sensations Félicité passively receives are described in spatial, visual terms. The different metaphoric significances of the varying descriptions of the holy spirit she hears—"a bird," "a fire," "a breath" ("oiseau," "un fou," "un souffle"[71]) —are unrecognizable to her, as is any positive temporal difference among their mentions, whose disconnected repetition over time is all Félicité is reported to note: "He was not only a bird but sometimes, a fire, and others times, a breath" ("il n'était pas seulement oiseau, mais encore un feu, et d'autres fois un souffle."[72]). In the novella's most daring negation of the very concept of subjective internalization, the elevated notions of spirit and spiritual redemption, personified ritualistically in the "holy spirit," are transferred by Félicité to a pet who literally parrots what it hears outside it, and whose dead body she preserves and keeps to serve as subject of her own rites.

From beginning to end, as the novella's introductory, entirely external description of her makes clear, the "interiority" of "Félicité"—central, unconceiving "subject" of the novella whose very name bears with it the external, allegorical tag of the "happiness" of non-reflection—is, first and last, the subject of exteriority:

> Son visage était maigre et sa voix aiguë. À vingt-cinq ans, on lui en donnait quarante. Dès la cinquantaine, elle ne marqua plus aucun âge;—et, toujours silencieuse, la taille droite et les gestes mesurés, semblait une femme en bois, fonctionnant d'une manière automatique.
>
> [Her face was thin and her voice shrill. At twenty-five years old, she looked forty. From her fifties, she no longer marked any age and, always silent, with erect figure and measured gestures, she seemed to be a woman made out of wood working automatically.]

By identifying the story about Félicité with Félicité, which is to say, an "always silent" subject whose apparently ageless "erect figure" and "measured gestures" resemble those of a "woman made out of wood working automatically," Flaubert confronts the reader with a material, nonhistorical subject whose own only meaningful face-to-face interactions occur with a beatified stuffed parrot in process of decomposing, another "happy" subject, lacking all animating subjectivity, whose residual status mirrors hers—"holy spirit" indeed. It is the reader, who, confronted with Flaubert's style, must look "the negative in the face" and "tarry" with it.[73] While the diverse viewpoints articulated in Richardson's epistles in the "lively *present-tense* manner"[74] of writing bring diachronic negations of subjective impressions of representations, and, ultimately, explicit allegorization in their wake, Flaubert's incorporations of twin inactive subjects, time and Félicité, into the very textual fabric of his novella brings with it, at every moment, the "tremendous power of the negative,"[75] and with that power, an inability to narrate a story based in the representation of dramatic actions.[76] If, in Flaubert's "realist" writing—in which, divorced from referents made meaningful by their subordination to plot, all that remains of "story" is the "style" that creates and enforces that divorce—the only "history" "really" ("wirklich"[77]) narrated is, in Hegel's terms, that of thinking in its generative power to negate, this is also the power that Hegel identifies with the Subject alone.[78] In this sense negative narration is its own dramatic action.

Notes

1 Samuel Richardson, *Clarissa, or, The History of a Young Lady*, ed. Angus Ross (London: Penguin, 2004), 882. (Emphasis in text) All further citations from *Clarissa* from this edition unless noted otherwise.

2 The latter description of the discursive style of the novel, provided by Richardson in his Preface (1759), is later echoed within the novel as Lovelace describes his penchant for "writing to the moment" (see following note). See Samuel Richardson, *Clarissa, or, The History of a Young Lady*, ed. George Sherburn (Boston: Riverside, 1962), xx.

3 Richardson, *Clarissa*, 721.

4 John Keats, *Complete Poems and Selected Letters of John Keats* (New York: Modern Library, 2001), 365.

5 Richardson, *Clarissa*, 1373.

6 Richardson, *Clarissa* (1962), xx.

7 Ibid., xxi.

8 Ibid.

9 See endnote 2, this essay.

10 Richardson, *Clarissa* (1962), xxi.

11 Ibid., xx.

12 Richardson, *Clarissa*, 351.
13 Ibid., 86.
14 Ibid., 416.
15 Ibid., 355.
16 Ibid., 416.
17 Ibid., 1233. In the abridged Riverside edition edited by Sherburn, the expression is capitalized as "Father's House." See Richardson, *Clarissa* (1962), 433.
18 Richardson, *Clarissa*, 1368.
19 Ibid., 1373.
20 Ibid., 1374–75.
21 Cf. Terry Eagleton, *The Rape of Clarissa: Writing, Sexuality, and Class Struggle in Samuel Richardson* (Minneapolis: University of Minnesota Press, 1982), 12. "Richardson half-converts himself from 'author' to the focal point of his readers' own writings."
22 Richardson, *Clarissa*, 883.
23 See Watt's discussion of the different tempo that Richardson establishes by way of his epistolary technique. Ian Watt, *The Rise of the Novel: Studies in Defoe, Richardson, and Fielding* (Berkeley: University of California Press, 1957), 209–11. See also Lois Bueler, *Clarissa's Plots* (Newark: University of Delaware Press, 1994), 149:

> The key to Richardson's hybrid form is the fact that a letter has both the immediateness of drama and the recursive possibilities of narrative. Thus the letters duplicate the unmediated point of view of a play: the reader receives the language of the writers directly, with no intervening consciousness. . . . Each character writes not only the present but *her* present. Even when recounting events of the past, of another's past, she is engaged in a performance of her present. And above all, that performance is for another.

24 Richardson, *Clarissa*, 1486.
25 Ibid.
26 Ibid., 1488.
27 Couched within a complaint about postmortem expenses incurred, de la Tour's report of Lovelace's final words, "LET THIS EXPIATE," empties them of their dramatic force in a manner reminiscent of Benjamin's observation of the "banality" that "issues" when "dramatic structure is emptied" and allegory "become[s] a hollow façade." See Walter Benjamin, *The Origin of German Tragic Drama*, trans. John Osborne (New York: Verso, 2009), 212–23:

> The obstacle of meaning and intrigue loses its weight, and both operatic plot and operatic language follow their course without encountering any resistance, issuing finally into banality. With the disappearance of the

obstacle the soul of the work, mourning, also disappears, and just as the dramatic structure is emptied, so too is the scenic structure, which looks elsewhere for its justification, *now* that allegory, where it is not omitted, has become a hollow façade. (Emphasis mine).

28 Clarissa writes of Lovelace's reputation as "a great plotter" in Richardson, *Clarissa*, 50. Later, Lovelace refers to himself in a letter to Belford as "the most plotting heart in the world" (Emphasis in text). See Richardson, *Clarissa*, 558. For references to Clarissa's "allegory," see Richardson, *Clarissa*, 1031, 1043, 1297, 1302, et. al.

29 G. W. F. Hegel, *Phenomenology of Spirit*, trans. A. V. Miller (Oxford: Oxford University Press, 1977), 59–60.

30 Hegel, *Phenomenology*, 63.

31 Ibid., 64.

32 G. W. F. Hegel, *Hegel's Aesthetics: Lectures on Fine Art*, trans. T. M. Knox (1975; Oxford: Oxford University Press, 2010), 8.

33 G. W. F. Hegel, *Vorlesungen über die Ästhetik*, vols. XIII–XV of Hegel, *Theorie Werkausgabe*, ed. E. Moldenhauer and K. M. Michel, XX vols. (Frankfurt, a. M.: Suhrkamp, 1977), XIII: 23. Translation adapted from Hegel, *Lectures*, 8.

34 Paul de Man, "Reading and History," in *The Resistance to Theory* (Minneapolis: University of Minnesota Press, 1986), 68.

35 See Hegel's discussion on "also" in "Perception" in Hegel, *Phenomenology*, 73–74.

36 G. W. F. Hegel, *Phänomenologie des Geistes*, vol. III of Hegel, *Theorie Werkausgabe*, ed. E. Moldenhauer and K. M. Michel, XX vols. (Frankfurt, a. M.: Suhrkamp, 1977), III: 83.

37 Hegel, *Phenomenology*, 59.

38 Ibid., 85.

39 Ibid., 267 (emphasis added).

40 Ibid., 149.

41 See Jacques Derrida, "Ousia and Grammē: Note on a Note from Being and Time," *Margins of Philosophy*, trans. Alan Bass (Chicago: University of Chicago Press, 1982), 29–67.

42 De Man, *Resistance*, 68.

43 Ibid., 56, 64. A recent essay that calls Clarissa's posthumous letters her posthumous presence is a case in point. See James Bryant Reeves, "Posthumous Presence in Richardson's *Clarissa*," *SEL Studies in English Literature 64 1500-1900 53*, no. 3 (2013): 617: "Relying on a traditional Christian conception of time as non-linear, Richardson thus opens an interpretive space in which is readers can experience the vividness of Clarissa's posthumous presence."

44 Hegel, *Phenomenology*, 19.

45 Cf. Theodor Adorno, *Aesthetic Theory*, trans. Robert Hullot-Kentor (Minneapolis: University of Minnesota Press, 2006), 6–7:

> The great epics, which have survived even their own oblivion, were in their own age intermingled with historical and geographical reportage. . . . The history of art as that of its progressive autonomy never succeeded in extirpating this element, and not just because the bonds were too strong. At the height of its form, in the nineteenth century, the realistic novel had something of what the theory of so-called socialist realism rationally plotted for its debasement: reportage, the anticipation of what social science would later ascertain. The fanatic linguistic perfection of Madame Bovary is probably a symptom of precisely this contrary element; the unity of both, of reportage and linguistic perfectionism, accounts for the book's unfaded actuality.

46 Richardson, *Clarissa*, 882.

47 Marcel Proust, "A propos du style de Flaubert," in *Chroniques*, ed. Robert Proust (Paris: Éditions de la Nouvelle Revue Francaise, 1927), 193, 196. "Par l'usage entièrement nouveau et personnel qu'il a fait du passé défini, du passé indéfini, du participe présent, de certains pronoms et de certaines prépositions, a renouvelé presque autant notre vision des choses que Kant, avec ses Catégories, les théories de la Connaissance et de la Réalité du monde extérieur." "La révolution est accomplie; ce qui jusqu'à Flaubert était action devient impression." ("By the entirely new and personal usage that he made of the definite past tense, of indefinite past, of present participle, of certain pronouns and of certain propositions, he renewed our vision of things almost as much as Kant did with his categories, the theories of knowledge and of reality of the external world." "The revolution is accomplished; that which had been action until Flaubert became impression.")

48 Gustave Flaubert, *Trois Contes*, ed. Christian Michel (Paris: Larousse, 2008), 49. (All translations mine).

49 Cf. Kathryn Oliver Mills, *Formal Revolution in the Work of Baudelaire and Flaubert* (Newark: University of Delaware Press, 2012), 140. "The first line of '*Un Cœur Simple*' . . . indicates that the narrator has adopted the superior vantage point of a historian."

50 Flaubert, *Trois Contes*, 81:

> Puis des années s'écoulèrent, toutes pareilles et sans autres épisodes que le retour des grandes fêtes: Pâques, l'Assomption, la Toussaint. Des événements intérieurs faisaient une date, où l'on se reportait plus tard. Ainsi, en 1825, deux vitriers badigeonnèrent le vestibule; en 1827, une portion du toit, tombant dans la cour, faillit tuer un homme. L'été de 1828, ce fut à Madame d'offrir le pain bénit; Bourais, vers cette époque, s'absenta mystérieusement; et les anciennes connaissances peu à peu s'en allèrent: Guyot, Liébard, Mme Lechaptois, Robelin, l'oncle Gremanville, paralysé depuis longtemps. Une nuit, le conducteur de la malle-poste

annonça dans Pont-l'Evêque la Révolution de Juillet. Un sous-préfet nouveau, peu de jours après, fut nommé.

[Then the years passed, each similar and without any episodes than the recurrence of big festivals: Easter, the Assumption, All Saints' Day. Some minor domestic events marked a milestone that would be carried over later. Thus, in 1825, two glaziers colourwashed the vestibule; in 1827, a portion of the roof, falling in the courtyard, almost killed a man. The summer of 1828, it was Madame who offered the blessed bread; around that time, Bourais was mysteriously absent; and the old acquantainces went away little by little: Guyot, Liébard, Mme Lechaptois, Robelin, Uncle Gremanville, who was paralyzed for a long time. One night, the mailman announced the July Revolution in Pont-l'Evêque. Few days later, a new subprefect was named.]

51 Flaubert, *Trois Contes*, 49.

52 Ibid., 81.

53 Cf. Mills, *Formal Revolution*, 160. "Although she is situated in her century, ultimately Félicité's heart is more important than the sociopolitical events."

54 Flaubert, *Trois Contes*, 55.

55 Cf. Victor Brombert, *The Novels of Flaubert: A Study of Themes and Techniques* (Princeton: Princeton University Press, 1966), 170: "Flaubert is probably the first major novelist to understand that the novel is essentially an experience *in time*, and who proceeded to exploit this tragic potential" (Emphasis in text).

56 Cf. Alison Finch, "The stylistic achievements of Flaubert's Fiction," in *The Cambridge Companion to Flaubert*, ed. Timothy Unwin (Cambridge: Cambridge University Press, 2004), 149. "The present is the main tense of lyric verse in the nineteenth century and earlier; by bringing the imperfect into prominence in prose fiction, Flaubert is creating the novel's equivalent of this poetic present."

57 Compare Jakobson's understanding of poetics: "The poetic function projects the principle of equivalence from the axis of selection into the axis of combination. Equivalence is promoted to the constitutive device of the sequence" (Roman Jakobson, "Linguistics and Poetics," *Language in Literature* [Cambridge: Belknap Press, 1987], 71), with that of Lukács: "From the point of view of the writer every quality of every human being is an accident and every object merely a piece of stage property, until their decisive interconnections are expressed in poetic form, by means of some action" (Georg Lukács, *Studies in European Realism; A Sociological Survey of the Writings of Balzac, Stendhal, Zola, Tolstoy, Gorki, and Others*, trans. Edith Bone [London: Merlin Press, 1989], 57.

58 Georg Lukács, *The Theory of the Novel: A Historico-philosophical Essay on the Forms of Great Epic Literature*, trans. Anna Bostock (Cambridge, MA: M.I.T. Press, 1982), 124.

59 Flaubert, *Trois Contes*, 57.
60 Ibid., 51.
61 Ibid., 50.
62 Ibid.
63 Ibid., 67.
64 Ibid., 68.
65 Ibid.
66 Ibid.
67 Ibid., 67.
68 Ibid.
69 Ibid., 68.
70 Ibid., 67.
71 Ibid., 68.
72 Ibid.
73 Hegel, *Phenomenology*, 19.
74 Richardson, *Clarissa*, 882. (Emphasis in text).
75 Hegel, *Phenomenology*, 19.
76 Cf. Erich Auerbach, *Mimesis: The Representation of Reality in Western Literature*, trans. Willard Trask (Princeton: Princeton University Press, 2003), 486.
   [Flaubert's] role is limited to selecting the events and translating them into language; and this is done in the conviction that every event, if one is able to express it purely and completely, interprets itself and the persons involved in it far better and more completely than any opinion or judgment appended to it could do. Upon this conviction—that is, upon a profound faith in the truth of language responsibly, candidly, and carefully employed—Flaubert's artistic practice rests.
77 Hegel, *Phänomenologie*, 24.
78 See Hegel, *Phenomenology*, 19. "This power is identical with what we earlier called the Subject, which by giving determinateness an existence in its own element supersedes abstract immediacy, i.e. the immediacy which barely is, and thus is authentic substance: that being or immediacy whose mediation is not outside of it but which is this mediation itself." See also Proust, *Chroniques*, 197. "Le subjectivisme de Flaubert s'exprime par un emploi nouveau des temps des verbes, des prépositions, des adverbes, les deux derniers n'ayant presque jamais dans sa phrase qu'une valeur rythmique. Un état qui se prolonge est indiqué par l'imparfait." ("Flaubert's subjectivity is expressed through a new use of verb tenses, prepositions, adverbs, the last two almost never have in his sentence but a rhythmic value. A state that is prolonged is indicated by the imperfect.")

Bibliography

Adorno, Theodor. *Aesthetic Theory*. Translated by Robert Hullot-Kentor. Minneapolis: University of Minnesota Press, 2006.

Auerbach, Erich. *Mimesis: The Representation of Reality in Western Literature*. Translated by Willard Trask. Princeton: Princeton University Press, 2003.

Benjamin, Walter. *The Origin of German Tragic Drama*. Translated by John Osborne. New York: Verso, 2009.

Brombert, Victor. *The Novels of Flaubert: A Study of Themes and Techniques*. Princeton: Princeton University Press, 1966.

Bueler, Lois. *Clarissa's Plots*. Newark: University of Delaware Press, 1994.

Culler, Jonathan. *Flaubert: The Uses of Uncertainty*. Ithaca: Cornell University Press, 1974.

De Man, Paul. "Reading and History." In *The Resistance to Theory*. Edited by Wlad Godzich. Minneapolis: University of Minnesota Press, 1986.

Derrida, Jacques. "Ousia and Grammē: Note on a Note from Being and Time." In *Margins of Philosophy*, translated by Alan Bass, 29–67. Chicago: University of Chicago Press, 1982.

Eagleton, Terry. *The Rape of Clarissa: Writing, Sexuality, and Class Struggle in Samuel Richardson*. Minneapolis: University of Minnesota Press, 1982.

Finch, Alison. "The stylistic achievements of Flaubert's Fiction." In *The Cambridge Companion to Flaubert*, edited by Timothy Unwin, 145–64. Cambridge: Cambridge University Press, 2004.

Flaubert, Gustave. *Trois Contes*. Edited by Christian Michel. Paris: Larousse, 2008.

Hegel, G. W. F. *Hegel's Aesthetics: Lectures on Fine Art*. Translated by T. M. Knox. 1975; Oxford: Oxford University Press, 2010.

Hegel, G. W. F. *Phenomenology of Spirit*. Translated by A. V. Miller. Oxford: Oxford University Press, 1977.

Hegel, G. W. F. *Werke II*. Edited by E. Moldenhauer and K. M. Michel. Frankfurt: Suhrkamp, 1977.

Israel-Pelletier, Aimée. "Flaubert and the Visual." In *The Cambridge Companion to Flaubert*, edited by Timothy Unwin, 180–95. Cambridge: Cambridge University Press, 2004.

Jakobson, Roman. *Language in Literature*. Cambridge: Belknap Press, 1987.

Keats, John. *Complete Poems and Selected Letters of John Keats*. New York: Modern Library, 2001.

Lessing, Gotthold Ephraim. *Laocoön: An Essay on the Limits of Painting and Poetry*, translated by Edward Allen McCormick. Baltimore: Johns Hopkins University Press, 1984.

Lukács, Georg. *Studies in European Realism; a Sociological Survey of the Writings of Balzac, Stendhal, Zola, Tolstoy, Gorki, and Others*, translated by Edith Bone. London: Merlin Press, 1989.

Lukács, Georg. *The Theory of the Novel: A Historico-philosophical Essay on the Forms of Great Epic Literature*. Translated by Anna Bostock. Cambridge, MA: M.I.T. Press, 1982.

Mills, Kathryn Oliver. *Formal Revolution in the Work of Baudelaire and Flaubert.* Newark: University of Delaware Press, 2012.
Proust, Marcel. *Chroniques.* Edited by Robert Proust. Paris: Éditions de la Nouvelle revue Francaise, 1927.
Reeves, James Bryant. "Posthumous Presence in Richardson's *Clarissa.*" *SEL Studies in English Literature 1500-1900* 53, no. 3 (2013): 601–21.
Richardson, Samuel. *Clarissa, or, The History of a Young Lady.* Edited by Angus Ross. London: Penguin, 2004.
Richardson, Samuel. *Clarissa, or, The History of a Young Lady.* Abridged and edited by George Sherburn. Boston: Riverside, 1962.
Watt, Ian. *The Rise of the Novel: Studies in Defoe, Richardson, and Fielding.* Berkeley: University of California Press, 1957.

6 UNEXPECTED YET CONNECTED: ON ARISTOTLE'S *POETICS* AND ITS HETERODOX RECEPTIONS

Karen Feldman

1 Introduction

Canonical readings of Aristotle's *Poetics*, going back at least to Lessing but also prominent throughout modern literary theory and philosophy, suggest that the value of tragedy lies variously in one or more of the following: the ability to purge us of the emotions of fear and pity and/or to render us more sensitive to human foibles by evoking fear and pity in us; the insight into our own finitude it provides, most particularly by representing a climactic plot that turns on an unexpected conjunction of events; and/or its ability to teach universal truths.

In the following pages I will consider how several noncanonical, even heterodox, readings of the *Poetics* over the last few decades effectively deflate these lofty claims made about the *Poetics*, and, by extension, reflect on the functions of literature. My analysis will focus on the different ways in which events are understood to be connected to one another and on the significance of these various principles of connection. The goal is not to adjudicate among the readings, but to examine their implications for our beliefs about literature itself. In this I follow the insight of Peter Szondi that "the history of modern poetics is the history of [Aristotle's] reception and influence," including its "adoption, expansion, and systematization, as well as misunderstanding and critique."[1] The heterodox responses to Aristotle described below turn out to unsettle a post-Enlightenment reception history that tends to emphasize the didactic and metaphysical aspects of the *Poetics,* and to illuminate the particularity of literature per se.

2 Heterodox katharsis

In canonical interpretations of the *Poetics*, as exemplified most clearly in Lessing, the course of the tragic action is seen to evoke fear and pity in the audience, and the climactic revelation of the connection of the events of the drama, to produce a release of those same emotions.[2] This "purgation" (*katharsis*) of fear and pity has been seen as a valuable, restorative, and particularly important way of healing or rectifying a pathology. Out of this central reference to the evocation and catharsis of fear and pity there also developed in the eighteenth century a canonical belief that literature evokes especially important emotions in an especially valuable way. Tragedy came to be seen as a means of sentimental education, making us more sympathetic to the plight of others. On this reading fear and pity are closely connected because we pity the tragic hero but are fearful insofar as we recognize that we could be similarly met by such an unpleasant fate. We thus both identify with the hero, and hence pity him, and fear for ourselves, all of which makes us more empathic and humane, and increases our sense of fellowship with all human beings. Literature is seen in this light to make us better people because it renders us more sympathetic to others and more sensitive to the frailties of our own moral intentions and actions.

The question of whether this effect arose from an emotional sensitization to the plight of others or a rational recognition of our own finitude was of course central to eighteenth-century thinking about poetics and literature in general. Lessing's *Hamburgische Dramaturgie* suggests that fear and pity are not in fact separate emotions for Aristotle. Pity is, by its very nature, fearful because it involves a recognition of sameness between the one who pities and the one who is pitied. For this reason Lessing lambasts the German translations of Aristotle in which *phobos* is translated as *Schrecken* instead of *Furcht*.[3] Lessing argues that the phrase "fear and pity" must be understood in effect as a hendiadys—that is, as a matter, rather, of "fearful pity," *mitleidiges Schrecken*, in which pity would involve an element of fear.[4] Lessing insists, against Moses Mendelssohn, that Aristotle is describing not fear for the hero but rather a form of displaced self-pity.[5] That is, tragedy calls on a recognition already present in the emotions themselves of our shared human finitude and proneness to disaster. While the capacity for such recognition was significant in the eighteenth-century reception of the *Poetics*, the degrees and combination of rationality and emotion were disputed. The connection between fear, pity, and self-pity reappears in the twentieth century—hence Brecht criticizes Aristotle for the prescription that stimulates an identification of the audience with the character, instead of a distance that allows for critical consciousness.

But what if purging the audience's fear and pity is not central to tragedy at all, and hence katharsis is not a matter of emotional cleansing, nor of sentimental education, nor even of our recognition of our kinship with the hero in his finitude? In Owen Hardison's interpretation and Leon Golden's translation, katharsis does not refer to the purgation of emotions. Rather katharsis is seen to constitute the achievement of a *clarification*, not a *purgation*; and what is clarified are the *incidents* that form the plot of the tragedy. It is not the case, according to Golden and Hardison, that emotions get purged. Instead katharsis refers to how incidents are clarified *in their connections to each other*. Hence, rather than relating katharsis to the psychology of the spectator and the purging of emotions, Hardison argues that the katharsis *of incidents* involves an enhanced depiction of a necessary and probable course of events, a depiction, in other words, of maximal connection of events.[6] If katharsis is at the center of Aristotle's definition of tragedy, then on Golden and Hardison's reading that center is not primarily emotional; it is a matter of clarifying connection in the movement of a necessary and probable course of events. This is consistent with Aristotle's emphasis throughout the *Poetics* on the primacy of the *muthos*, such that nothing may mitigate the connections that are depicted in the course of the tragic drama. With the emphasis on the inexorable unfolding of events, this reading downplays the importance of subjectivity—both that of the hero and of the audience. This reading of katharsis is therefore far less humanistic or anthropocentric in orientation than readings that emphasize fear, pity, and the psychology of the tragic characters. What is at stake instead is the automatism of a system or sequence of events that operate beyond human control, intention, or teleology.

Claudio William Veloso argues in a different vein for the centrality of the events above all, on the basis of a philological argument that katharsis does not appear in the *Poetics* in the first place, neither as purgation nor clarification. According to Veloso, the phrase *pathematon catharsin* was interpolated in a misreading of an earlier manuscript and should properly be read as *pragmaton sustasin*, the arrangement of incidents.[7] Veloso's revision of this key spot in which Aristotle names the goal of tragedy would put the arrangement of fearful and pitiful incidents at the center of the tragedy. Veloso points out that this is entirely fitting with Aristotle's emphasis on plot and the lack of further reference to katharsis in the *Poetics*. The events themselves, rather than the emotions they evoke, are thereby stated once again to be the point of tragedy. With Golden/Hardison's and Veloso's readings, sentimental education by way of emotional purgation, and the lofty recognition of our common humanity and shared frailty are left aside in favor of the bare connection of tragic events to one another.

3 Didacticism and universals

The Golden/Hardison interpretation, and the Veloso interpretation, with their emphasis on the sheer connection of events, speak against Lessing's suggestion that the *Poetics* involves the capacity for human solidarity in tragedy's evocation of fear and pity. A somewhat separate Enlightenment legacy in the reception of the *Poetics* can also be found in twentieth-century representations of the *Poetics* as offering philosophical reflections on universal truths. Indeed Aristotle famously contrasts poetry and history, claiming that "Poetry ... is more philosophical and more significant than history, for poetry is more concerned with the universal, and history with the individual."[8] Based on this reference to universals, twentieth-century philosophical readings of the *Poetics* have found in it a cornerstone of a large-scale ethical theory; Martha Nussbaum, for instance, suggests that tragedy shows us what our human values are.[9]

The prominence of the term "universal" (*katholou*) in the *Poetics* lends itself to such philosophical and ethical interpretations, rather than literary ones, in which by extension literature per se is seen as dealing with broader, wider-reaching truths than any other kind of writing. There are, however, interpretations of Aristotle's references to universals that downplay or contradict the notion that the *Poetics* is concerned with didacticism or even philosophical insight at all. J. M. Armstrong's heterodox reading of what Aristotle means by universals offers a much more modest philosophical yield from tragedy. Armstrong suggests that the universals Aristotle refers to in the *Poetics* are not universal truths, nor anything metaphysical. Rather, universals are a matter of general *types,* and have to do, more modestly, with types of events above all. Armstrong examines Aristotle's statement that "A universal is the sort of thing that a certain sort of person happens to say or do according to likelihood or necessity, which is what poetry aims at, although names [of characters] are added."[10] He interprets this passage as suggesting that universals in Aristotle's context are simply types of events, which in turn fit with types of characters.

In Armstrong's rendition, "universal" is not a matter of an abstract or metaphysical truth or value. Instead it is a sheerly literary designation regarding genre or event-type for the purposes of inventing a plot to be peopled with particular characters, deeds, and incidents. Types, genre, character—these are not Platonic forms nor truths of a higher sort; they are structural relations that condition our knowledge of connections between actions and characters, hence our knowledge of the world as such, not as metaphysical universals but as types that are intelligible to us, most obviously in tragedy.

4 Pleasure and aesthetics

Perhaps most deflationary of all when it comes to anti-didactic readings of the *Poetics* and the role of universals in Aristotle's definition of the tragic genre is the interpretation of G. R. F. Ferrari. He suggests, following Dorothy Sayers and against the canon of didactic readings, that tragedy is purely a matter of the art of suspense.[11] The "universality" of the plot is, in Ferrari's interpretation, not a matter of the insight it provides, and the "universality" of the tragedy has no moral or educative function; it is instead simply a matter of the likelihood that connects the events.[12] What, then, could Aristotle find "more philosophical" "and "more serious" about poetry than about history in this understanding of universals? What is "universal" here, in Ferrari's reading, is the understanding of plausibility and likelihood in the connection of tragic events that is required for the production of a properly tragic plot. This understanding of plausibility is a more philosophical task than history-writing, which does not require such an understanding because it is tied to actual events rather than fabulated ones. Hence universals are not a metaphysical matter at all but a literary one, for Aristotle is exclusively concerned with "the qualities of what we would now call 'literature' and . . . what makes a literary work of art successful in its own special terms—with tragic drama, the consummate literary form, selected for particular attention."[13]

Ferrari emphasizes that within Aristotle's genre prescriptions, "philosophical" ability is only at stake for the poet. That is, the poet's task is philosophical, insofar as the process of plot creation requires an understanding of universals. Nonetheless "that the *task* [of the poet] is more philosophical, however, does not mean that its *product* is any kind of philosophy, or aims at any kind of teaching."[14] The *tragedian* must be philosophical, but not the tragedy itself, since in Ferrari's view, "Tragedy is plot for plot's sake."[15] Likewise, the relentless inevitability of succession of events in the tragedy is "a fictional creation of the dramatist's," it is not a matter of teaching us about fate, finitude, universals, or human values.[16] Ferrari resists at each turn a didactic, moral interpretation of the *Poetics;* in his reading Aristotle writes a recipe for suspenseful—and only for that reason "good"—literature.

Key to Ferrari's argument is his translation of Aristotle's statement about the unexpectedness of the events of the tragedy. Lines 1452a4-5 are usually translated to mean "contrary to expectation [and yet] because of one another." Ferrari emphasizes, however, that most translations include an adversative—the "but" or "and yet"—which indicates that there is a conflict between the causal connection of the events (because of one another) and the unexpected character of those events (contrary to expectation).[17] The adversative in "contrary to expectation *and yet/but* because of one another" (emphasis added) suggests a mismatch between the flaunting of our expectations regarding what happens and the tight causal connections that lead to those happenings. For Ferrari, this translation gives rise to quasi-existential readings of tragedy as turning on a divide between our human expectations and fate. But Aristotle's Greek, Ferrari shows, does not contain the adversative in the first place. Thus instead of "contrary to expectation *and yet* because of one another," which again suggests a conflict between the audience's expectation and the necessity of events, Ferrari argues for the translation, "against expectation *because of* one another," with no adversative. In other words, what is contrary to expectation is not the events themselves but that they occur because of one another, that is, what is surprising is that they are causally connected.

For Ferrari the heart of tragedy is this surprising causal connection, and nothing else. Such an unanticipated linkage of cause and effect is striking in its effect. It is striking to the characters above all, who are themselves surprised by the reversals that turn out to be contained in the confluence of events. It is of course also striking to audience members unacquainted with the story. Yet even for audience members familiar with the story, the unfolding of that story can produce pleasure, owing to "that capacity we all have to find a novel thrilling even on second, third, fourth readings."[18] Even when the fact of that connection is known in advance, its representation is the source of the pleasure. Hence, Ferrari treats the likelihood that connects the tragic events as an aesthetic rather than a moral or metaphysical term.[19] It is not a *metaphysical* inevitability that connects the tragic events, rather it is a "*writerly* inevitability."[20]

5 Pleasures of the unexpected

As we have seen, the "writerly inevitability" represented in the connection of tragic incidents is what produces proper tragic pleasure in Ferrari's interpretation of Aristotle's prescriptions for the pleasure of tragedy. While other critics puzzle over Aristotle's references to probability, necessity, likelihood, and plausibility in the connection of tragic events, Ferrari's point is that the looseness of Aristotle's terms reflects a concern for connectedness per se, "and never mind exactly how."[21] The causal connection simply must be surprising and unexpected, regardless of whether that causality is necessary or probable or plausible. What is significant for the purposes of tragedy is that, in an always surprising aesthetic sense, "the pieces unexpectedly come together," and hence what is marvelous is "the emergence of the unexpected from its causal nexus."[22]

For when events occur because of one another and yet their relationship, even when known, appears to us as unexpected, this is for Aristotle "more marvelous" than sheer chance (152a59). The events in a good plot "defeat expectation *by virtue of* resulting from one another,"[23] with that virtue ("vir" or "strength") residing in the artifice of its construction. The marvelousness to which Aristotle refers is a matter of "the intricacies of the plot, and the winding-up and subsequent release of suspense."[24] Things unexpectedly fit together in tragedy, and that is the source of the great pleasure. This pleasure in unexpected fit is clarified in Ferrari's reading of the Mitys anecdote in which, Aristotle reports, the murderer of the king Mitys was himself killed when a statue of the dead Mitys fell on him (1452a). Ferrari suggests that Aristotle's reference to the Mitys anecdote shows that even the mere appearance of extreme coincidence—without an actual causal connection—produces a great pleasure in both tragedy and in life. Hence the story of Mitys' killer "seems. . . . Too good to be true; seems, as we might also say, just like a story."[25]

For Ferrari, the revelation of connections between events is key because it produces the requisite amazement and pleasure in the audience. The whole point of Aristotle's treatment of plot is the maximization of properly tragic pleasure; but, in contrast to a tradition that sees tragedy as teaching us universal truths, that proper pleasure is not for Ferrari related to learning, insight, edification, or existential recognition of human finitude. The pleasure, in Aristotle's prescriptions for the genre of tragedy, is of simple suspense and release, as evoked by the audience's sympathy for the hero. What is "philosophical" here is the poet's understanding of how to maximize the pleasure by producing a surprisingly connected set of events.

In effect Ferrari expands on Armstrong's view that considerations rightly pertaining to "philosophy" are on the side of the poet who must discern what makes for the right type of action and hence plausible connections between events. Ferrari, however, emphasizes that the deployment of this discernment serves no purpose other than that of producing greater pleasure by way of greater suspense and release. Katharsis is, in this model, not a purgation of anything intrinsic to the audience, no "preexisting pathological condition," nor is anything essential at work here[26]; the play produces pity and fear through artful construction just as it purges them. The tragedian must have insight about producing proper plots; this is Armstrong's view as well. But the purpose of such plots is neither to produce learning, nor an identification with the tragic hero, a recognition of our human finitude, or a conflict between expectation and likelihood. Ferrari's only "larger" take on tragedy is that tragic plot (as in the Oedipus story) "effects a match between the machinations of the gods and those of the human mechanic who makes the whole thing run—the playwright."[27] Tragedy is not about evoking philosophical insights on the part of the audience either, and this holds true for literature as well: "for every drama and literary fiction tout court . . . The human dramatist plays god in the little world he has created."[28]

Ferrari's anti-existential, anti-didactic reading rejects the idea that with the reversal of fortune that is tied to recognition, a tragedy should illuminate our own existence within finitude, chance, and inexorability. Rather, despite Aristotle's claims in the earlier chapters of the *Poetics* about the pleasures of learning from imitations, the pleasure we get from tragedy is exclusively caused by the tension and subsequent release therefrom generated by the mechanisms of its plot. It is not a matter of intelligibility and meaning; fear and pity are not existentially more important than other emotions; in fact, Ferrari even suggests anger and shame as other possible emotions that tragedy might arouse.[29] Fear and pity are significant for the simple reason that they are effective ingredients for maximal suspense and release in the audience.[30] Hence in contrast to Enlightenment readings and philosophical interpretations, Ferrari argues that the *Poetics* offers purely literary prescriptions for properly tragic pleasure, with no existential, intellectual, edifying implications. Tragedy does not give the audience a "universal" understanding in contrast to history, according to Ferrari. For Ferrari, rather than offering us any higher pleasure of learning, Aristotle is instead analyzing and describing the most effective means of heightening "the *lowest* common denominator of the pleasure we take in fictions."[31]

6 Conclusion: Allegories of reception

For Ferrari, philosophical readings of the *Poetics* that focus on its didactic qualities and claim that tragedy offers insights into universals neglect the specifically literary character both of the genre and of Aristotle's prescriptions. In a different register, David Ferris views the *Poetics* itself as performing an occlusion of the specific question of literature, and literary criticism in general as repeating this avoidance of the literary.[32] Specifically, Ferris argues that the shift within the *Poetics* from the topic of mimesis, in its first five chapters, to the prescriptions for tragedy in those that follow, constitutes an evasion of the central literary question of mimesis. Ferris concludes that the history of literary theory recapitulates the break in the *Poetics* where the question of mimesis is dropped and instead the genre prescriptions for tragedy become the focus. The question of what mimesis is and how it works haunts the history of literary theory, which continues to evade that question in its emphasis on prescriptions and genre debates.

The question of the literary character of the *Poetics* in Ferrari's and Ferris's readings and, in very different ways, the readings of Armstrong, Veloso, and Golden and Hardison, focus on the connections of events in tragic plot in place of any of the didactic, metaphysical or otherwise "lofty" functions that philosophers attribute to tragedy. Such widely divergent receptions of Aristotle offer an allegory of sorts for the uncertain relationship of didacticism and moral enlightenment to literature per se: Does literature make us wiser, better, more moral? Traditional readings of the *Poetics* see it in terms of the insights gained, the moral functions accomplished, the edification of the audience, including the identification of our own potential moral flaws. In such didactic readings, it is the effect on the audience rather than the prerequisites for the writer that are at issue. For Armstrong, the writer's insight into universals understood as *types* of events is the closest the *Poetics* comes to philosophy. For Golden and Hardison, the emotions of fear and pity are not purged so much as the connection of events is clarified. If there is a didacticism in this, it is simply the exposure to the inexorability of such connections. For Veloso, there is no katharsis in the first place, only the unfolding of actions.

For Ferrari, the didactic readings obscure Aristotle's straightforward concern for tragic pleasure in suspense and release. In different ways, the philosophical, didactic, and "universalizing" readings, in Ferrari's words, put "more moral and existential weight on the girders of Aristotle's structure than they were designed to bear."[33] On the other hand, the receptions of the *Poetics* that focus on the didactic function of tragedy, the revelation of metaphysical universals, and the purgation of fear and pity in the audience—which in modernity comes to us by way of Lessing and others—cannot be shed as if they were an old skin. Whether or not we find any of the heterodox (and incompatible) readings of the *Poetics* convincing, we can ask, in any case, why the canonical reception of Aristotle developed and prevailed to begin with; how and why tragedy came to be attributed a moral weight, and insight, privileged in its reception; why, since the Enlightenment, theory upon theory has presumed an edifying function for tragedy instead of a sheerly pleasurable one.

There is a desire for morality in the reception of Aristotle's *Poetics*, in other words, that may not be present in the *Poetics* itself. Where did this desire for morality come from and how does it pertain to the form of the tragedy? That last question comes in effect from Hayden White, who applies literary analysis of plot to historiography but ends up with large-scale accounts of ideology critique.[34] For White, the desire for narrative closure in historiography corresponds to a wish for completeness in stories that does not exist in life itself. The closure of the story in the form of the narrative fulfills, albeit only partially and temporarily, the desire for such completeness. Reception is of course also a historical phenomenon, but is inseparable from the formal aspects of what is received. In other words, the historical phenomenon of the moralizing receptions of the *Poetics* seek their support in the form of tragedy that Aristotle prescribes. Even though Aristotle's prescriptions for the connections between tragic events are formal, they nonetheless evoke historical understandings in the legacy of the *Poetics*' reception. That legacy involves didacticism and metaphysical universals, but also rejections of these in favor of a formal approach to the connections of the *Poetics*. If, as Ferris writes, all literary theory recapitulates the avoidances enacted in the *Poetics*, then the tangle of receptions reviewed here properly demonstrates the impossibility of separating the formal level of critique from the historical object it examines.[35]

Notes

1 Peter Szondi, *An Essay on the Tragic,* trans. Paul Fleming (Stanford: Stanford University Press, 2002), 1.

2 Aristotle, *Poetics,* 1449b10-11.

3 Gotthold Ephraim Lessing, *Hamburgische Dramaturgie,* in *Werke,* vol. 6, ed. Herbert G. Göpfert (Munich: Hanser, 1979), §74, 265.

4 Lessing, "Dramaturgie," §§74–78, 264–77.

5 "Es ist die Furcht, welche aus unserer Ähnlichkeit mit der leidenden Person für uns selbst entspringt; es ist die Furcht, dass die Unglücksfälle, die wir über diese verhänget sehen, uns selbst treffen können; es ist die Furcht, dass wir der bemitleidete Gegenstand selbst werden können. Mit einem Worte: diese Furcht ist das auf uns selbst bezogene Mitleid" [It is the fear for ourselves which originates from our similarity with that of the sufferer; it is the fear that the misfortunes that we see are impending for the sufferer could also befall ourselves; it is the fear that we ourselves could become the object of such pity. In a word, this fear is pity that is directed toward ourselves.] (Lessing, "Dramaturgie," §75, 267).

6   Leon Golden, Owen Hardison, *Aristotle's Poetics: A Translation and Commentary for Students of Literature*. Translated by Leon Golden. Commentary by Owen Hardison (Tallahassee: Florida State University Press, 1981), 113–20.

7   Claudio William Veloso, "Aristotle's *Poetics* without Katharsis, Fear or Pity," *Oxford Studies in Ancient Philosophy* 33 (Winter 2007), 268.

8   Aristotle, *Poetics,* trans. Leon Golden (Tallahassee: Florida State University Press, 1981), 17.

9   Martha Nussbaum, *The Fragility of Goodness: Luck and Ethics in Greek Tragedy and Philosophy* (Cambridge: Cambridge University Press, 1986), 378–94.

10 J. M. Armstrong, "Aristotle on the Philosophical Nature of Poetry," *The Classical Quarterly* 48, no. 2 (1998): 450.

11 See Sayers, Dorothy L. "Aristotle on Detective Fiction," *English* 1, no. 1 (1936): 23–35.

12 "The universality at which poetry aims is not its ultimate goal but something it must look to if its plots are to be properly constructed . . . . Poetry 'says what is universal' not by making universal statements but by fulfilling the task that Aristotle assigned to the poet . . . [i.e.] of saying 'what could be expected to happen'" (G. R. F. Ferrari, "Aristotle's Literary Aesthetics," *Phronesis* 64, no. 3 [1999]: 181–98).

13 Ferrari, "Aristotle's Aesthetics," 181.

14 Ibid., 188.

15 Ibid., 183.

16 Ibid., 188.

17 Translations of the *Poetics* differ somewhat but the following selection indicates that they include what Ferrari points to as the "adversative" element, the "but" or "yet": "contrary to expectation yet still on account of one another" (Halliwell, Aristotle. *Poetics*. Translated by Stephen Halliwell [Chicago: University of Chicago Press, 1998]. 63); "unexpectedly, yet because of one another" (Golden, Leon, "Aristotle, Frye, and the Theory of Tragedy," *Comparative Literature* 27, no. 1 [1975]: 47–58); "contrary to expectation but because of one another" (Janko, Aristotle. *Poetics*. Translated by Richard Janko. [Indianapolis: Hackett Publishing Co., 1987], p. 13).

18 Ferrari, "Aristotle's Aesthetics," 192.

19 Ibid., 188.

20 Ibid., 187, emphasis added.

21 Ferrari, "Aristotle's Aesthetics," 189.

22 Ibid., 192.

23 Ibid., 191.
24 Ibid., 186.
25 Ibid., 192.
26 Ibid.
27 Ibid., 193.
28 Ibid.
29 Ibid., 194.
30 The fear and pity that are evoked by tragedy are not for ourselves, in Ferrari's reading, and do not teach us about our own vulnerability. The tragedy evokes our fear and pity on behalf of the hero of the play. In contrast to the *Rhetoric*, in which Aristotle is concerned with how to motivate an audience to action or commitment, and thus fear for themselves must be produced by the speaker (II.v.15), the tragic poet's job is instead to engage the audience in the fiction he has created. We care about, and thus fear for and pity, the tragic hero. We do not fear for ourselves or reflect on ourselves and katharsis involves the pleasure of relief when suspense is heightened and released.
31 Ferrari, "Aristotle's Aesthetics," 185 (emphasis added).
32 See David Ferris, *Theory and the Evasion of History* (Baltimore: The Johns Hopkins University Press, 1993).
33 Ferrari, "Aristotle's Aesthetics," 190.
34 Hayden White, "The Value of Narrativity in the Representation of Reality," in *The Content of the Form* (Baltimore: The Johns Hopkins University Press, 1987), 1–25.
35 Ferris, "*Theory*," 2.

Bibliography

Aristotle. *Poetics*. Translated by Leon Golden. Tallahassee: Florida State University Press, 1981.

Aristotle. *Poetics*. Translated by Richard Janko. Indianapolis: Hackett Publishing Co., 1987.

Aristotle. *Poetics*. Translated by Stephen Halliwell. Chicago: University of Chicago Press, 1998.

Aristotle. *Art of Rhetoric*. Translated by J. H. Freese. Cambridge: Harvard University Press, 2006.

Armstrong, J. M. "Aristotle on the Philosophical Nature of Poetry." *The Classical Quarterly* 48, no. 2 (1998): 447–55.

Brodsky, Claudia. "Lessing and the Drama of the Theory of Tragedy," *MLN* 98 (1983): 426–53.

Campe, Rüdiger. "Presenting the Affect the Scene of Pathos in Aristotle's *Rhetoric* and Its Revision in Descartes' *Passions of the Soul*." In *Rethinking Emotion: Interiority and Exteriority in Premodern, Modern, and Contemporary Thought*, edited by Julia Weber and Rüdiger Campe, 36–57. Berlin: De Gruyter, 2014.

Ferrari, G. R. F. "Aristotle's Literary Aesthetics." *Phronesis* 64, no. 3 (1999): 181–98.

Ferris, David. *Theory and the Evasion of History*. Baltimore: The Johns Hopkins University Press, 1993.

Golden, Leon. "Aristotle, Frye, and the Theory of Tragedy." *Comparative Literature* 27, no. 1 (1975): 47–58.

Golden, Leon and Hardison, Owen. *Aristotle's Poetics: A Translation and Commentary for Students of Literature*. Translated by Leon Golden. Commentary by Owen Hardison. Tallahassee: Florida State University Press, 1981.

Lessing, Gotthold Ephraim. *Hamburgische Dramaturgie*. *Werke*, vol. 6. Edited by Herbert G. Göpfert. Munich: Hanser, 1979.

Nussbaum, Martha. *The Fragility of Goodness: Luck and Ethics in Greek Tragedy and Philosophy*. Cambridge: Cambridge University Press, 1986.

Sayers, Dorothy L. "Aristotle on Detective Fiction." *English* 1, no. 1 (1936): 23–35.

Szondi, Peter. *An Essay on the Tragic*. Translated by Paul Fleming. Stanford: Stanford University Press, 2002.

Veloso, Claudio William. "Aristotle's *Poetics* without Katharsis, Fear or Pity." *Oxford Studies in Ancient Philosophy* 33 (Winter 2007): 255–84.

White, Hayden. *The Content of the Form*. Baltimore: The Johns Hopkins University Press, 1987.

7 THE CAUSAL ECONOMY OF THE SUBJECT IN KANT, HEGEL, AND MARX: BEING IN TIME AND EXTERNALIZATION

Irina Simova

With the recent insurgence of speculation on the special being of objects and "theological niceties"[1] of things, meditations on the question of mediation do not appear untimely. Attempts to return to a pre-critical discourse claiming to speak directly for the enchanted being of objects aim both to recast the objective as pure gift of *physis* and to escape their own structures of meaning-production by equating these with the immediately given, things-in-themselves whose distance from reflective representation has been reduced to an absolute minimum. As if included within that reduction, the subject performing it appears to vanish even while projecting its own capability to produce knowledge and signification ever more exclusively upon objects.

As is well known, it was precisely by theoretically bracketing off all such notions of unmediated being that Kant enacted a radical break in the history of metaphysics, re-orienting the focus and presumed basis of philosophical speculation from a pure, transcendent origin of knowledge to an hypothesis of strictly limited knowledge produced and constructed by *a priori*, subjective mediations. The resulting object perceptions and epistemology represent not subjectively held "ideas" of "things-in-themselves" but things as they appear to us empirically. What is less well known and will serve as point of departure for the present paper is Kant's explicitly temporal predication, in the *Critique of Pure Reason*, of the "internal" existence of the subject upon its own relation to externality. For, Kant remarks, "experience... would not even be possible internally if it were not also at the same time, in part, external" ("wenn sie nicht [zum Teil] zugleich äusserlich wäre"[2]). Just as he rejects ideational mythologies of objects purporting to report on presence unmediated by the parameters of perception, Kant rejects all mythologies of subjectivity as "internal," foundational locus whose "existence" precedes "external" perception. By relating the internality of subjective experience inextricably to externality, Kant instead suggests that the subject, too, is constructed of materially mediated acts of apperception. Not only as a purveyor of knowledge but as an identity and being subject to experiential causality, the subject, Kant argues, is instantiated through an ongoing, dialectical praxis of negotiating her relation to the external.

My aim in this essay is to disturb the traditional division between idealism and materialism and reevaluate both components in this dichotomy as they are represented in the work of Kant, Hegel, and Marx. On the one hand, I reconstruct a line in Western ("idealist") metaphysics that thinks the subject, along the lines suggested by Kant, as a construct grounded upon a process of self-actualization within a field of signifying practices. Such practices—including perception, conceptualization, desire, deployment, utilization, and creation of the empirical—relate subjects to objects as these interact *in time*. This transactional logic, already articulated in brief at the outset of the *First Critique* and extensively developed by Hegel, contests the entrenched identification of all Enlightenment philosophy with a conception of the subject as self-revealing metaphysical essence or a supra-experiential scheme predating all historical figuration. My analysis suggests instead that for Kant and Hegel the subject is a form that first emerges from "the labour of the negative"[3] and is organized around a constitutive break—a productive fissure radically lacking in point of origin.

On the presumed other end of the spectrum, I argue that Marx's conception of historical materialism also questions the epistemological purity of the idealism-materialism schism. In this, the goal of replacing both the aim and outcome of philosophy, by irrevocably altering its real and conceptual bases, that Marx, famously, expressly advocated—"The philosophers have only *interpreted* the world in various ways; the point, however, is to *change* it"[4]—can be understood to derive as much from the heterogeneity of the sources of reflection espoused by both Kant and Hegel as from the object of reversing their purported purposes. For Marx's pathbreaking, historical-theoretical enactment of the temporal structure of negation itself effectively alters the very Hegelian paradigms—of subject-, history-, and concept-construction—from which it departs. With Marx, these become the central critical premise of a materialist theory of the history of capital and historical production of alienated labor as agent and subject of social praxis. Yet, the effectivity of Marx's own theory, it can be argued, owes in no small measure to its enactment of—and subjection to—what Paul de Man calls a "rhetoric of blindness," according to which one thinker's insight sometimes "seems to have been gained from a negative moment . . . an unstated principle that leads [the critic's] language away from its asserted stand," while in fact "it is this negative, apparently destructive labor that led to what could legitimately be called an insight."[5]

Thus, even as Marx insists that dialectical materialism constitutes a radical break from abstract Enlightenment epistemological schemata by shifting the focus of theoretical analysis to embodied social agents, he remains "blind"—de Man would argue, inadvertently—to the positive force exercised upon his very process of thinking by the antecedent insights he de facto negates. In other words, Marx is oblivious to the powerful possibility for thinking that Kant's and Hegel's critical theories of subjects—first instantiated by their relation to externality, in the form of objects, praxes, or norms—provide. Thus, Marx's theoretization of historical materialism disavows certain historical-critical aspects of previous "idealist" thinking (reducing Hegel's *Begriff*, for example, to a disembodied mystification) and even can be seen to relapse into a form of pre-Kantian idealism, one that predicates the subject upon a primary emergence of pure being and understands alienation as a secondary and reversible process.

Finally, the reevaluation of the materialist strain in Enlightenment thought provided in this analysis uncovers the inherent instability at the core of any subject's accession to a situated selfhood that Hegel's model of externalization and dialectical paradigm of work *as action*—of object-production and subject-formation—first exposes and Marx's critique of philosophical "idealism" largely ignores. For both Kant and Hegel, this analysis argues, the experiential fact of existence in time (*Dasein in der Zeit*) at once precludes any foundational notion of identity and produces actual historical subjectivity as a form of belatedness.

1 The subject as temporal relation: Kant's model of *Dasein in der Zeit*

In a footnote to the Preface to the second edition of the *Critique of Pure Reason* refuting the idealist view that the external (or permanent, as he calls it) might be subjectively contrived, Kant states:

> But this permanent cannot be an intuition in me. For all the determining grounds of my existence [*meines Daseins*] which can be found in me, are representations, and, as such, do themselves require a permanent, distinct from them, which may determine my existence in relation to their changes, that is, my existence in time, wherein they change.[6]

This assessment of the relation between the perception of external permanence and "my existence" is itself based upon a radical departure from the history of metaphysics, a definition of subjective existence unlike any preceding it, including, most notably, Descartes's. Kant elaborates:

> But I am conscious, through internal *experience*, of my *existence in time* [*Dasein in der Zeit*] (consequently, also, of the determinability of the former in the latter), and that is more than the simple consciousness of my representation. It is, in fact, the same as the *empirical consciousness of my existence*, which can only be determined in relation to something, which, while connected with my existence, is *external to me*. This consciousness of my existence in time is, therefore, identical with the consciousness of a relation to something *external to me* [emphasis mine], and it is therefore, experience, not fiction, sense, not imagination, which inseparably connects what is external to me with my internal sense.[7]

The basis for Kant's claims in these passages, as Claudia Brodsky has argued,[8] lies in his understanding of time as a nonempirical conception, which, *as such,* is unavailable to phenomenal perception. Brodsky observes: "Every reference to time as a line is a figure of speech upon which we ... rely—but *only* a figure of speech on which we rely—because, as such, time is equally unavailable to wholly empirical experience and purely 'intellectual intuition'."[9] As a "*pure* form of *sensuous* intuition,"[10] that is, an internal form for the construction of external cognitions by all subjects, time does not adhere in things, but determines the relations informing our representations of things. Not only is time not externally observable: it cannot even be represented *figuratively* nor itself serve as form for representation without first being related by us to external objects of experience. For the same reason, our consciousness of our own existence, as "being in time" ("Dasein in der Zeit"), can only be determined in relation to given externals whose perception by us (as representation) has the effect of first rendering time itself perceptible (in the contrasting modes of "permanence," "contemporaneity" and "succession"[11]). In other words, the subject can neither perceive nor have any conception of either time or her own "existence in time" independent of empirical data; in fact, as Brodsky maintains: "the only way we can understand time *is* analogically, i.e., based on experience, but that experience is of phenomenal objects *in* time, not 'empty' or 'unified' time itself."[12] Thus, the conditions of possibility of *Dasein in der Zeit* require, according to Kant, an "I" related to the external world by the "analogies of experience"[13] or modi of temporal organization that formalize our perceptions of relations between material things. The constant relating of externality to its perception by the subject is, Kant states, "identical with" the subject's "consciousness" of its own "being in time."[14] Therefore the internal agency of the subject, her consciousness, does not precede but rather depends on its experiential relation to the objective world.

This dynamic model of the subject as temporal nexus between the internal and the external indicates that underlying Kant's architectonic model of empirical cognition are *practices* relating a subject to the objects of which she is aware. When viewed through this lens, Kant's and Hegel's understanding of subject formation appears to operate on a similar structural principle: that of consciousness produced in acts of mediation relating subjects with the empirically given in time. Indeed, the "concept," as Hegel conceives it anew, is no longer a merely nominal tool of cognition, but rather the *content of subject-object relations* first rendered explicit to and by consciousness.

2 Hegel's subject and concept as historical formations

In direct contrast to entrenched metaphysical readings of his work, this analysis identifies in Hegel's epistemology an explicitly historical development of the structural framework of Kant's *Dasein in der Zeit*. Recent commentators of Hegel, from Pippin to Žižek, who have suggested that subjectivity in the *Phenomenology* is not a pre-factual, self-identical substance merely expressed differently at different moments of historical unconcealment, align with the view developed in this analysis that the subject first becomes herself in acceding to a situated selfhood via purposive activities in which she engages with regard to the empirical.[15]

On this account, the subject is in fact a potentially active because "empty," that is, previously undetermined, signifier: a grammatical and semantic placeholder whose content is defined only within and by the subject's history of practices of perceiving, mediating, and acting upon the experientially given. It is precisely in this—in her own ongoing predication upon object relations—that the subject *qua* subject comes into being as such *in time*. For, this critical re-interpretation of Kant's and Hegel's subject, I argue (*pace* Marx), contradicts the essentially atemporal logic of unilateral—whether object- or subject-based—epistemologies by including temporality within its understanding of the active, work-based production of experience, knowledge, and history as such. In so doing, this critical turn within philosophy paves the way for a shift from an essentialist understanding of subjectivity to a philosophy of subjective praxis in which historically situated and embodied agents participate in and are modified by a system of socially signifying practices.

In traditional interpretations of the structural causality of the subject in Hegel, an initial projection of the self into the realm of the objective (i.e., our perceiving, cognizing, and acting in the world) is recuperated into the subject through her appropriation of objectivized content. The standard account of this model insists on the essentially disembodied nature of the self and the conceptual apparatus it produces, an understanding that, on my reading, fails to account for the fundamental rift between interiority and exteriority and the material practices of mediation at the core of Hegel's model of individuation and articulated knowledge. As Hegel states of the foundational act of relating any subject to its other, "the identification of Subject and Predicate" "in philosophical proposition[s]" "is *not* meant to destroy the difference between them."[16]

Hegel's famous statement in the Preface to the *Phenomenology* that everything hinges on "expressing the True [i.e. the actual] not *only*[17] as *Substance*, but equally as *Subject*,"[18] does not presuppose a simple principle of self-identity, through which an essentially abstract subject/spirit emerges redoubled, as the traditional "idealist-subjectivist" reading of his work suggests. Indeed, Hegel's dialectical method is itself an elaborate critique of the "monochromatic" formalism of the Absolute, whose failure to produce distinctions of any kind, he famously remarks, results only in a "night in which, as the saying goes, all cows are black."[19] Thus, Hegel's epistemology is aligned with Kant's approach, in which subjectivity becomes aware of itself not as an immediate given, but *in its relation* to externality, that is, relations themselves *produced*, on Hegel's view, through a host of necessarily temporal—perceptual and cognitive—practices of interaction with the objective. The "concepts" resulting from such a praxis of cognition, as Robert Brandom has argued,[20] contain rather than efface the meaning and history of the mediating acts of their production.

Hegel's model of concept formation is spelled out—objectified or exemplified—in his discussion of our use of such deictic or indexical terms as "This," "Here" and "Now" in the opening chapter of the *Phenomenology*, "Sense-Certainty: or the 'This' and 'Meaning'."[21] Purposefully employing everyday instances of perception, Hegel begins his discussion by hypothetically equating a present moment, "Now," with "Night,"[22] that is, the actual, specifically demarcated objectification of time he is experiencing "now." Commenting that, like any valid cognitive perception, this one should not be impaired merely by being "written down,"[23] Hegel narrates that, having so transcribed his perception, he looks again and finds instead that, "Now" has become "*this noon*."[24] Through its external relation to two perceptibly distinct moments in time, the content of the concept, "Now," is internally differentiated and thus constructed and cognized to possess general meaning. If the "Night" of "Now" had not been preserved as a previous content of the concept, comparable to another that succeeds and negates it experientially, the applicability of the concept, "Now," *as* concept, to an infinite number of particular spatio-temporal contents would have been impossible to cognize.

Such conceptual cognition requires mediation, or as Hegel states: "This self-preserving Now is, therefore, not immediate, but mediated; for it is determined as a permanent and self-preserving Now *through* the fact that something else, viz. Day and Night, is *not*."[25] Yet, in Hegel's narrative of the production of the concept, "Now," the empirical actuality of the individual context serves not only as particular grist for the greater mediation of the concept, as traditional interpretations of Hegel would have it (i.e., that of immediate experiences dialectically negated by mediation that transcends them ideationally). By preserving the specific spatio-temporal moments upon which it depends, Hegel's narrative model of conceptualization instead renders the concept indisassociable from an historical praxis. Hegel's concept carries its history with it: the product of empirical differentiation and its mediation performed by a cognizing subject, it also departs historically from its postulation as *a priori* category of knowledge within Kant's epistemology.

On this reading, the concept starts out like an indexical, a general linguistic form or "empty beginning,"[26] which is to be filled with content in the process of its application, becoming "actual knowledge" "only in the end of the proposition"[27] in which it partakes. The *Begriff* in this epistemological framework becomes a sublated form of the history of its own production. In other words, according to Hegel, Kant's model of being in time is not only a mode of subject formation, but is also reflected in the structures of cognition, foregrounding an understanding of the subject as shaped by her perceptual, inferential, and practical interaction with the objective. It thus opens up a theoretical mode for the inclusion of the social in epistemology as the terrain in which such perceptual, inferential, and practical activities are embedded and enacted.[28] This paradigm shift toward a philosophy of praxis is therefore already enacted *in nuce* in Hegel's work long before Marx's famous contention in the *German Ideology* that: "The production of ideas, of conceptions, of consciousness, is at first directly interwoven with the material activity and the material intercourse of men—the language of real life."[29] In fact such historical-processual resignification of epistemology would itself have been unthinkable without Hegel's mediation.

3 Alienation as a principle of subject formation in Hegel

As already suggested, Hegel understands the subject as a fundamental decentering: the split between subject and substance is foundational and subjectivity accedes to a stabilized selfhood only as a temporary derivative effect of its relating of itself to externality. As Žižek argues, "The subject has no substantial actuality, it comes second, it emerges only through the process of separation, the overcoming of its presuppositions and the presuppositions are also just the retroactive effect of the same process of their overcoming."[30] Hegel's well-known lord-bondsman dialectic can be understood in the same manner—it is not so much a narrative of struggle and liberation of a formed but subjugated consciousness as it is an epistemological account of the construction of the self. With it, it can be argued, Hegel endeavors to demonstrate how the coming into being of a self-conscious subject is always already a form of *Nachträglichkeit*: like the concept, the subject is a reconstruction of past activities of meaning and self-expression. It is precisely this feature of Hegel's understanding of subject formation that Marx in his own dialectical enactment of blindness and insight overlooks while reappropriating the lord-bondsman model.

In the origin myth of the lord-bondsman dialectic,[31] as presented by Hegel, the self is initially "the universal, indestructible substance, the fluid self-identical essence"[32] and all external reality is for this self an "inessential, negatively characterized object."[33] Thus while this primordial, "fluid" self possesses *subjective* certainty regarding the authenticity and absoluteness of its self-representation, in order to confirm to itself this representation *objectively*, it has to confront and negate all "inessential" external objectivity.

According to Hegel's paradigmatic narrative, when two such self-positing instantiations of subjectivity come into contact, a struggle for domination ensues, whereby the defeated self, the bondsman, has to reconstitute its self-representation as one coterminous with "thinghood."[34] A new economy of self-identification emerges in this process, as the bondsman accepts the subjective representations[35] of the lord as normative and perceives his own essential nature as being for another. The lord, for his part, can only relate to the bondsman as to an entity affirming his own identity, while annihilating any other objectivity, as it contests his status as a self-sufficient and autotelic consciousness.

The lord's rapport to externality is therefore mediated through the bondsman who, as separate self-consciousness, relates negatively to the object, but, as dominated self, cannot completely annul that object's independence. The bondsman's negation of his object then becomes his work on it, which incorporates the object in the lord's web of authoritative and self-affirming desires and thus makes it available to the lord as an entity verifying the lord's identity. Yet, the lord realizes that his confirmation as a form of autonomous selfhood is in fact produced only through the mediating intervention of the bondsman's consciousness and work and thus "the inessential consciousness is for the lord the object, which constitutes the *truth* of his certainty of himself."[36] The lord as a subject-signifier does not coincide with his purported signified (autonomy)—his ostensibly self-sufficient subject position turns out to be a thwarted and impossible identification, while the bondsman is instantiated as an authentic and autonomous self-consciousness confirmed in the externalized form of his work.

This model of subject construction regards conceptualizations of the self both as a hermetic self-formation and as an unconcealing of pure origin (the lord's "fluid self-identical essence"[37]) as forms of mystification. Hegel views the production of subjectivity not as an act of unmediated self-positing, but as a process that needs to be objectivized in a form of action in order to be substantiated and cognized by a subject (of knowledge). Self-positing is nothing but self-fabulation, whereas identity in Hegel's view is produced by active differentiation vis-à-vis concrete sociohistorical reality. The "I" accedes to selfhood through the modes of mediation in which it is engaged. It is a produced effect negotiating a constitutive fissure of experience: properly actualized self-consciousness is for Hegel "a being-for-self which is for itself only through another."[38]

This paradigm of externalization in identity-affirming practices, however, reveals, in addition, the belated temporality of subjectivity: alienated in the other of its material activity, it is only subsequently reincorporated in its concept of self. For Hegel it is first at the end of this two-part movement that the subject emerges and does so provisionally, in a process of being redefined in yet a further objectification. Marx, on the other hand, does not see objectification as a decisive moment of rupture, but as a form of self-expression that can only secondarily be estranged from a punctual and self-same subject, and so eschews the processual nature of Hegel's negative.

4 Alienation and misrecognition as the structural causality of the social

This paradigm of externalization in Hegel is not relegated only to the sphere of subjectivity. Since Hegel's model includes both normative and conceptual content, it provides a basis for understanding all forms of objectification, including the construction of the social, and of cultural practices and institutions. Hegel's assertion that "[this world's] existence is the *work* of self-consciousness"[39] is not simply an epistemological statement about the mediated form of perception and cognition, but also a claim about reality as a web of particular, subject-produced, normative scripts for action and representation performed by cognizing subjects. As the Antigone chapter[40] ("The True Spirit and the Ethical Order") of the *Phenomenology*, examined at the end of this discussion, reveals, Hegel sees the social as structured by historical agents engaging in practical interaction both with their objective and self-generated and administered (social) context.

Yet, inasmuch as the world is a product of the work of the subject on Hegel's account, "it is also an alien reality already present and given, a reality which has a being of its own and in which it does not recognize itself."[41] Consciousness, for Hegel, constantly oscillates between the recognition of its world-structuring activities and their immediate perception as objective alterity. Since both the subject and the social are not organic forms of self-organization or simple unity, a *being-given*, the perpetual mediation of the constitutive cut of the subject can never be fully reduced nor can it serve to reduce the distance between representation and its source to an absolute epistemological minimum. That this ongoing process will always result in effects of alienation both owes to the structural belatedness of the "I" and reflects a fundamental premise of Hegel's *Logic*. In his interpretation of Hegel's epistemology, Robert Brandom[42] draws attention to a foundational feature of Hegel's conception of judgment formation. Cognizing subjects will always enter into relations of contradiction in the course of producing and endorsing inferential commitments while adjudicating and applying determinate concepts in practice. In Hegel's view, this has to do with the nature of thinking itself as explicated at the beginning of the *Logic*: "To see that thought is by its very nature dialectical, and that, as understanding, it *must* [emphasis added] fall into contradiction—the negative of itself—will form one of the main lessons of the logic."[43]

Hegel introduces the subject into the field of immanence as a disrupting force capable of mediating substance and producing its own notional and social content in the relations with substance it forms. Yet, at the same time as it does this, the subject of knowledge is marked by a constitutive lack, the fallibility and error that are the driving forces of cognition itself. The diversions of reason from itself, and the processes embedded in its attempt to resolve its internal inconsistencies, are the motor both of rationalizing experience and of the production of meaning.

In this cognitive model, a different form of causality emerges: one that is not grounded in necessity, but in the mediating powers of the self. Human cognition introduces contingency into the system of its world-constructing and normative representations and the network of social relations becomes a causally incomplete field, one in which error and fallibility remain constitutive operational possibilities. On the one hand, then, Hegel's epistemology opens up the space for agency (Hegel's causality is cognitively and socially constructed, not necessitarian, and is therefore opposed to models based on blind necessity, such as Spinoza's philosophy). Yet, on the other hand, autonomous agency is also necessarily embedded in and restricted by a system of contradictions emerging from its own conditions of possibility.

Thus, Hegel's epistemological model of *Dasein in der Zeit*, a subjectivity predicated upon its network of relational practices, is involved in a double bind in which its main structural premise of externalization (its nonidentity with its historically manifested activity) is in reality a form of alienation. In other words, the subject is nothing but her own belatedness, never coinciding with her objectifications, be it temporally or cognitively. Objectifications are cognized as congealed external forms disposable to their own integration into mystifying and purportedly non-conflictual meta-narratives, and thus also *productive* of falsely conciliatory social representations concealing deeper forms of estrangement recognizable as such at yet another historical moment (the commodity form is one example of such a process).

In fact, Hegel's *Phenomenology* is precisely the history of such alienating objectifications: a retrospective reconstruction of the deficiencies and fissures in the different formations of consciousness and the resulting structural representations of the world that Hegel's historical epistemology describes.[44] Hegel views all societal paradigms he examines in the *Phenomenology*—including that of Ancient Greece, then considered the most harmonious—as unable to read the constructedness of their own performative scripts and normative roles, and for that reason continuously engaged in formal inconsistency and internal contradictions.

In Hegel's argument, Greek *Sittlichkeit* or morality is exposed as a form of obfuscation containing a fundamental internal conflict. As Molly Farneth describes, this purportedly harmonious social formation produces differentiations of its ethical substance that cannot be reconciled. For, Greek ethics is actualized in two spheres—divine and human law—posited by self-consciousness; yet, this split marks divine law as a transcendental other whose reality as a social normative construct is never rendered legible:

> It [ethical essence] splits itself up into distinct ethical substance, into a human and divine law. Similarly, the self-consciousness confronting the substance assigns to itself according to its nature one of these powers, and as a [mode of] knowing, is on the one hand ignorant of what it does, and on the other knows what it does, a knowledge which, for that reason, is a deceptive knowledge.[45]

Thus, human law is rationalized as a product of human consciousness, albeit perceived as immediately given, while divine law, which is not subject to critical self-consciousness, is equally neutralized as "the simple and immediate essence of the ethical sphere."[46] This dual substance of Greek ethical life is further divided socially into two politically differentiated and gendered spaces: the public life of the polis (in which male agency and social law intersect) and the private life of the family (the locus of both female agency and divine law). Thus, both divine and human law are socially realized in the distinct spheres of Greek society, with each sphere containing a distinct combination of either gender and either status (human or divine). Since in both cases, gender and status are *not* conceptualized as constructs, they are instead immediately internalized as authentic ethical consciousness, that is, as duty.

While a detailed analysis of Hegel's discussion in the *Phenomenology* of the concrete ethical practices realized in the two distinct spheres of Ancient Greek life is beyond the scope of this paper, what logically emerges from Hegel's analysis of the forms of Greek social being as such is that the gender-normative behaviors of Antigone (as defender of the divine law of burial) and Creon (as defender of the human law of political reason) must indeed inevitably enter into irreconcilable conflict. In other words, Greek ethical life, or *Sittlichkeit*, is self-contradictory in nature precisely because of the untheorized identities (female, male; divine, human) of its subjects and the scripts for action available to them. Based on the immediate identifications that structure it, the conflict between Creon and Antigone is irresolvable by human means, which is to say, tragic.

An important ramification of this analysis is the historical-practical orientation of Hegel's model. Hegel's reading of the texture of the social superstructure prefigures the understanding of "material action" "governed" by a "material ideological apparatus" Althusser would later describe: "the existence of the ideas of [the subject's] belief is material in that *his ideas are his material actions inserted into material practices governed by material rituals which are themselves defined by the material ideological apparatus from which derive the ideas of that subject.*"[47] Anticipating and paving the way for later developments in dialectical materialism, Hegel already sees the work (or, alternatively, the predetermined—in Althusser's words, ideologically governed—role-playing) of the subject as constituting the entire panoply of a society's cultural, institutional, and identity-constructing norms as these are realized and performed by historical agents. Yet *historically,* or in the long run, the subject, like the culture the subject makes, is constituted by the work of the negative, a self-differentiation to the other inscribing division, reunification, and thus temporality into identity.

5 Blindness and insight. Marx's reappropriation of the model of externalization

While following closely on the footsteps of Hegel's argument, Marx positions his own argument differently, describing the production of the subject and the social as taking place in the context of a concrete set of pathological circumstances. On the one hand, in the early *Economic and Philosophical Manuscripts,* he analyzes work in clearly Hegelian terms as the dialectical production of self and object:

> In his fashioning of the objective . . . man really proves himself to be a *species-being*. Such production is his active species-life. Through it nature appears as *his* work and his reality. The object of labor is therefore the *objectification of the species-life of man*: for man reproduces himself not only intellectually, in his consciousness, but actively and actually, and he can therefore contemplate himself in a world he himself has created.[48]

Yet, on the other hand, Marx views the subject's life-structuring capabilities as exclusively materially substantiated in products of labor[49] rather than in a belated reconstruction of the "I" through cognitive mediation of the constitutive split of subjectivity. Hegel's externalization is for Marx the productive, thetic aspect of objectification, an experience of differentiation and negation undergone in the course of the expression of the self in labor. Thus, Marx differs from Hegel in that externalization and alienation are not coterminous—externalization in his model is an immediate confirmation of the subject's conscious and spontaneous activity.[50]

While both Marx and Hegel associate externalization with temporally differentiated agency expressed in interactions (cognitive and practical) with concrete material contexts, for Marx alienation occurs only secondarily, as a derivative of labor. The subject's labor, whose estranged product is the commodity, positions the subject in a complex system of economic exchange in which her subjectivity and the commodity emerge as homologous *things*. Subjectivity as produced by work is reified: "political economy regards labor abstractly as a thing; labor is a commodity."[51] The realization of work is introduced in a cycle of abstract interchangeable values and thus labor becomes divorced from its concrete sensuous form. Under these circumstances, the product of the subject's labor is experienced as "*something alien*, as a power *independent* of the producer,"[52] in that it is neither produced for nor causally conditioned by her, but rather, by and on behalf of the capitalist system of exchange (and its privileged, or non-laboring subject, or capital as such).

Marx's critique of alienation remains one of the central foci of his work, as he famously develops his concepts of surplus value[53] and commodification, in which estranged subjects are mystified by the metaphysical dimension, or "theological niceties,"[54] of the commodity form. For, the alienation of the subject of labor equals her inability to identify and perceive the transference of the social dimension of her work onto the objects she produces and exchanges for wages. While Marx's later work (*Capital*, in particular) remains more diagnostic and descriptive of this process, his early writings prescribe models for superseding self-estrangement[55] that identify the relations of production (division of labor and private property) as the primary causal factors for alienation. Subjectivity on this account can restore the equivalence between self-realization and objectification, achieving a "complete restoration of man to himself" and "true resolution of the conflict between existence and being, objectification and self-affirmation,"[56] by modifying a set of economic relations culpable of the disjuncture in the primary relationship between the subject and her work. Even Marx's later writings, albeit less revolutionary in content, effectively sustain the notion of the historical feasibility of unalienated forms of subject and social production (under the right economic circumstances), finding its precedent in precapitalist societies.[57] To put it another way, in contradistinction to Hegel's model, Marx's account is haunted by the specter of pre-representational, undifferentiated subjectivity.

6 Conclusions

The arc of development of theories of the subject described in this analysis challenges the epistemological purity of cognitive and theoretical models predicated upon a linear notion of progression—from more abstract, less historicized paradigms of experience to a full-fledged dialectical materialism—of the kind normative accounts of the history of Western philosophy present.

This intervention in the standard narrative of philosophy of ideas retraces a concept of the material and historical production of *Dasein in der Zeit* that is at the core of "idealist" philosophy, one whose very conditions of possibility are based squarely upon the relationality of subjectivity to empirical externality. The subject (as well as the social) on this account is not an organic unity or a primordial essence disclosed in an ahistorical apophantic moment. Instead, as we have seen, subjectivity and all cognitive forms of concept formation—including theoretical ones—are strategic constructs organized around a constitutive fissure and retroactively reflecting the history of their own production. This decidedly antiessentialist paradigm, grounded in material signifying practices, however, does not cancel out the nondialectical schematic tendencies in the founding hypothesis of a subjectively produced composite of *a priori* forms and experiential, empirical matter informing Kant's representational epistemology in particular. Neither does it erase Hegel's overall treatment of history as a collective singular, that is, a repeating structure working both within and between periods of historical development to link material formations of consciousness externally and exhibit internally an identical set of deficiencies, contradictions, and future-oriented developments.

Upon closer inspection, this analysis argues, the work of Marx, the avowedly antimetaphysical, "materialist" thinker, demonstrates the same kind of conceptual ambiguity. For, while Marx produces a far more internally differentiated and heterogeneous understanding of the social as a collective plural marked by forms of uneven development, the radical division between philosophical conceptions of the subject, on the one hand, and historical-material reality, on the other, upon which that understanding of the social is based, conforms in large measure to that presupposed by the very "idealism" it critiques. In opposition to that, the work of Kant and Hegel is in fact focused precisely on an attempt to mediate this schism. At the same time, in a De Manian double bind of blindness and insight, even as it denies and opposes[58] the purportedly "hollow abstraction" of Hegelian consciousness, Marx's materialist theory may be seen both to underscore and demonstrate the critical potential of the Enlightenment models. For these models already contain the framework for a fully developed turn to *historical reason* as realized in the practical activity of socially determined agents.

Furthermore, that double bind binds, as it were, Marx to the very blindness he describes. For Marx's dialectical materialism exhibits remnants of an essentialist philosophy of the subject, according to which the subject expresses a primary consolidated identity and alienation is considered reversible. Marx fails to recognize that an enduringly productive feature of Hegelian epistemology is its exposure of the structure of necessary delay and belatedness intertwined with the process of alienation. Indeed, self-estrangement is an insurmountable effect of the production of subjectivity in this model: the subject's activity is not a natural and immediate instantiation of an originary, reconciled self ("essential being"[59]) only secondarily split from itself in the inscription of its work in the identity-perpetuating representations of the other (the lord or capital). Work for Hegel is instead a form of self-generating and grounding alienation in and of itself.

The internal differentiation and contradictions of the conceptual premises of the thinkers presented in this analysis call for a more nuanced understanding of the traditional notional affiliations in the history of ideas. As the concept of a unilinear, homogenous, and progressive unfolding of historical processes is revealed as a fallacy, a reexamination of entrenched divisions and identities in modern (Enlightenment) philosophy not surprisingly reveals a much more complex web of influences, conceptual attachments, uneven development, delays, leaps, and lapses, belonging to multiple epistemological temporalities—small wonder that both psychoanalytic and postmodern theories of the subject find structural homologies with Hegel's thought, when trying to think with, while moving beyond Marx. Despite its long tradition of interpretation, it might even be the case that—to borrow Benjamin's term—the "Now of cognizability" of the Enlightenment has not arrived yet.

Notes

1. Karl Marx, *Capital* (New York: Vintage Books, 1977), 163.
2. Immanuel Kant, *Critique of Pure Reason*, trans. J. M. D. Meiklejohn (London: J. M. Dent & Sons, 1934), B XLI, 23; Immanuel Kant, *Kritik der reinen Vernunft*, Hrsg. Wilhelm Weischedel (*Werkausgabe in 12 Bänden*) Bd. 3. (Frankfurt: Suhrkamp, 1992), Anm. B XLI, III: 39.
3. Georg Wilhelm Friedrich Hegel, *The Phenomenology of Spirit* (Oxford: Oxford University Press, 1977), 10.
4. Karl Marx, *Theses on Feuerbach*, in Karl Marx and Friedrich Engels, *Collected Works*, 47 vols. (London: Lawrence & Wishart, 1975-), V: 8.
5. Paul de Man, *Blindness and Insight. Essays in the Rhetoric of Contemporary Criticism* (Minneapolis: University of Minnesota Press, 1983), 103.
6. Kant, *Critique* B XL, 22.
7. Ibid., 22.
8. Claudia Brodsky, *Response to Rei Terada* (Annual Conference in Comparative Literature: "Constructions; History and Narrativity," Princeton University, October 23-24, 2015).
9. Brodsky, *Response*, 6.
10. Kant, *Critique* B 48, A 32, 48.
11. See the section on the analogies of experience in Kant, *Critique* B 218-65, 140-65.
12. Brodsky, *Response*, 8.
13. See Kant, *Critique* B 218-65, 140-65.
14. Kant, *Critique*, B XL, 22.
15. Whether the subject's purposive activities are absolutely and immediately legible is a different question and one that this essay will address shortly.
16. Hegel, *The Phenomenology*, 38 (emphasis added).
17. Emphasis mine.
18. Hegel, *The Phenomenology*, 10.
19. Ibid., 8.
20. In his discussion of Hegel's model of construction and application of empirical concepts in "Some Pragmatist Themes in Hegel's Idealism," in *Tales of the Mighty Dead. Historical Essays in the Metaphysics of Intentionality* (Cambridge, MA: Harvard University Press, 2002), 233-34,

Robert Brandom draws attention to the historical component in the process of concept as perceived by Hegel:

> Hegel's pragmatism, I have claimed, consists in his commitment to understanding determinately contentful empirical conceptual norms as instituted by *experience*, the process of *using* those concepts by applying them in practice: making judgments and performing actions.... This is the recognitive structure of *tradition*, which articulates the normative structure of the process of *development* by which concepts acquire their contents by being applied in experience.

21 Hegel, *The Phenomenology*, 58–66.
22 Ibid., 60.
23 Ibid.
24 Ibid.
25 Ibid.
26 Ibid., 12.
27 Ibid.
28 A certain strain of Hegel scholarship represented by scholars such as Robert Pippin, Robert Brandom, Terry Pinkard, and Jeffrey Stout has foregrounded an interpretation of Hegel's work which reads the history of the formations of consciousness in the *Phenomenology* as an account of the activity of fully embodied social subjects of knowledge endowed with agency within an interpretative community. This explication of Hegel's system argues for a transition from a focus on individual and isolated consciousness to a system of situated historical self-legislating reflexive agents engaged in activities encompassing both external objects of perception and the subjects' own attitudes. These scholars see the *Phenomenology* as Hegel's historical account of such activities and their conditions of possibility—premises, normative standards, deficiencies, development, and other criteria of success. For a detailed explication of this line of interpretation, see Terry Pinkard, *Hegel's Phenomenology. The Sociality of Reason* (Cambridge: Cambridge University Press, 1996) and Jeffrey Stout, "The Spirit of Pragmatism. Burstein's Variations on Hegelian Themes," *Graduate Faculty Philosophy Journal* 33, no. 1 (2012): 185–246.
29 Karl Marx and Frederick Engels, *The German Ideology*, in *Collected Works*, V: 36.
30 Slavoj Žižek, *Less Than Nothing. Hegel and the Shadow of Dialectical Materialism* (London: Verso, 2012), 259.
31 The form of the story of the production of the self is a fictional narrative, an origin myth, as Hegel is presented with the double bind of having to talk about a subject (the lord and the bondsman) that has to always already have been recognized by another self-consciousness and interpolated into its subject position in order to have become a self in the first place; that

is, Hegel needs to address a pre-factual situation and thus uses his lord-bondsman narrative as a propaedeutic for the actual argument he makes. Similar to Althusser's model of interpolation, the formation of the subject is not a story of historical or temporal development. Rather, history starts with the fact of subjectivity.

32 Hegel, *The Phenomenology*, 110.
33 Ibid., 113.
34 Ibid., 115.
35 My approach is indebted to Terry Pinkard's analysis of the introduction of the bondsman's work into the model of the self-asserting desire of the lord in *Hegel's Phenomenology*, 53–63.
36 Hegel, *The Phenomenology*, 116.
37 Ibid., 110.
38 Ibid., 115.
39 Ibid., 294 (original emphasis).
40 Ibid., 266–90.
41 Ibid., 294.
42 Robert Brandom, "Sketch of a Program for a Critical Reading of Hegel. Comparing Empirical and Logical Concepts," *Internationales Jahrbuch des Deutschen Idealismus* 3 (2005): 145–46.
43 Georg Wilhelm Friedrich Hegel, *Hegel's Logic* (Oxford: Oxford University Press, 1975), 15.
44 In fact, scholars such as Brandom and Stout locate in the notion of Absolute Knowing not a termination of the dialectical reversals of cognition, but the final recognition of these reversals as driven and structured by the (ever failing) attempts of thought to overcome its internal contradictions as manifested in the production of socially signifying practices (i.e., to decipher its social hieroglyphic). See Stout, "The Spirit of Pragmatism," 230–33. Hegel inscribes all formations of consciousness he theorizes in *The Phenomenology* in some form of mystification. See Pinkard, *Hegel's Phenomenology*, 135–345.
45 Ibid., 268.
46 Ibid.
47 Louis Althusser, *Lenin and Philosophy and Other Essays* (New York: Monthly Review Press, 1971), 169 (original emphasis).
48 Karl Marx, *Early Writings* (London: Penguin Books, 1992), 329.
49 Cf. Marx, *Early Writings*, 328: "The whole character of a species, its species-character, resides in the nature of its life-activity, and free conscious activity constitutes the species-character of man."
50 See previous endnote.

51 Marx, *Early Writings*, 293.
52 Ibid., 324.
53 For the difference between the totality of labor-time performed by the worker and part of her labor-power compensated through wages, see Marx, *Capital*, 283–320.
54 Marx, *Capital*, 163.
55 See, for instance, the chapter, "Private Property and Communism," in *The Economic and Philosophical Manuscripts*, in Marx, *Early Writings*, 345–58 and "The Necessity, Preconditions and Consequences of the Abolition of Private Property" in "Part I. Feuerbach. Opposition of the Materialist and Idealist Outlook," *The German Ideology*, in Marx and Engels, *Collected Works*, V: 87–89.
56 Marx, *Early Writings*, 348.
57 See Marx, *Capital*, 169–73.
58 Cf. Marx, *Early Writings*, 396–97:

> Because Hegel equates man with self-consciousness, the estranged object, the estranged essential reality of man is nothing but consciousness, nothing but the thought of estrangement, its *abstract* and hence hollow and unreal expression, *negation*. The supersession of alienation is therefore likewise nothing but an abstract hollow supersession of that hollow abstraction, *the negation of negation*. The inexhaustible vital, sensuous, concrete activity of self-objectification is therefore reduced to its mere abstraction, *absolute negativity*, an abstraction which is then given permanent form as such and conceived as independent activity, an activity itself. Since this so-called negativity is nothing more than the *abstract*, *empty* form of that real living act, its content can only be a *formal* content, created by abstraction from all content.

59 Marx, *Early Writings*, 329.

Bibliography

Althusser, Louis. *Lenin and Philosophy and Other Essays*. New York: Monthly Review Press, 1971.

Brandom, Robert. "Sketch of a Program for a Critical Reading of Hegel. Comparing Empirical and Logical Concepts." *Internationales Jahrbuch des Deutschen Idealismus* 3 (2005): 131–61.

Brandom, Robert. *Tales of the Mighty Dead: Historical Essays in the Metaphysics of Intentionality*. Cambridge, MA: Harvard University Press, 2002.

Brodsky, Claudia. *Response to Rei Terada*. Delivered at "Constructions: History and Narrativity," Comparative Literature Conference, Princeton University, Princeton, NJ, October 23–24, 2015.

De Man, Paul. *Blindness and Insight. Essays in the Rhetoric of Contemporary Criticism*. Minneapolis: University of Minnesota Press, 1983.

Farneth, Molly. "Gender and the Ethical Given. Human and Divine Law in Hegel's Reading of the Antigone." *Journal of Religious Ethics* 41, no. 4 (2013): 643–67.

Hegel, Georg Wilhelm Friedrich. *Hegel's Logic*. Oxford: Oxford University Press, 1975.

Hegel, Georg Wilhelm Friedrich. *The Phenomenology of Spirit*. Oxford: Oxford University Press, 1977.

Kant, Immanuel. *Kritik der reinen Vernunft*. In *Werkausgabe*, 12 Bde. Hrsg, Wilhelm Weischedel. Wiesbaden: Suhrkamp, 1992.

Kant, Immanuel. *Critique of Pure Reason*, Translated by J. M. D. Meiklejohn. London: J. M. Dent & Sons, 1934.

Marx, Karl. *Capital*. New York: Vintage Books, 1977.

Marx Karl and Frederick Engels. *Collected Works*, 47 vols. London: Lawrence & Wishart, 1975–.

Marx, Karl. *Early Writings (Economic and Philosophical Manuscripts)*. London: Penguin Books, 1992.

Pinkard, Terry. *Hegel's Phenomenology. The Sociality of Reason*. Cambridge: Cambridge University Press, 1996.

Stout, Jeffrey. "The Spirit of Pragmatism. Burstein's Variations on Hegelian Themes." *Graduate Faculty Philosophy Journal* 33, no. 1 (2012): 185–246.

Žižek, Slavoj. *Less Than Nothing. Hegel and the Shadow of Dialectical Materialism*. London: Verso, 2012.

PART THREE

JUDGMENT

8 THE MAN WITHIN THE BREAST: SYMPATHY, DEFORMITY, AND MORAL SUBJECTIVITY IN ADAM SMITH'S *THE THEORY OF MORAL SENTIMENTS*

Paul Kelleher

He is a bold surgeon, they say, whose hand does not tremble when he performs an operation upon his own person; and he is often equally bold who does not hesitate to pull off the mysterious veil of self-delusion, which covers from his view the deformities of his own conduct.

—**ADAM SMITH,** The Theory of Moral Sentiments

Each of us has a disabled other who cannot be acknowledged.
—**HENRI-JACQUES STIKER,** A History of Disability

In this essay, I explore a mode of experience that is an abiding concern in both eighteenth-century British moral philosophy and contemporary disability studies: the intersubjective bonds of sympathy. There is no question that considerable differences—historical, cultural, and discursive—separate the forms of thought that characterize moral philosophy and disability studies. Nevertheless, when read by one another's lights, significant cross-historical relays emerge between the moral-philosophical speculations of the eighteenth century and the relatively recent critiques of ableist ideology. Moreover, while disability studies generally have tended to focus on nineteenth-, twentieth-, and twenty-first-century contexts, groundbreaking work by scholars such as Lennard J. Davis, Felicity Nussbaum, Helen Deutsch, and David M. Turner, among others, has revealed the eighteenth century to be an important chapter—perhaps even a decisive turning point— in the history of conceptions of "disability," not only as an historically defined and redefined set of physical phenomena, conditions, or characteristics, but as these are deeply intertwined with theories of nonphysical or "moral" judgment and sensibility.[1] Scholarship on eighteenth-century disability has interrogated how a society ostensibly devoted to "enlightenment" represented, taxonomized, judged, excluded, and (too often) brutalized disabled individuals and populations. More recently, there has been an effort to recover and to theorize the lived, subjective experience of the disabled in the eighteenth century—and more broadly still, to understand what Deutsch refers to as "the history of the link between disability and subjectivity" as such.[2] It will be my contention that eighteenth-century moral philosophy's sustained inquiry into the process of sympathy—how it works, why it often fails, and who does and does not deserve the balm of fellow-feeling—played a vital, but little examined, role in fashioning both disabled and nondisabled forms of subjectivity. Indeed, I will suggest that disability enabled the philosophical constitution of the subject as such.

Although my analyses largely focus on the eighteenth century, I draw inspiration from contemporary critiques of sympathy's impact on the lives of the disabled. For instance, Joseph P. Shapiro's trenchant history of the disability rights movement, *No Pity*, makes clear that the lived experience of disability is normatively defined—often painfully and oppressively—by the experience of being pitied. Shapiro stresses that when the disabled claim forms of sociopolitical agency and power, or undertake acts of culture-building predicated on positively inflected notions of disabled identity, the first order of business is calling into question the historically overdetermined relationship between disability and pity (and pity's seemingly less patronizing counterparts, such as sympathy, compassion, and empathy). In addition to intervening in the arenas of legislation and policy-making, politicizing disability requires us to challenge the cultural politics of the "poster child," the spectacularized image-parade of Tiny Tims and "supercrips" who are offered up respectively as objects of pity and sources of "inspiration"—but who, at the end of the day, embody the nondisabled population's fear of atypical mental and bodily states.³ Lennard J. Davis reinforces this point, and broadens its theoretical import, in his editor's introduction to the groundbreaking volume, *The Disability Studies Reader* (1997). Most "normals," Davis suggests, assume they can intuitively understand what disability entails, and he ventriloquizes their attitude thus: "What could be simpler to understand? One simply has to imagine the loss of the limb, the absent sense, and one is half-way there. Just the addition of a liberal dose of sympathy and pity along with a generous acceptance of ramps and voice-synthesized computers allows the average person to speak with knowledge on the subject."⁴ However, in Davis's reckoning, if sympathy seemingly affords the "normal" individual spontaneous and immediate access to the life experience of the disabled, this promise of intersubjective connection across the divide of difference is an illusion at best and a disguised form of discrimination at worst. "Pity and empathy do not lend themselves to philosophy, philology, or theoretical considerations in general"; indeed, as Davis stresses, those working in disability studies explicitly work against pity and empathy, in order to "articulat[e] and theoriz[e] a political, social, and ideological critique."⁵

I take seriously Shapiro's and Davis's assessments of the distorting—indeed oppressive—effects that sympathy has on the ways that disabled minds and bodies, lives and experiences, are conceptualized and represented.⁶ There is no question that appeals to sympathy have been used to reaffirm the ideological distinction between the so-called "normal" and the disabled. However, while these contemporary critiques of the ideological pretensions of sympathy are vitally necessary, in this essay I explore other aspects of the historical relationship between sympathy and disability, ones that nuance and complicate our sense that sympathy, across the centuries, merely has aided and abetted an oppressive dispensation in which "normal" subjects pity—and thereby objectify and marginalize—disabled minds and bodies. I qualify Davis's position by arguing that sympathy does in fact have the potential to provoke general philosophical and theoretical considerations. By reconsidering eighteenth-century theorizations of sympathy from the vantage point of contemporary disability studies, I argue that a critical engagement with sympathy affords new strategies for mounting the kinds of "political, social, and ideological critique" that Davis and other disability scholars advocate.

To this end, I focus on what is without question the eighteenth century's most influential philosophical treatment of sympathy: Adam Smith's

The Theory of Moral Sentiments (1759). More specifically, I demonstrate that Smith's exploration of the workings of sympathy is thoroughly enmeshed, both conceptually and rhetorically, in an ambivalent relationship with figures of disability. On the one hand, when he turns his attention to disabilities that affect the mind or the body, disability seems to provide just another empirical example through which Smith will articulate the ways that an individual forms a conception of the thoughts and passions of other individuals. References to the mad, to "idiots," or to men who have lost a leg sit alongside discussions of aggrieved lovers, generous benefactors, and fictional heroes, suggesting, it would seem, that figures of disability bear no special explanatory power within Smith's account of the formation of the sympathetic subject.[7] On the other hand, these discrete appearances of the disabled within *The Theory of Moral Sentiments* are only one—and perhaps the most superficial—way that disability informs Smith's philosophical enterprise.

Even as he appears merely to reproduce the commonplace attitudes of his contemporaries when he renders scenes in which spectators sympathize with the disabled body or the disordered mind, Smith uses the rhetoric of disability to articulate the internal workings of sympathy and the instantiation of moral subjectivity. It is true that the term *disability* does not explicitly appear in *The Theory of Moral Sentiments*, but as David M. Turner has shown, a writer in Smith's historical moment certainly would have been familiar with the terms *disability*, *disabled*, and *able-bodied*.[8] In the absence of a direct reference to *disability*, what we do find in the twists and turns of Smith's philosophical exposition is the language of *defect*, *excess*, and *deformity*, a cluster of terms that function as figurative or conceptual counterparts to the more materially inflected notions of *disabled* and *able-bodied*. I pay particularly close attention to the ideological work that deformity performs in *The Theory of Moral Sentiments*, and further, I show how Smith's philosophical system renders the notion of self-interested "partiality" a form of moral disability.

In Smith's hands, the rhetoric of disability underwrites the logic of sympathy, and by extension, his understanding of moral subjectivity and affective interiority (what he calls the "man within the breast" [130]) is constitutively entwined with the ostensible "otherness" of the disabled. Thus, within the pages of *The Theory of Moral Sentiments*, when sympathetic spectators engage in affectively charged encounters with disabled minds and bodies, these "normals" (to recall Davis's term) are not simply pitying the disabled "other"; rather, they are on the verge of recognizing what Smith calls the "precariousness of human life," the shared human condition of being unavoidably exposed to the vicissitudes—that is, the calamities, disorders, and deformations—of embodied life and subjective experience (136). As we will further see, the force of Smith's philosophical speculations and playful rhetoric repeatedly brings his own text to the verge of a moral deformation, in which the brand of subjectivity he seeks to theorize and formalize (the moral subject as "natural," "proper," "reasonable," and Stoic—in a word, "manly" [48]) begins to slip away from the ideological framework of *The Theory of Moral Sentiments*.

1 Face to face

Before going further, I want to touch on some of Smith's key arguments and formulations regarding how sympathy operates. Early on, he broadens more familiar understandings of "sympathy." Whereas pity and compassion typically "signify our fellow-feeling with the sorrow of others," Smith will use "sympathy" to "denote our fellow-feeling with any passion whatever" (10). In other words, while the idea of sympathizing with another's grief or distress is common enough, and is perhaps even today what most readily comes to mind when we speak of sympathy, Smith will be equally interested in thinking about how we come to sympathize with passions that do not arise from hardship or pain, such as the passion of joy. In addition to expanding what it means and how it functions, from the beginning Smith conceptualizes sympathy as a form of moral judgment. The alignment of sympathy and judgment brings us to the "impartial spectator," the theoretical centerpiece of *The Theory of Moral Sentiments*. The "impartial spectator" signifies an internalized figure of judgment, the "great inmate of the breast," whose calculus of the proper and the improper determines how we perceive and assess the feelings and the conduct of others (134). Our capacity to feel sympathy for another is, according to Smith, entirely bound up with our capacity to judge, approve and disapprove of the causes and the effects of his or her passions.[9] As he phrases it, "To approve of the passions of another . . . as suitable to their objects is the same thing as to observe that we entirely sympathize with them; and not to approve of them as such, is the same thing as to observe that we do not entirely sympathize with them" (16).

Before Smith equates sympathy and judgment, in the opening pages of *The Theory of Moral Sentiments* he briefly entertains the possibility of unchecked sympathetic connection:

> Upon some occasions sympathy may seem to arise merely from the view of a certain emotion in another person. The passions, upon some occasions, may seem to be transfused from one man to another, instantaneously, and antecedent to any knowledge of what excited them in the person principally concerned. Grief and joy, for example, strongly expressed in the look and gestures of any one, at once affect the spectator with some degree of a like painful or agreeable emotion. A smiling face is, to every body that sees it, a cheerful object; as a sorrowful countenance, on the other hand, is a melancholy one. (11)

However, as the careful qualifications in this passage begin to suggest, while *The Theory of Moral Sentiments* offers the eighteenth century's most elaborate meditation on sympathy, Smith's moral punch line ultimately is *we sympathize, but only imperfectly, and it is a good thing, too*. From the perspective of the spectator, the incompleteness of sympathy makes judgment both possible and essential. As the moral spectator, I sympathize only to the extent that I approve or disapprove of the other's feelings or conduct; my approval or disapproval is guided by how I imagine the impartial spectator would approve or disapprove of the scene before me. When I find myself in the position of the one whose feelings or conduct are being viewed and judged, my previous experiences as a spectator (and my own internalization of the impartial spectator) already have taught me that sympathy is incomplete. Consequently, my desire for the spectator's sympathy is checked, and in order to secure some modicum of sympathy, I call upon my powers of self-discipline; these for Smith are the lessons learned in the Stoic school of self-command. By lowering the pitch of my passions, I achieve the moral self-composure that will be judged as a "proper" reaction to life's vicissitudes. In this way, I become a proper object of sympathy; the spectator's sympathetic approval, and my own self-approval, conform as closely as possible to the expectations and the dictates of the abstract impartial spectator that thoroughly inform this moral drama.

Smith often describes the intersubjective connection formed between spectator and spectatee (so to speak) as a face-to-face encounter, a scene of seeing and being seen, but as he makes clear, the formation of the impartial spectator within the human subject is only possible within the broader context of civil society. Without the presence of others, who en masse constitute a social realm of passion, action, and thought beyond the self, the impartial spectator would remain unrealized and, in some sense, so too would the human subject itself. Unlike Rousseau, who explicitly invented and extensively theorized a primordial, inherently historically unavailable, "hypothetical," "natural," or "savage man" for the comparative purpose of demonstrating the defining sociability of actual historical man, Smith does not elaborate at length a philosophical fiction in which a conjecturally figured "man" exists prior to or apart from society. "Man," he asserts, "can subsist only in society" (85).[10] At the same time, though, he does find it philosophically useful to imagine briefly that which could never be:

> Were it possible that a human creature could grow up to manhood in some solitary place, without any communication with his own species, he could no more think of his own character, of the propriety or demerit of his own sentiments and conduct, of the beauty or deformity of his own mind, than of the beauty or deformity of his own face. (110)

By entertaining for a moment the fiction of a human creature developing alone, apart from others, Smith has no intention of entering into a debate regarding a pre-social state of nature. His purpose, rather, is to reaffirm the naturalness and the propriety of the aesthetic criteria—the beautiful and the deformed—that structure his philosophical account of how self and other enter into and sustain a system of moral relationality.[11] Smith does not believe that a human creature can reach "manhood" alone, either physically or morally. And when he speaks of "manhood" in *The Theory of Moral Sentiments*, he most often has in mind a Stoic version of masculinity, one that privileges self-command and self-sacrifice and strives to achieve a reasoned and restrained relationship to external events and misfortunes in order to cultivate and preserve a "tranquility" of mind that best predisposes one to feel and act virtuously (151).[12] The Stoic concern with regulating how external phenomena impact our internal state—and how our internal state, when properly developed, assumes a kind of mastery over external phenomena—informs Smith's introduction of aesthetic criteria into his moral philosophy. Simply put, the relation of outside to inside, and inside to outside, is important to both Stoic and aesthetic discourse. Smith's conflation of these two discourses accounts for a great deal of the rhetorical power of his text; at the same time, this discursive conflation, as we will see, introduces a set of problems, both ideological and moral, that trouble some of Smith's central premises and thereby make his text available for counterreadings and reappropriations from the perspective of contemporary disability studies.

In the fictional state of nature that Smith briefly invokes and quickly discards, a solitary human creature has no occasion to contemplate the beauty or deformity of his own face or his own mind. "All these are objects which he cannot easily see, which naturally he does not look at, and with regard to which he is provided with no mirror which can present them to his view" (110). The deformed face and the deformed mind, Smith seems to suggest, do exist in a pre-social state (albeit a conjectural one), but in the absence of other human creatures, their existence has no empirical or moral consequences. Differently put, whatever material form they may take, this materiality is virtually nonexistent, there and not there at the same time—but importantly, deformity always is waiting in reserve. Once the scene becomes populated with other people, once the human creature is brought into society, "he is immediately provided with the mirror which he wanted [that is, lacked] before" (110). Of what does this figurative mirror consist? Echoing a similar image in David Hume's *Treatise of Human Nature* (1739–40), Smith asserts that this mirror is "placed in the countenance and behaviour of those he lives with, which always mark when they enter into, and when they disapprove of his sentiments" (110).[13] Society and judgment simultaneously spring into being as the faces and bodies of others embody a visceral moral calculus. Smith exploits the connotations of this figurative mirror, in which the once-solitary human creature "first views the propriety and impropriety of his own passions, the beauty and deformity of his own mind" (110). By apprehending himself in others, and seeing there a reflection of his own beauty and deformity, the human creature becomes a social being. He becomes acutely aware that others judge his appearance, his sentiments, and his conduct; in return, he will learn to exercise the same form of judgment in his perceptions and assessments of others.

Judging those with whom he shares the realm of civil society, though, is predicated on a certain intensification and deepening of what we now would call "interiority." By reading the approval or disapproval of others in their faces and bodies, the socialized human creature not only comes under the sway of moral judgment. He also is subjected, and subjects himself, to a new economy of the passions. Moral judgment and the inner life of the passions develop alongside—and indeed, depend on—one another. The fictional "man who from birth was a stranger to society" possesses a limited range of passionate attachment and intellectual deliberation (110). The "external bodies which either pleased or hurt him" engross him thoroughly and exhaust his concern with the external world (110). Even the most insistent passions would lose some of their power because, despite their strength, they would be fleeting. The things "most immediately present to him," the sources of his pleasures and pains, "could scarce ever be the objects of his thoughts" (110). In society, though, the passions are not only more intensely engaged. Importantly, they are themselves multiplied and diversified. "Bring him into society," Smith observes, "and all his own passions will immediately become the causes of new passions" (111). Desire breeds new desire, joy and sorrow give rise to new joys and sorrows. This profusion of new passions is set into motion by "our first ideas of personal beauty and deformity," which are "drawn from the shape and appearance of others"; this process is then accelerated and compounded when we "become sensible . . . that others exercise the same criticism upon us" (111).

2 Beauty and deformity

According to Smith's own terms, it would not be an overstatement to suggest that the experience of becoming cognizant of our own beauty and deformity (and the beauty and deformity of others) is the condition of possibility for morality itself. Accordingly, we would be right to say that Smithean civil society is underwritten, from first to last, by an ideological dispensation that divides the beautiful from the deformed. Smith inherits the binary of "beauty" and "deformity" from the moral philosophy of his teacher, Francis Hutcheson, who in turn derives it from the work of Anthony Ashley Cooper, the third earl of Shaftesbury.[14] Looking forward, the aesthetic ideology that informs eighteenth-century moral philosophy lays the groundwork for, and is recapitulated in, the ideology of the normal and the abnormal, which begins in the nineteenth century and continues unabated into the contemporary moment.[15] The notions of normality and abnormality have been recruited to identify, classify, and pathologize atypical bodies and minds, frequently, of course, to disastrous ends. As we already have seen, Smith freely applies the criteria of beauty and deformity to describe the external (appearance and conduct) and the internal (thoughts and passions) characteristics of the human creature. He moves easily and without comment from discussions of pleasing and displeasing bodies to pleasing and displeasing actions. An almost comic scene is offered in which "we," newly sensitized to the aesthetic effects of personal appearance, rush to an actual mirror after having regarded ourselves in the figurative mirror of society. "We become anxious to know how far our appearance deserves either their blame or approbation," and so we "examine our persons limb by limb, and by placing ourselves before a looking-glass, or by some such expedient, endeavour, as much as possible, to view ourselves at the distance and with the eyes of other people" (111–12). Those lucky few who discover that they are "tolerably handsome" are afforded in the future a kind of psychological buffer, whereby they will be better able to withstand the "most disadvantageous judgments of others" (112). Unfortunately, those who discover that they are the "natural objects of distaste" must ready themselves for a lifetime of criticism and anxiety, given that every sign of another's disapprobation will trigger in them a mortification "beyond all measure" (112).[16]

Smith follows these scenes of bodies examined and judged with a discussion of how these social processes carry over into judgments regarding our character and our conduct. As before, "we" find ourselves before a mirror, and begin to "examine our own passions and conduct" (112). "We suppose ourselves," Smith writes, "the spectators of our own behaviour, and endeavour to imagine what effect it would, in this light, produce upon us" (112). But unlike the moment of self-examination in which we scrutinized our bodies, there is no mirror that can reflect back to us the image of our behavior other than the mirror found in other people. "This is the only looking-glass by which we can, in some measure, with the eyes of other people, scrutinize the propriety of our own conduct" (112). Also as before, some will like what they see and others will not. Those who are "tolerably satisfied" when they behold their moral character through the eyes of others will grow "indifferent" to applause, and perhaps even despise the "censure of the world" should they be "misunderstood or misrepresented," because comfort will be found in the knowledge that they are "the natural and proper object of approbation" (112). And those who have reason to doubt how their moral characters appear will grow "more anxious" for approbation, and will feel every instance of "censure" with a "double severity" (112).

Over a period of time that Smith does not specify, the repeated act of routing our self-perception and self-understanding through the minds and bodies of others consolidates the power of the impartial spectator. The virtual eyes of the impartial spectator, we come to feel, are always upon us, and this experience of becoming habituated to the scrutiny of moral spectatorship transforms the shape of our thoughts and passions. Indeed, we are not only internally transformed but also internally divided. The circuit established between self and society, in which seeing and being seen constitute our apprehension of the proper and the improper, fashions a split social subject. As Smith phrases it,

> When I endeavour to examine my own conduct, when I endeavour to pass sentence upon it, and either approve or condemn it, it is evident that, in all such cases, I divide myself, as it were, into two persons; and that I, the examiner and judge, represent a different character from that other I, the person whose conduct is examined into and judged of. (113)

The first "I" is the impartial spectator, a "particular point of view" that also represents a general and abstract point of view. The second "I" is the "person whom I properly call myself" (113). In this somber scene of judgment, Smith does not suggest that any sort of communication occurs between these two selves. The one sees and judges, the other remains silent and accepts whatever judgment is handed down. Smith underscores the absolute divide that must remain in place when he refutes, in advance, the idea that these two selves might collapse again into one undivided person. This would be as impossible, he claims, as discovering that cause and effect were one and the same (113).

The strict opposition Smith wishes to maintain between these two selves, I would argue, draws inspiration from what he claims is the absolute and immediately recognizable difference between beauty and deformity. If morality depends on our ability to divide ourselves in two, this resonates with Smith's penchant for drawing on the discourse of aesthetics to articulate the workings of morality. In other words, the internal scene of judgment in which one "I" confronts another "I" should be read as precisely that: a *scene*, one which bears all the marks of aesthetic construction.[17] The aesthetic ideology that informs *The Theory of Moral Sentiments* privileges the classical idea of beauty as that which is synonymous with symmetry, order, and harmony.[18] Throughout his text, Smith applies this vision of beauty to matters large and small. His frequent appeals to Nature stress the beneficial orderliness of what he will designate as "natural" and thus attempt to render inarguable. "The rules which [Nature] follows are fit for her," he writes, "those which [man] follows for him: but both are calculated to promote the same great end, the order of the world, and the perfection and happiness of human nature" (168). When Smith turns his attention to more local matters—for instance, in his discussion of how we assess the passions of others (and ourselves) as being either "proportionate" or "disproportionate" to their causes—he implicitly aestheticizes both the language and the process of moral judgment. And so, when he invites his reader to imagine that each human subject who has properly internalized the impartial spectator does so through a process of self-division, we can read this self-division as a recapitulation within the human subject of the providential order manifested in Nature more generally. By erecting and preserving within ourselves a scene of orderly opposition, in which "I" faces "I," we participate in the "order of the world." At the same time, I would suggest, by staging this scene of self-judgment, we also internalize and reaffirm the binary of the beautiful and the deformed. Aligned with the principles of beauty, the impartial spectator examines the accused, looking closely and carefully for traces of deformity. Were this moral drama played out in a real courtroom, one might reasonably consider the possibility that the accused will be found not guilty. But when we recall Smith's earlier observation that "no human conduct ever did, or ever can come up to" the "idea of complete propriety and perfection," we realize that this scene of judgment will necessarily find something to condemn, and thus repeat once again the moral and aesthetic deprecation of deformed minds and bodies (26).

3 Imagining morality

As I suggested above, the opposition between beauty and deformity is fundamental to the philosophical enterprise of *The Theory of Moral Sentiments*, and so it comes as no surprise that Smith consciously works to diminish the possibility that this opposition will be called into question. He is particularly vigilant, as we will see, when he discovers that he himself has introduced a troublesome and potentially destabilizing element into his text. After the passage in which the eyes of other people are figured as the "looking-glass" in which we "scrutinize" our own behavior, Smith notes the following:

> Unfortunately, this moral looking-glass is not always a very good one. Common looking-glasses, it is said, are extremely deceitful, and by the glare which they throw over the face, conceal from the partial eyes of the person many deformities which are obvious to every body besides. But there is not in the world such a smoother of wrinkles as is every man's imagination, with regard to the blemishes of his own character. (112)

This short passage appears only in the first edition of *The Theory of Moral Sentiments*; all subsequent editions eliminate these lines and move immediately to the discussion of self-division and self-judgment. Why, we might ask, would Smith remove this passage? To my mind, it reads as both a witty and realistic aside about the vagaries of moral life. And throughout the text, Smith amply demonstrates a sardonic familiarity with the foibles and lapses that plague even the best-intentioned moral subjects.

Smith rethinks the wisdom of this observation, I argue, because it explicitly threatens to undermine the status of the imagination in his text, and more particularly, the role that the imagination plays in bringing us into relation with others and thus into the sphere of morality. On the opening page of *The Theory of Moral Sentiments*, Smith both acknowledges and partially refutes the conventional wisdom that humans are inherently selfish. Yes, he concedes, humankind may be naturally inclined to gratify self-interested desires. But at the same time, they are animated by other principles, such as the active desire to see, to be aware of, and thereby to become "interested" in the fortunes of others (9). Even when faced with the spectacle of another's distress, we derive a "pleasure" merely from "seeing it" (9). As an example of this sort of pleasure, he refers to "pity or compassion, the emotion which we feel for the misery of others, when we either see it, or are made to conceive it in a very lively manner" (9). The phrase "or are made to conceive it" signals the work of the imagination. "As we have no immediate experience of what other men feel," he notes, "we can form no idea of the manner in which they are affected, but by conceiving what we ourselves should feel in the like situation" (9). It goes without saying that Smith invokes the act of seeing everywhere; but without the imagination, without this capacity to project beyond the confines of our experience and "conceive" ourselves as another, sight would never give rise to the intersubjective realm of morality.

In order to make his vision of the imagination rhetorically powerful and to set firmly in place the moral dynamic of imaginatively trading places with another, Smith conjures up a famously lurid scene of torture:

> Though our brother is upon the rack, as long as we ourselves are at our ease, our senses will never inform us of what he suffers. They never did, and never can, carry us beyond our own person, and it is by the imagination only that we can form any conception of what are his sensations. Neither can that faculty help us to do this any other way, than by representing to us what would be our own, if we were in his case. It is the impressions of our senses only, not those of his, which our imaginations copy. By the imagination we place ourselves in his situation, we conceive ourselves enduring all the same torments, we enter as it were into his body, and become in some measure the same person with him.... His agonies, when they are thus brought home to ourselves, when we have thus adopted and made them our own, begin at last to affect us, and we then tremble and shudder at the thought of what he feels. (9)

One of the ironies of this scene, which certainly provides one of the most memorable openings of any philosophical work, is that Smith will progressively temper the immediacy and intensity of feeling we have before us here. As we move forward in *The Theory of Moral Sentiments*, much importance will be given to the fact that we *cannot*, in fact, feel another's pain as sharply as he does. This, as I have discussed earlier, teaches us to moderate the expression of our pain, thus enabling a sympathetic onlooker to share our passion, albeit in a lower register and to a lesser degree. Nevertheless, this remains a sensory connection between the self and the other, and as Smith explains, when we attempt to conceive within ourselves what the impassioned situation of another feels like, the imagination "copies" the impressions of our own senses and "excites some degree of the same emotion" (9). Smith needs the imagination to operate with a considerable amount of fidelity as it performs its work of copying, for only through the imagination is it possible to "become in some measure the same person" as the suffering person we contemplate.

A great deal depends on the imagination serving the cause of moral order.[19] Were the imagination chronically or constitutionally prone to making inaccurate or infelicitous sensory reproductions, the moral subject would be imprisoned within the boundaries of the self and the entire system of intersubjective relationality would either dissipate or, perhaps worse, would become a tangled web of improper—not to say, deformed—correspondences. Thus, when Smith remarks in the excised passage how the imagination is an extraordinary "smoother of wrinkles" and a deft concealer of the "blemishes" of our character, he introduces precisely this possibility. Just as the glare of a "common looking-glass" helps to disguise the "deformities" our "partial" eyes wish to ignore, imagination, as Smith momentarily figures it, is a force through which we enact another kind of trading of places, an improper exchange of beauty and deformity. This is the reason, I argue, that Smith, when it came time for a second edition of his treatise, eliminated this unflattering depiction of the imagination. Correct moral perception depends on the imagination being a reasonably reliable relay between my senses and those of another; it also depends on the imagination being a faculty that does *not* habitually undo the distinction between the beautiful and the deformed. With this textual revision, Smith prevents the imagination as such from becoming allied with partiality and deformity. He does, however, leave in place his condemnation of a cast of characters—the "woman who paints," the "foolish liar," and the "important coxcomb"—whose self-deluding "vanity arises from so gross an illusion of the imagination, that it is difficult to conceive how any rational creature should be imposed upon by it" (115). The moral power of the imagination, somewhat paradoxically, is thus shored up by Smith's admission that it is "difficult" for the philosopher "to conceive"—that is, to imagine—how and why the imagination can be so grossly abused.

4 A stronger love

The rhetoric of deformity, as we have seen, is indissociable from Smith's philosophical account of how the individual enters into and assumes the moral duties entailed by civil society. Having fashioned the contours of his moral subject, Smith continues to deploy the trope of deformity as he refines and specifies the ways that sympathy sustains the relationship between self and other. For instance, in a chapter entitled "Of the Influence and Authority of Conscience," Smith considers how individuals are able to make "any proper comparison" between their own interests and the interests of others (135). Only by consulting the impartial spectator, Smith tells us, can we see our self-interest in its "proper shape and dimensions" (134). At first, our desires and concerns appear urgent and imposing. But this perception is analogous to the optical tricks a person experiences when viewing a landscape. Just as "to the eye of the body," the greatness and smallness of objects is determined by the distance between the object and the viewer, so to "the natural eye of the mind," the interest closest to hand—that is, our own self-interest—appears great and the interests furthest from us—that is, the interests of others—appear small (134, 135). As Smith argues, both of these organs—"the eye of the body" and "the natural eye of the mind"—are inherently imperfect and flawed and their respective "defects" are corrected in similar fashion (135). The person beholding a landscape and the person calculating his own self-interest are both taught by "habit and experience" to imaginatively assume the position and adopt the eyes of a "third person" (135). Only by aligning ourselves with the perspective of this third person, this impartial spectator who embodies an ideal form of moral perception, can we properly judge and correct our seemingly congenital tendency to see and judge improperly. Smith understands habit and experience as, in a sense, prosthetic devices that correct the perceptual defects that are inherent in the human creature. Be it the eye of the body or the eye of the mind, the formation within ourselves of the impartial spectator promises to replace our "improper" forms of seeing with a form of moral spectatorship that "correct[s] the otherwise natural inequality of our sentiments" (136).

From here, Smith immediately turns to one of the most striking, indeed shocking, philosophical thought exercises in *The Theory of Moral Sentiments*. He asks us to entertain in our mind's eye the following catastrophe: "Let us suppose that the great empire of China, with all its myriads of inhabitants, was suddenly swallowed up by an earthquake, and let us consider how a man of humanity in Europe, who had no sort of connexion with that part of the world, would be affected upon receiving intelligence of this dreadful calamity" (136). How does this man of humanity react?[20] As Smith tells us, "He would, I imagine, first of all, express very strongly his sorrow for the misfortune of that unhappy people, he would make many melancholy reflections upon the precariousness of human life, and the vanity of all the labours of man, which could thus be annihilated in a moment" (136). However, these sorrowful feelings and somber meditations quickly enough come to an end. "And when all this fine philosophy was over," he regretfully observes, "when all these humane sentiments had been once fairly expressed, he would pursue his business or his pleasure . . . with the same ease and tranquillity, as if no such accident had happened" (136). And then Smith really raises the moral stakes:

> The most frivolous disaster which could befal [sic] himself would occasion a more real disturbance. If he was to lose his little finger to-morrow, he would not sleep to-night; but, provided he never saw them, he will snore with the most profound security over the ruin of a hundred millions of his brethren, and the destruction of that immense multitude seems plainly an object less interesting to him, than this paltry misfortune of his own. (136–37)

The philosophical question that follows is disconcerting, but given Smith's assumption that the uncorrected human creature tends to indulge in morally defective judgments, the question is also inevitable: would this so-called man of humanity, who has been tossing and turning over the prospect of losing a finger, sacrifice the lives of millions of Chinese men, women, and children in order to avoid being bodily mutilated? The answer of course is a resounding *no*—or in any case, it *should* be a resounding *no*—for "human nature startles with horror" at such a thought. "When our passive feelings are almost always so sordid and so selfish, how comes it," Smith asks, "that our active principles should often be so generous and so noble?" (137). Here again the impartial spectator—variously glossed as "reason, principle, conscience, the inhabitant of the breast, the man within, the great judge and arbiter of our conduct"—intervenes to save us from our imperfect and defective selves (137):

> It is he who, whenever we are about to act so as to affect the happiness of others, calls to us, with a voice capable of astonishing the most presumptuous of our passions, that we are but one of the multitude, in no respect better than any other in it; and that when we prefer ourselves so shamefully and so blindly to others, we become the proper objects of resentment, abhorrence, and execration. It is from him only that we learn the real littleness of ourselves, and of whatever relates to ourselves, and the natural misrepresentations of self-love can be corrected only by the eye of this impartial spectator. It is he who shows us the propriety of generosity and the deformity of injustice; the propriety of resigning the greatest interests of our own,

for the yet greater interests of others, and the deformity of doing the smallest injury to another, in order to obtain the greatest benefit to ourselves. (137)

Smith here recapitulates the moral drama of a self divided into accuser and accused. The "man within," the impartial spectator, sternly hails the self that presumptuously—albeit "naturally"—follows the dictates of self-love. It is important to note that Smith explicitly draws on the trope of blindness in this passage. Shame covers those who "blindly" prefer their own interest to the interest of others; the self is morally disabled by the blindness that encourages the undisciplined individual to embrace the partial and the deformed. Only the eyes of the impartial spectator can correct the disabling effects of self-love. And yet, having chastened us for our predisposition toward moral defect and deformity, Smith takes away a bit of his argument's sting by opening before us a path toward a higher kind of love:

> It is not the love of our neighbour, it is not the love of mankind, which upon many occasions prompts us to the practice of those divine virtues. It is a stronger love, a more powerful affection, which generally takes place upon such occasions; the love of what is honourable and noble, of the grandeur, and dignity, and superiority of our own characters. (137)

However, without saying so explicitly, Smith, I would argue, has outlined a moral-philosophical rationale for how our self-love can be both transcended *and* preserved. We are being invited to indulge not our undisciplined, uncorrected, deformed, and deforming self-love, but rather a love of the "superiority of our own characters," which is made possible by the moral intervention of the impartial spectator.

In short, then, treating others properly mens loving ourselves properly. And loving ourselves properly is a moral accomplishment grounded in habit and experience—specifically, the habit and experience of overcoming our deformities and adopting the ideal, undeformed perspective of the impartial spectator. But as we ascend the heights of moral grandeur, we must remember that impartiality can only be fashioned through partiality, and propriety can only be fashioned through deformity. In other words, disability is the condition of possibility for Smithean sympathy and morality. We also must remember, no less importantly, that Smith's appropriation of the language of disability, although it is often pitched at the level of the abstract and the figurative, takes for granted the existence and experience of those disabled minds and bodies for whom a morally transcendent self-love is often an exceedingly challenging proposition.

By way of closing, I want to consider the suggestive echoes between Smith's *The Theory of Moral Sentiments* and one of the most illuminating contributions to disability studies: Rosemarie Garland-Thomson's *Staring: How We Look* (2009), her incisive exploration of "uncivil attention."[21] In their respective ways, Smith and Garland-Thomson offer an anatomy of the bodily and moral phenomena that arise when we behold the other with our eyes, especially the other who disrupts our everyday expectations of how men and women should look and behave. Further, both Smith and Garland-Thomson direct our attention to the particular challenges facing the other whose appearance in the social landscape constitutes a spectacular display of self—indeed, an often unintended self-spectacularization that draws seer and seen, starer and staree, into a fraught and disorienting (but potentially transformative) intersubjective and intercorporeal relationship.

Staring, Garland-Thomson suggests, is a physiological impulse keenly attuned to variations in our shared social and cultural landscape. Startled by an unforeseen and unforeseeable image of bodily difference—and she asks us to understand the disabled body as the "exemplary form of the unforeseen"—the starer's eyes are fixated by the irruption of novelty within a visual field shaped by modernity's efforts to normalize our conception of the human body.[22] Novelty interrupts the habituated forms of seeing that quickly, smoothly scan and sort the scenes and objects that come before the eyes. In this sense, novelty triggers inquiry and speculation. Understood as an "interrogative gesture," Garland-Thomson stresses that staring "demands a story," a story that will piece together again the starer's momentarily shattered expectations of how the human body appears—and how the human body *appears* in two senses: the physiological shape and postural disposition of the body, as well as the presence and persistence of the body within the public sphere.[23]

To be sure, the implicit demand issued from starer to staree—in short, explain who or what you are—can easily choreograph a scene in which the staree is made intelligible by being re-objectified according to a calculus of the normal and the pathological. Garland-Thomson, of course, is keenly aware of the ideological quandaries associated with the topic of staring, and she carefully traces how the dynamic initiated between starer and staree can reassert the dominance of the norm (for instance, when the starer looks away in disgust) or intensify the disenfranchisement of the disabled (for instance, when the staree is pitied, studiously ignored, or simply compelled to retreat from the realm of visibility). Nevertheless, because the connection—however brief—forged between starer and staree is so intense and intensely disorienting, staring keeps open the possibility that *something may happen* that exceeds or confounds the powers of normalization. Domination and disgust may be the outcomes of a staring encounter, but staring is also capable of catalyzing other, more generative reactions, including "adoration, curiosity, surprise, allegiance, wonder, befuddlement, and openness."[24] By developing the generative potential of staring, Garland-Thomson proposes that we reconsider our devotion to the forms of ideology critique that, for decades now, have been the preferred currency of critical theory—particularly those theories of visuality that have concentrated their efforts on exposing and interrupting the power of the gaze. Whereas the gaze fixes, subordinates, and disciplines its object, the stare troubles the ideological dispensation of subject and object, starer and staree. "The task of the modern individual," Garland-Thomson argues, "is to move appropriately and effectively from disengaged spectator to attentive perceiver in order to slide easily into the social order. The starer, in contrast, is an undisciplined spectator."[25]

How does this process of becoming an undisciplined spectator unfold, according to Garland-Thomson? Surprised and curious, the spectator is caught off guard by the sight of an extraordinary body that deviates from the everyday protocols of visual conformity. As surprise and curiosity grow, the spectator's staring eyes initiate an experience of absorption that radiates across the face and quickly takes over the now-starer's body. Given that staring is typically considered an impolite, if not improper form of seeing, the starer's absorption in a seemingly "improper" human figure transforms the starer, in some sense, into an improper human figure. In short, staring re-embodies the starer, reminds the starer that he or she is simply one (unavoidably) imperfect body among other imperfect bodies. The subject bearing the gaze becomes, however briefly, a transfixed object. As the taken-for-granted privileges of being the unseen seer dissolve in the staring encounter, the starer's demand to the staree—tell me the story of who you are—turns against itself. Curiously seeking to make sense of the extraordinary body, the starer instead finds the prosthetic armor of the gaze slipping away. Staring disables the gaze, thereby making possible the re-apprehension of a collective story:

namely, our shared bodily experience of being constitutively exposed, susceptible, and vulnerable; our shared experience of undergoing the "changes in our function and form that we think of as disabilities" but that are, in fact, the common, unavoidable effects of simply being alive. As Garland-Thomson succinctly phrases it: "If we live long enough, we will all become disabled."[26]

Perhaps it will be unsurprising to learn that, although Smith offers us seemingly countless scenarios in which complex acts of seeing and being seen take place, explicit scenes of staring are hard to come by in *The Theory of Moral Sentiments*. And for good reason: unlike Garland-Thomson, who is concerned with bringing to our attention and cultivating the ethical transformation of starers into "undisciplined spectators," Smith's most obvious intention is to develop a persuasive philosophical account of how, in his words, our "untaught and undisciplined feelings" are corrected through the agency of the "impartial spectator" (148). What prevents Smith's moral spectator from becoming, so to speak, an (im) moral starer is precisely the ever-vigilant surveillance of the impartial spectator, which serves to triangulate the dynamic that unfolds between spectator and spectatee. In other words, Smith's impartial spectator supplies the filter of moral abstraction that guards against the kinds of disorienting absorption described by Garland-Thomson.

This, in any case, is Smith's moral ideal. However, as we look more closely at *The Theory of Moral Sentiments*, certain conceptual openings become apparent, ones that promise to productively unsettle the smooth functioning of the impartial spectator. Specifically, I have in mind the tension between story and judgment in Smith's treatise. Shortly after suggesting that the mere appearance of grief or joy, "upon some occasions," may transfuse these passions between spectator and spectatee, Smith adds the following: "General lamentations, which express nothing but the anguish of the sufferer, create rather a curiosity to inquire into his situation, along with some disposition to sympathize with him, than any actual sympathy that is very sensible. The first question which we ask is, What has befallen you?" (11). Smith's spectator, much like Garland-Thomson's starer, demands a story. Moral spectatorship, as an interrogative gesture, seeks to piece together and to make intelligible the spectacle of grief or joy that has interrupted the everyday business of the civil society that forms the background of Smith's treatise. Presumably, once the situation that occasions the spectatee's passion is made comprehensible, this passion can then come before the tribunal of the impartial spectator, where it will be judged as either a proper or improper reaction to the situation at hand. But in order to be judged, both the passion and the situation must be rendered abstract, that is, fixed and interchangeable with other seemingly comparable passions and situations. In other words, the story of the spectatee must be drained of its temporal and physical particularity, and to recall Garland-Thomson, by abstracting away the experience of the spectatee, the Smithean moral spectator guards against the knowledge of his own temporal, bodily implication in the world.

However, an unforeseen, generative outcome might also be possible. Despite his thorough exposition of how the impartial spectator functions to morally temper our "untaught and undisciplined feelings," Smith acknowledges that the empirical spectator's internalization of (and identification with) the impartial spectator is—like sympathy itself—imperfect and incomplete (25–26). This imperfection and incompleteness, I would suggest, sharpens the poignancy of Smith's moral philosophy, especially when seen from the perspective of disability studies, for it leaves open the possibility that, in the moment of demanding the story behind the spectatee's passion, the spectator may begin to interrogate—that is, to temporalize, to re-embody, to make productively precarious—the story behind moral subjectivity as such.

Notes

1 See Lennard J. Davis, *Enforcing Normalcy: Disability, Deafness, and the Body* (New York and London: Verso, 1995) and Davis, *Bending over Backwards: Essays on Disability and the Body* (New York: New York University Press, 2002); Helen Deutsch, *Resemblance and Disgrace: Alexander Pope and the Deformation of Culture* (Cambridge, MA: Harvard University Press, 1996); Felicity Nussbaum, "Feminotopias: The Pleasures of 'Deformity' in Mid-Eighteenth-Century England," in *The Body and Physical Difference: Discourses of Disability*, ed. David Mitchell and Sharon L. Snyder (Ann Arbor: University of Michigan Press, 1997), 161–73; Helen Deutsch and Felicity Nussbaum, eds., *"Defects": Engendering the Modern Body* (Ann Arbor: University of Michigan Press, 2000); and David M. Turner, *Disability in Eighteenth-Century England: Imagining Physical Impairment* (New York and London: Routledge, 2012).

An earlier version of this essay appeared as "The Man Within the Breast: Sympathy and Deformity in Adam Smith's *The Theory of Moral Sentiments*," *Studies in Eighteenth-Century Culture* 44 (2015): 41–60.

2. Helen Deutsch, "The Body's Moments: Visible Disability, the Essay, and the Limits of Sympathy," *Prose Studies* 27, no. 1–2 (April-August 2005): 14. Chris Mounsey, for instance, calls for more detailed explorations of the "immediacy of individual lived experience"; further, he stresses that we need to attend to how individuals with the "same" disability are, in fact, both "same" and "different"—not least because disabilities exhibit synchronic and diachronic variation. See Chris Mounsey, "Introduction: Variability: Beyond Sameness and Difference," in *The Idea of Disability in the Eighteenth Century*, ed. Chris Mounsey (Lewisburg: Bucknell University Press, 2014), 18.

3. Joseph P. Shapiro, *No Pity: People with Disabilities Forging a New Civil Rights Movement* (New York: Three Rivers Press, 1994), 30, 38.

4. Lennard J. Davis, "Introduction," in *The Disability Studies Reader*, ed. Davis (New York: Routledge, 1997), 2.

5. Davis, "Introduction," 2–3.

6. Elsewhere, Davis observes that "by narrativizing an impairment, one tends to sentimentalize it, and link it to the bourgeois sensibility of individualism and the drama of the individual story" (Davis, *Enforcing Normalcy*, 11). David T. Mitchell and Sharon L. Snyder elaborate on Davis's position as follows:

   > The personal narrative expands the boundaries of our understanding of disability on an individual level, but its attendant social and political contexts tend to be overshadowed by the emotions of pity and/or sympathy evoked by the reader's identification with the narrator's personal plight. Consequently, first person narratives cannot singularly provide the interpretive paradigms needed to revise cultural understandings of disability.

   David T. Mitchell and Sharon L. Snyder, "Introduction: Disability Studies and the Double Bind of Representation," in *The Body and Physical Difference: Discourses of Disability*, ed. David T. Mitchell and Sharon L. Snyder (Ann Arbor: University of Michigan Press, 1997), 11. From the perspective of disability studies, Smith's *Theory of Moral Sentiments* represents as an important chapter in the history of conceptions of disability, affect, and self-narration. More specifically, *The Theory of Moral Sentiments* philosophically narrates the ideological instantiation of the "first person" moral subject, and along the way, reveals how sympathy—the capacity to think and feel intersubjectively—is indissociable from the social and political contexts that give rise to the "first person."

7. Adam Smith, *The Theory of Moral Sentiments*, ed. D. D. Raphael and A. L. Macfie (Indianapolis: Liberty Fund, 1984), 12, 148 and 260–61. All further references will be to this edition and cited parenthetically in the text.

8. See Turner's first chapter, "Defining Disability and Deformity," in *Disability in Eighteenth-Century England*, 16–34.

9   See Hina Nazar, *Enlightened Sentiments: Judgment and Autonomy in the Age of Sensibility* (New York: Fordham University Press, 2012), for a consideration of how Enlightenment notions of judgment are grounded in (rather than merely repudiate or transcend) the aesthetics and ethics of sentimentalism. Her discussion of *The Theory of Moral Sentiments* (e.g., 24–25, 52–56) highlights the determinative role Smith accords to affective experience and social relations in the formation of moral duty. James Chandler offers a brilliant reading of Smithean sympathy in relation to sentimentalism's revolutionizing of literary form, communication, and perception in *An Archaeology of Sympathy: The Sentimental Mode in Literature and Cinema* (Chicago: University of Chicago Press, 2013). For other discussions that situate Smith's theory of sympathy within Enlightenment debates regarding reason and sentiment, see Charles L. Griswold Jr., *Adam Smith and the Virtues of Enlightenment* (Cambridge: Cambridge University Press, 1999); Pierre Force, *Self-Interest Before Adam Smith: A Genealogy of Economic Science* (Cambridge: Cambridge University Press, 2003); and Michael L. Frazer, *The Enlightenment of Sympathy: Justice and the Moral Sentiments in the Eighteenth Century and Today* (Oxford: Oxford University Press, 2010), 89–111.

10 See Jean-Jacques Rousseau, *Discours sur les sciences et les arts; Discours sur l'origine et les fondements de l'inégalité parmi les hommes* (Paris: Flammarion, 1992 [Paris: Plissot, 1751; Geneva, 1755]), para. 6, p. 169. Throughout this essay, I typically will use male or masculine pronouns and references, in order to remain consistent with Smith's linguistic habits. It goes without saying that Smith's philosophical thought is tendentiously grounded in a gender ideology that opposes, in conventional and often facile ways, male and female forms of thought, feeling, and action.

11 Disability studies scholars have begun to interrogate the ways that aesthetic ideology historically aids and abets the pathologization of the so-called abnormal or anomalous. See, for instance, Ato Quayson, *Aesthetic Nervousness: Disability and the Crisis of Representation* (New York: Columbia University Press, 2007), and Tobin Siebers, *Disability Aesthetics* (Ann Arbor: University of Michigan Press, 2010).

12 For considerations of masculinity and Stoicism in Smith, see Stewart Justman, *The Autonomous Male of Adam Smith* (Norman: University of Oklahoma Press, 1993), 24–81; and Julie Ellison, *Cato's Tears and the Making of Anglo-American Emotion* (Chicago: University of Chicago Press, 1999), 10–12, 69–73. Additionally, Wendy Motooka offers a suggestive reading of masculinity in *The Theory of Moral Sentiments* in *The Age of Reasons: Quixotism, Sentimentalism and Political Economy in Eighteenth-Century Britain* (London and New York: Routledge, 1998), 205–20.

13 As Hume writes,

> The minds of men are mirrors to one another, not only because they reflect one another's emotions, but also because those rays of passions,

sentiments and opinions may be often reverberated, and may decay away by insensible degrees. Thus the pleasure, which a rich man receives from his possessions, being thrown upon the beholder, causes a pleasure and esteem; which sentiments again, being perceiv'd and sympathiz'd with, encrease the pleasure of the possessor; and being once more reflected, become a new foundation for pleasure and esteem in the beholder.

David Hume, *A Treatise of Human Nature*, ed. David Fate Norton and Mary J. Norton (Oxford: Oxford University Press, 2000), 236. Hume conceives of sympathy as a fairly immediate form of emotional communication, even contagion, whereas Smith stresses that sympathy typically involves a spectator's assessment of an emotional "situation," in which emotional immediacy is subordinated to and tempered by considerations of propriety and impropriety, merit and demerit. Sympathy, Smith observes, "does not arise so much from the view of the passion, as from that of the situation which excites it" (12). Nevertheless, when he imagines the human creature first encountering others of his kind, Smith seems to imply that physical deformity is immediately sensed and identified, whereas moral deformity only becomes possible within a social system of comparative perceptions and assessments.

14   References, both explicit and implicit, to "deformity" are everywhere to be found in Shaftesbury's *Characteristics of Men, Manners, Opinions, Times* and Hutcheson's *An Inquiry into the Original of Our Ideas of Beauty and Virtue*. For Shaftesbury, see Anthony Ashley Cooper, Third Earl of Shaftesbury, *Characteristics of Men, Manners, Opinions, Times*, ed. Lawrence E. Klein (Cambridge: Cambridge University Press, 1999), 93, 172–73, and 415. For Hutcheson, see Francis Hutcheson, *An Inquiry into the Original of Our Ideas of Beauty and Virtue*, ed. Wolfgang Leidhold (Indianapolis: Liberty Fund, 2004), 25, 61, 92, 124, 139, and 168. Elsewhere, I have considered how the notion of deformity is central to Shaftesbury's moral philosophy. See Paul Kelleher, "Defections from Nature: The Rhetoric of Deformity in Shaftesbury's *Characteristics*," in *The Idea of Disability in the Eighteenth Century*, ed. Chris Mounsey (Lewisburg: Bucknell University Press, 2014), 71–90.

15   For an incisive account of the rise of "normality" in the nineteenth century and its relationship to conceptions of disability, see Davis, *Enforcing Normalcy*, in which he draws on Michel Foucault's critique of the norm. See especially, Foucault, *The History of Sexuality, Vol. 1: An Introduction*, trans. Robert Hurley (New York: Vintage, 1990) and Foucault, *Abnormal: Lectures at the Collège de France, 1974-1975*, trans. Graham Burchell (New York: Picador, 2003).

16   Smith's description of the individual's disorienting encounter with his own deformity, which in some sense functions as the primal scene of moral subjectivity, resonates with Lennard J. Davis's definition of "physical disability" as "a disruption in the sensory field of the observer." Disability, for Davis, "is located in the observer, not the observed, and is therefore

more about the viewer than about the person using a cane or a wheelchair." Davis, "Dr. Johnson, Amelia, and the Discourse of Disability in the Eighteenth Century," in *"Defects"*, ed. Deutsch and Nussbaum, 56.

17 In *The Figure of Theater: Shaftesbury, Defoe, Adam Smith, and George Eliot* (New York: Columbia University Press, 1986), 167–92, David Marshall offers a subtle discussion of how Smith's conception of sympathy relies extensively on the tropes of theatricality.

18 See Terry Eagleton, *The Ideology of the Aesthetic* (Oxford, UK: Blackwell, 1990).

19 Drawing on Michel Foucault's well-known discussion of panopticism in *Discipline and Punish*, John Bender argues that the moral order envisioned by Smith is at the same time a social order that enacts discipline and control through sympathetic spectatorship. See Bender, *Imagining the Penitentiary: Fiction and the Architecture of Mind in Eighteenth-Century England* (Chicago: University of Chicago Press, 1987), 218–28.

20 For a rigorous consideration of Smith and the challenges of enacting sympathy in a global context, see Fonna Forman-Barzilai, *Adam Smith and the Circles of Sympathy: Cosmopolitanism and Moral Theory* (Cambridge: Cambridge University Press, 2011).

21 Rosemarie Garland-Thomson, *Staring: How We Look* (New York: Oxford University Press, 2009), 35.

22 Garland-Thomson, *Staring*, 38.

23 Ibid., 3.

24 Ibid., 39.

25 Ibid., 21.

26 Ibid.

Bibliography

Bender, John. *Imagining the Penitentiary: Fiction and the Architecture of Mind in Eighteenth-Century England*. Chicago: University of Chicago Press, 1987.
Chandler, James. *An Archaeology of Sympathy: The Sentimental Mode in Literature and Cinema*. Chicago: University of Chicago Press, 2013.
Cooper, Anthony Ashley (Third Earl of Shaftesbury). *Characteristics of Men, Manners, Opinions, Times*. Edited by Lawrence E. Klein. Cambridge: Cambridge University Press, 1999.
Davis, Lennard J. *Bending over Backwards: Essays on Disability and the Body*. New York: New York University Press, 2002.
Davis, Lennard J. "Dr. Johnson, Amelia, and the Discourse of Disability in the Eighteenth Century." In *"Defects": Engendering the Modern Body*, edited by Helen Deutsch and Felicity Nussbaum, 54–74. Ann Arbor: University of Michigan Press, 2000.

Davis, Lennard J. "Introduction." In *The Disability Studies Reader*, edited by Lennard J. Davis, 1–8. New York: Routledge, 1997.

Davis, Lennard J. *Enforcing Normalcy: Disability, Deafness, and the Body*. New York and London: Verso, 1995.

Deutsch, Helen. "The Body's Moments: Visible Disability, the Essay, and the Limits of Sympathy." *Prose Studies* 27, nos. 1–2 (April-August 2005): 11–26.

Deutsch, Helen, and Felicity Nussbaum, eds. *"Defects": Engendering the Modern Body*. Ann Arbor: University of Michigan Press, 2000.

Deutsch, Helen. *Resemblance and Disgrace: Alexander Pope and the Deformation of Culture*. Cambridge, MA: Harvard University Press, 1996.

Eagleton, Terry. *The Ideology of the Aesthetic*. Oxford, UK: Blackwell, 1990.

Ellison, Julie. *Cato's Tears and the Making of Anglo-American Emotion*. Chicago: University of Chicago Press, 1999.

Force, Pierre. *Self-Interest Before Adam Smith: A Genealogy of Economic Science*. Cambridge: Cambridge University Press, 2003.

Forman-Barzilai, Fonna. *Adam Smith and the Circles of Sympathy: Cosmopolitanism and Moral Theory*. Cambridge: Cambridge University Press, 2011.

Foucault, Michel. *Abnormal: Lectures at the Collège de France, 1974-1975*. Translated by Graham Burchell. New York: Picador, 2003.

Foucault, Michel. *The History of Sexuality, Vol. 1: An Introduction*. Translated by Robert Hurley. New York: Vintage, 1990.

Frazer, Michael L. *The Enlightenment of Sympathy: Justice and the Moral Sentiments in the Eighteenth Century and Today*. Oxford: Oxford University Press, 2010.

Garland-Thomson, Rosemarie. *Staring: How We Look*. New York: Oxford University Press, 2009.

Griswold Jr., Charles L. *Adam Smith and the Virtues of Enlightenment*. Cambridge: Cambridge University Press, 1999.

Hume, David. *A Treatise of Human Nature*. Edited by David Fate Norton and Mary J. Norton. Oxford: Oxford University Press, 2000.

Hutcheson, Francis. *An Inquiry into the Original of Our Ideas of Beauty and Virtue*. Edited by Wolfgang Leidhold. Indianapolis: Liberty Fund, 2004.

Justman, Stewart. *The Autonomous Male of Adam Smith*. Norman: University of Oklahoma Press, 1993.

Kelleher, Paul. "Defections from Nature: The Rhetoric of Deformity in Shaftesbury's *Characteristics*." In *The Idea of Disability in the Eighteenth Century*, edited by Chris Mounsey, 71–90. Lewisburg: Bucknell University Press, 2014.

Marshall, David. *The Figure of Theater: Shaftesbury, Defoe, Adam Smith, and George Eliot*. New York: Columbia University Press, 1986.

Mitchell, David T., and Sharon L. Snyder, "Introduction: Disability Studies and the Double Bind of Representation." In *The Body and Physical Difference: Discourses of Disability*, edited by David T. Mitchell and Sharon L. Snyder, 1–31. Ann Arbor: University of Michigan Press, 1997.

Motooka, Wendy. *The Age of Reasons: Quixotism, Sentimentalism and Political Economy in Eighteenth-Century Britain*. London and New York: Routledge, 1998.

Mounsey, Chris. "Introduction: Variability: Beyond Sameness and Difference." In *The Idea of Disability in the Eighteenth Century*, edited by Chris Mounsey, 1–27. Lewisburg: Bucknell University Press, 2014.

Nazar, Hina. *Enlightened Sentiments: Judgment and Autonomy in the Age of Sensibility*. New York: Fordham University Press, 2012.

Nussbaum, Felicity. "Feminotopias: The Pleasures of 'Deformity' in Mid-Eighteenth-Century England." In *The Body and Physical Difference: Discourses of Disability*, edited by David T. Mitchell and Sharon L. Snyder, 161–73. Ann Arbor: University of Michigan Press, 1997.

Quayson, Ato. *Aesthetic Nervousness: Disability and the Crisis of Representation*. New York: Columbia University Press, 2007.

Shapiro, Joseph P. *No Pity: People with Disabilities Forging a New Civil Rights Movement*. New York: Three Rivers Press, 1994.

Siebers, Tobin. *Disability Aesthetics*. Ann Arbor: University of Michigan Press, 2010.

Smith, Adam. *The Theory of Moral Sentiments*. Edited by D. D. Raphael and A. L. Macfie. Indianapolis: Liberty Fund, 1984.

Stiker, Henri-Jacques. *A History of Disability*. Translated by William Sayers. Ann Arbor: University of Michigan Press, 1999.

Turner, David M. *Disability in Eighteenth-Century England: Imagining Physical Impairment*. New York and London: Routledge, 2012.

9 JUDGING, INEVITABLY: AESTHETIC JUDGMENT AND NOVELISTIC FORM IN FIELDING'S *JOSEPH ANDREWS*

Vivasvan Soni

In *Joseph Andrews*, a forceful reaction against the sentimental, introspective, domestic novel epitomized by Samuel Richardson's *Pamela*, Henry Fielding diagnoses the advent of a "sociological" modernity and perceives that it poses an acute threat to our capacity for judgment. He responds by constructing a narrative whose intelligibility requires a constant practice of judging on the part of the reader. Indeed, Fielding recognizes in the emergent form of the novel a literary vehicle uniquely suited to foster judgment, though this promise was not fully realized until the extraordinary novels of Jane Austen nearly three-quarters of a century later.[1] At this early moment in the history of the novel, Fielding identifies its potential as a haven for judgment, finding in the distinctively modern literary form a remedy for one of modernity's characteristic and enduring problems, though it was a rare novelist who followed in his footsteps.

But how could judgment function as an antidote to a "sociological" modernity? Insisting on our capacity for judgment, as figures like Shaftesbury and Fielding do in the early eighteenth century, means taking a stand against the overwhelming sense of necessity and inevitability that dominates philosophical, psychological, sociological, and scientific accounts in the period, whether it be Newton's mechanics; Locke's and Mandeville's theories of motivation; Locke's purely external account of "freedom," in which freedom refers not to the will but only to the absence of external impediments to its execution; or nascent forms of social theory like Mandeville's, which led to the great historicisms of the nineteenth century and their sense of the historical inevitability and the necessary advent of modernity.[2] Where things are inevitable, there can be no judgment, only calculation and the brute prediction of outcomes. Fielding's novel, by contrast, demonstrates that our ability to make judgments is predicated on our capacity to imagine things otherwise. As Aristotle says about deliberation (which issues in a decision), judgment is about the things that can *be* otherwise, and a judgment can always be *made* otherwise or it is not a judgment in any meaningful sense.[3] It is precisely the sense of agency and judgment, the possibility of doing otherwise, that strong versions of inevitability or necessity found in certain sociological accounts of modernity would render unthinkable.[4]

To concede that judgment, if there is a cognitive act worthy of the name, can always be made otherwise, may sound elementary.[5] This is precisely what distinguishes a judgment from an infallible decision or an inevitable conclusion. But there are profound consequences to this observation that are usually overlooked. If a judgment can always, by definition, be made otherwise, then whatever the empirical matter under consideration, the judgment is not in principle determined by it but is a sentence passed on it; it is a judgment *on* rather than a judgment dictated by the empirical matter. In other words, the judgment is not epistemological: knowledge about the facts is indispensable, but it is never sufficient to issue in a judgment by itself. Knowledge, then, is not the concern or result of a judgment[6]; judgment in its fullest sense can only ever be ethico-existential, not epistemological.[7] There is always an evaluative or normative excess to judgment, which is why there is an irreducibly literary element to every judgment. This means, moreover, that it is *impossible* to speak of a judgment as right or wrong, correct or incorrect, however uncomfortable we may be with such a consequence, because to do so would place us back in the realm of epistemology.[8] Nevertheless, we recognize that there are "better" and "worse" judgments; if there were not, all judgments would be equally valid, and indistinguishable from opinions. If there is a kind of claim that we want to call a judgment, distinct from both knowledge and opinion, then it must be possible to assess it according to the criteria of "better" and "worse," even as we acknowledge that every judgment can be made otherwise. This is the paradoxical space that judgment inhabits. But how and by what authority can we declare a judgment that could be made otherwise better or worse? We can do so only by a further act of judgment, in a typical regress that affirms the priority and inevitability of judgment.[9]

Joseph Andrews begins as a mock-domestic novel of the *Pamela* type, with Joseph (Pamela's alleged brother) in the service of Lady Booby and subject to her sexual predations.[10] But true to its vocation as a "comic Epic-Poem in Prose,"[11] it almost immediately breaks free of the confines of domesticity, as Joseph is dismissed for refusing Lady Booby and strikes out into the English countryside, undertaking a journey reminiscent of the *Odyssey*'s narrative of homecoming (*nostos*).[12] Thus Fielding departs from the introspective, psychological novel that we find in Daniel Defoe's *Robinson Crusoe* or Richardson's *Pamela* and adopts the register of sociological observation and anatomization that is another of the novel's signal strengths.[13] The encounters of Joseph and his companion, Parson Adams, with characters from every walk of life furnish a variegated palette of social types that maps in impressive detail the social world of early-eighteenth-century England ("its Action being more extended and comprehensive; containing a much larger Circle of Incidents, and introducing a greater Variety of Characters" [*JA*, 3–4]). Naturally, it is not the world of the *Odyssey* or Greek romances, but it is also not a generic realistic portrait of early modern England. Surprisingly, it is instead a Hobbesian world, resembling not so much Hobbes's polity as his state of nature.[14] Social relations are shaped almost entirely by violence, fear, deceit, self-interest, and the abuse of power.[15]

The first incident on the road is emblematic. Joseph is robbed, stripped, beaten, and left for dead. His discovery by the passengers in a stagecoach prepares the way for an archetypal sentimental vignette, in which an anonymous victim's unmistakable suffering elicits the sympathy of observers. However, the ensuing conversation between the passengers reveals the utter failure of the "social affections," whether conceived in a Shaftesburian or a Richardsonian manner. Although they are "perhaps *a little* moved with Compassion at the poor Creature's Condition, who stood bleeding and shivering with the Cold" (*JA*, 46), their deliberations are shaped more by fear (of robbery or prosecution), self-interest (the wish to arrive at their destination on time, without blood on their clothes), and money (Joseph's seat in the coach would cost them). Wherever one turns in this world—to inns that refuse them hospitality, to predators who take advantage of their naïveté, or to those who delight in abusing their privilege and authority—a hermeneutics of suspicion dominates all social relations, and, it would seem, rightly so. Such a hermeneutics, still widespread today, insists that we view people as inevitably motivated by their own limited interests and concerns, unable to transcend the confines of their individual perspectives by acts of judgment relying on a shared or common sense (*sensus communis*).

There is an interpretive puzzle in Fielding's depiction of a Hobbesian social world structured by fear, distrust, and self-interest, with no place for the exercise of judgment.[16] Fielding is not a committed Hobbesian, since the exemplary characters of his novel cannot be construed as exhibiting a Hobbesian moral psychology.[17] And it is implausible to think, as Golden does, that Fielding simply vacillates between Hobbesian and Shaftesburian characters, since the Hobbesian nature of the social world encountered by Joseph and Adams appears so marked and consistent.[18] So what accounts for the systematically self-interested and distrustful character of social relations in this world, in which the exercise of judgment is unnecessary, or worse, dangerous? For Fielding, this world is neither merely accidental nor inevitably conditioned by human depravity. Rather, he presents it as the effect of a commercial modernity that produces the very hermeneutics of social relations that it then theorizes as the bedrock of all sociality. The monetization of social relationships, the central feature of this transformation, dictates that self-interest dominates the rich array of human interactions and that the relationship to things takes priority over the relationship to people.[19] In addition, social relations are conceived in increasingly contractual, legalistic, and litigious terms, as the preponderance and power of lawyers and legal reasoning in the novel demonstrate (*JA*, 46, 128–30).[20] The narrow specialization and professionalization required by a complexly articulated modern society result not only in the fragmentation and mutual unintelligibility of professional languages (46, 50, 128) but also in the dependence of individuals on performing a single task for their livelihoods, which makes them nearly incapable of charity or benevolence (as the example of innkeepers below shows). Finally, the growing mobility of populations, figured by Joseph and Adams's own journey through the landscape, fosters the anonymity, disconnectedness, and distrust that pervade social relations. If we should doubt that these are systematic effects of an incipient modernity, the example of Wilson's disoriented, disembedded life in the city clinches the point, as he capitalizes on undeserved credit ("Notwithstanding the Lowness of my Purse, I found Credit with them more easily than I expected" [176]), trades on the possibilities of anonymity to reinvent himself ("Here I soon got a fresh Set of Acquaintance, who knew nothing of what had happened to me" [178]), indulges monetized social relationships that have lost their narrative texture ("visited Whores" [179]), falls victim to pecuniary legal proceedings ("He then prosecuted me at Law, and recovered 3000 l. Damages" [184]), and encounters the ravages of professionalization when he turns hack writer (187–89). As Adams laments, in the city that is emblematic of the social space of modernity, life no longer has the structure of a narrative but turns into a series of discrete, disaggregated episodes: "Well, Sir, in this Course of Life I continued full three Years,— 'What Course of Life?' answered *Adams*; 'I do not remember you have yet mentioned any'" (177).

Abstraction characterizes all four ways in which modernity transforms social relations: monetization, legalization, professionalization, and mobility. People lose the rich, complex, narratively entangled, and embedded relationships found in earlier societies and confront each other as punctual subjects stripped of shared histories.[21] Commerce requires that we bracket the affective and ethical obligations that bind people to one another in order to focus on financial gain. The law treats people only as abstract legal persons. Professionalization reduces the web of goal-oriented activity in practical life to a single dimension whose narrative monotony becomes intolerable. And anonymous encounters between people are the archetype of abstract social relations devoid of shared narrative context, a condition that a sentimental ethics attempts without success to turn into a virtue.[22] In other words, under the conditions of modernity Fielding is diagnosing, the narratively embedded relations between people either actually erode or are bracketed for the sake of other considerations. Now, to the extent that judgment is possible only on the basis of experience garnered in the course of a narrative,[23] the abstraction of social relationships produced by a commercial modernity dissolves the very grounds we have for judgment. It is no wonder that judgments in the Hobbesian world of the novel are so unstable, unreliable, and capricious (*JA*, 57).

Modernity, that is, *almost* inevitably renders the social world Hobbesian. Joseph's visit to the first inn addresses the encounter with modernity via the question of whether the innkeeper will take in and offer hospitality to someone so destitute. Inns are a regular feature of

Fielding's fictional landscapes and are especially significant in the context of Joseph's epic *nostos*, which harks back to the hospitality that Odysseus is conspicuously offered at a number of stages during his journey. They allow us to track what happens to hospitality under the conditions of modernity. Fielding's inns exhibit three of the four features of modernity described above: monetization of social relationships, professionalization (the innkeeper depends for his livelihood on the "hospitality industry" of which he is a part), and anonymity.[24] (Odysseus may be a stranger to his hosts, but he is often extended hospitality on the basis of long-standing family connections.) For innkeepers, the ancient ethic of hospitality becomes all but unthinkable. After all, people who earn a living by keeping an inn would soon be out of business if they were hospitable to everyone who needed a room. Modern innkeepers, in contrast to the ancient *philoi* who welcome Odysseus, are conditioned by the hospitality industry to behave in self-interested and ungenerous ways. In this context, their behavior is eminently reasonable and beyond reproach; once hospitality has been monetized, any other judgment about how to act becomes implausible and indeed irrational. Putting a price on hospitality does not simply reveal the costs that were always implicit in being hospitable, as if making hospitality a marketable good were a neutral act; instead, it corrupts the very institution itself, rendering a hospitable relationship to others either unthinkable or irrational and producing a Hobbesian or Mandevillian psyche in the process[25]:

> "My Dear," cries *Tow-wouse*, "this Man hath been robbed of all he hath." "Well then," says she [Mrs. Tow-wouse], "where's his money to pay his Reckoning.... I shall send him packing..." "My Dear," said he, "common Charity won't suffer you to do that." "Common Charity, a F—t!" says she, "Common Charity teaches us to provide for ourselves, and our Families; and I and mine won't be ruined by your Charity, I assure you." (*JA*, 49)

C. B. Macpherson argues compellingly that the state of nature in Hobbes and Locke models not so much a natural condition as the bourgeois society of commercial modernity.[26] But *Joseph Andrews* and, implicitly, Mandeville's *Fable of the Bees* arrived at this diagnosis much earlier, recognizing that the Hobbesian world is not the inevitable result of an intractable, morally straitened human nature,[27] unable to transcend fear and self-interest, but *produced by* the conditions of modernity that make fear and self-interest reasonable responses to the game as it has been rigged. However, the Hobbesian condition is not celebrated in *Joseph Andrews*, as it is in Mandeville's *Fable*. A number of Fielding's exemplary characters are able to transcend the moral psychology that is otherwise so pervasive, although, significantly, most of them are only tenuously affected by modernity: the postilion, Betty, and, above all, Wilson in his deliberate retreat from the city. Even the second innkeeper, when Adams cannot pay him, notably refuses to act reflexively according to the imperatives of the profit motive and engages instead in a deliberative practice of reading Adams's character; as a result, he allows Adams to leave without paying, because he trusts him to pay later, an action that is unexpected and improbable within the frame of self-interest (*JA*, 155). This example reveals that judgment always remains possible, and enables us to act *otherwise*, even when the reigning social conditions appear to dictate that we act almost inevitably like abstract Hobbesian individuals. Our capacity for judgment can be concealed or misdirected, but it cannot be eradicated no matter what social or material changes we confront. We may judge badly, but if we lose the ability to judge, we cease to be human.

A critique of modernity by itself cannot suffice. If the advent of modernity and its concomitant social transformations were inevitable, immanent critique would amount to nothing more than railing against a hopeless fate. Instead, Fielding imagines an alternative and thereby passes judgment on modernity; he is not content merely to critique it.[28] In doing so, he rejects two other remedies for the predicament of social fragmentation that, by his lights, ultimately capitulate to their own logics of inevitability. These are the sentimentalism of Richardson's *Pamela* and the common or shared sense indicated by Shaftesbury's conception of "Sensus Communis."

Joseph Andrews is a concerted parody of nearly every aspect of *Pamela*, from its depiction of character to its class and gender politics to its sanctimony, and through this parody Fielding opens the way to a radically alternative conception of what the novel form could be. Many aspects of his innovations are well understood. But if we were not so conditioned to think of Fielding as a critic of Richardson, his hostility to sentimentalism should be surprising.[29] After all, in the philosophical discourse of the period (Shaftesbury, Francis Hutcheson, Adam Smith), sentimentalism was one of the most powerful responses to a Hobbesian modernity in which self-interest and anonymity threatened to shred the fabric of sociality. Sympathy and the other "social affections," it was argued, gave evidence of a primordial, nearly instinctual capacity for bracketing our own selfish concerns and for attending to the sufferings even of anonymous others. Why, then, should sentimentalism be so objectionable to Fielding?

Richardsonian sentimentalism, in which the reader goes "hand-in-hand" with the protagonist and sympathizes with her, is to Fielding nothing less than a form of seduction.[30] We are lured or even corralled into a single perspective, lacking the capacity to pause, reflect, consider, or judge.[31] Although some critics argue, with respect to *Clarissa*, that epistolary sentimentalism can foster the practice of judgment, Fielding finds that we become so identified with the character as to lose our ability to judge.[32] Although letters can provide characters with the space for reflection and deliberation, we readers are not granted similar privileges, as our sympathy aligns us strongly with a character's perspective. Perhaps most disconcerting for Fielding is the concealment of the figure of the narrator by the epistolary form, which creates the fiction of direct, transparent access to a character. Where Richardson collapses the reader and the character together in an immersive experience, eliminating the enlarged perspective that provides a vantage from which to judge, Fielding emphatically separates character, narrator, and reader but insists that each has an indispensable role to play in novel reading, indeed that each must be construed as a character *within* the novel.[33] From Locke and Shaftesbury to Friedrich Hölderlin and G. W. F. Hegel, this internal differentiation or self-division constitutes the condition of possibility of judgment, if not the very act of judgment, although in Fielding the provocation to judgment that this splitting produces takes an unexpected form. From the beginning, the narrator of *Joseph Andrews* is a personality, and not a likable one at that. Intrusive, cajoling, bullying, he hardly seems calculated to help us become good judges. "He is a sagacious Reader who can see two Chapters before him," he taunts (*JA*, 41). Explaining why he needs to write a preface to the novel, he demeans what is likely the majority of his audience: "As it is possible the mere *English* Reader may have a very different Idea of Romance with the Author of these little Volumes; and may consequently expect a kind of Entertainment, not to be found, nor which was even intended, in the following Pages; it may not be improper to premise a few Words" (3). He cultivates an air of authority and classical learning worn lightly, entirely in keeping with the book's ultimately patrician politics, as though to intimidate us by reminding us how little we know and to quell any urge toward autonomous judging on our part. But the effect of this narrative voice is very much the opposite, and I believe designedly so.[34] The narrator's patronizing tone is irritating, even deliberately alienating, provoking mistrust and a desire to judge for ourselves. The constant warnings about how little we will anticipate of the plot ("in which we prophesy there are some Strokes which every one will not truly comprehend at the first Reading" [36]),[35] and how little transparency there is in a good narrative or character ("It is an Observation sometimes made, that to indicate our Idea of a simple Fellow, we say, *He is easily to be seen through*: Nor do I believe it a more improper Denotation of a simple Book" [41]), remind us how much hermeneutic labor there is in reading and keep us on our toes instead of forcing us to submit to the narrator's authority. But perhaps most important with regard to the problem of judgment, the narrator does not imagine a homogeneous readership but interpellates different kinds of readers at various moments. We have already encountered the "sagacious Reader" and the "mere *English* Reader," but there is also the "judicious Reader" (29), "the Classical Reader" (4), and more. The effect must surely be to make us wonder which kind of reader we are, to make us reflect on our own reading practices, and, ideally, to make us develop reading practices that would align us more with the judicious, the classical, or even the sagacious reader than with the mere English reader, for instance. More than the stereotypical character portraits,[36] it is these characterizations of the reader that are designed "not to expose one pitiful Wretch, to the small and contemptible Circle of his Acquaintance; but to hold the Glass to thousands in their Closets, that they may contemplate their Deformity, and endeavor to reduce it, and thus by suffering private Mortification may avoid public Shame" (164). This practice of reflection and introspection is integral to the practice of judgment in Shaftesbury's "Soliloquy," as the emblematic mirrors of his carefully commissioned prefatory drawings reveal,[37] and it is perhaps surprisingly this quiet practice of judging ourselves and deciding what kind of readers we are or want to be that Fielding's loud and intrusive narrator seeks to provoke,[38] a judgment that requires not simply an arbitrary decision but a concomitant practice of self-cultivation.

If, in Fielding's novel, judgment is the antidote to Richardson's sentimentalism as much as it is a response to the Hobbesian social world produced by modernity,[39] then it is also a riposte to Shaftesbury's solution to the Hobbesian problem in "Sensus Communis." One might expect Shaftesbury's argument against Hobbes—that we have a shared sense or sense of the common operative alongside the instinct toward self-preservation—to be congenial to Fielding, who, in fact, invokes Shaftesbury's sense of judgment from "Soliloquy."[40] Moreover, the preface to *Joseph Andrews* claims agreement with Shaftesbury on the question of burlesque ("my Lord *Shaftesbury's* Opinion of Burlesque agrees with mine" [5]) and, more importantly, adopts as its own the method of ridicule proposed by Shaftesbury as the corrosive that will eat away at the dross of private opinion, leaving only the solid gold of common sense.[41] It might appear from the preface, then, that Fielding designed his novel as an exercise in Shaftesburian wit and humor.[42] Given the substantial overlap in their concerns and methods, and Fielding's openly acknowledged debt to Shaftesbury (as opposed to his avowed hostility to Richardson's *Pamela*), why might we suspect that Fielding finds Shaftesbury's aestheticizing response to Hobbes inadequate in *Joseph Andrews*?

For the Shaftesbury of "Sensus Communis," the ridiculous is an aesthetic category ("For nothing is ridiculous except what is deform'd" [*Characteristics*, 80]), albeit of a negative kind, operating with a compulsive force or inevitability that preempts deliberation and judgment. This differs significantly from his "Soliloquy," where, to counter Locke's account of action in chapter 2.21 of the *Essay concerning Human Understanding*, Shaftesbury made deliberation and reflective judgment integral to the practice of soliloquy. But in "Sensus Communis" common sense is an instinctive force equiprimordial with the drive for self-preservation, and when Shaftesbury turns to the aesthetic late in the essay, as a way of showing that even those who insist on their own pleasure as the only standard still have a sense of beauty, the language of force and compulsion asserts itself repeatedly. Thus Shaftesbury claims that "the Men of Pleasure, who seem the greatest Contemners of this philosophical Beauty, are *forc'd* often to confess her Charms" (*Characteristics*, 87; my emphasis) and insinuates that poets cannot deny "this Force of *Nature*" (85). In explaining why the "Man of thorow Good-Breeding [one of the essay's moral exemplars] . . . is incapable of doing a rude or brutal Action," Shaftesbury effectively conceives him as unthinking, and all the more virtuous for avoiding the doubts of the sophister or casuist: "He never deliberates in this case, or considers of the matter by prudential Rules of Self-Interest and Advantage. He acts from his Nature, in a manner necessarily, and without Reflection: and if he did not, it were impossible for him to answer his Character" (81). The aesthetic and the moral, it would seem, operate through the sheer force of necessity, unclouded by the free work of judgment.

The logic of ridicule is, if anything, even less promising where judgment is concerned. The problem is not simply that humor and ridicule appear to function in an immediate, reflexive way, without any mediation of judgment. Rather, if there are any individual judgments, they count for little or nothing, because the relevant judgment that reveals the common sense of the community takes place at the level of the social as an emergent effect that bears scant analogy to the labor of judgment. According to Shaftesbury's account, an early version of the marketplace of ideas or the logic of the public sphere, individuals must be granted the freedom to ridicule anything they want, no holds barred. Actions or behaviors that are ridiculous will then be shamed out of existence, while those that are not ridiculous will survive unscathed. By means of an agonistic process that epitomizes the dialectic of the social throughout this period, the commonsense judgment about what is ridiculous emerges not as any individual's labor of *phronesis* but as what remains when the conflict of competing opinions about what is ridiculous has temporarily subsided (*Characteristics*, 41–42). It is the "judgment" of society or history or the market, requiring no individual to have undertaken any exercise of judgment along the way. To discover what is common only by way of this clash of opposing views is, one suspects, to have conceded much, indeed far too much, to Hobbes's agonistic vision of society, as Shaftesbury's regular recourse to martial metaphors in the essay attests (46, 48, 71, 120). More than that, this agonistic model of an emergent social "judgment" displaces the potentially visionary agency of judgment, and its ability to imagine things otherwise, with a logic of inevitability that makes modernity, whether in its Hobbesian or its Shaftesburian guise, a foregone conclusion.[43]

Ridicule is an indispensable and dominant element in *Joseph Andrews*'s novelistic strategy, but it cannot suffice by itself, because it alone cannot point the way to an alternative.[44] Like all dialectical techniques, it functions only through negation, clearing the way for something else but sternly forbidden from saying what that something else might be. To discern how Fielding's novel resists the inevitability of a dialectical social process, as theorized by Shaftesbury or Mandeville, we must look for the rare passages that transcend the ridiculous. Undoubtedly, the most significant is the story of Wilson, perhaps the only character entirely above ridicule. This story initially appears to be just one more lengthy digression in a frequently digressive novel.⁴⁵ When the travelers encounter Wilson, the narrative pauses for his entire life story, from his wayward existence in the city to a detailed description of his reform and retreat into the idyllic countryside. The importance of this narrative digression is signaled only later, when it turns out that Wilson is Joseph's father.⁴⁶ The class politics of this plot twist are clearly legible, since it means that Joseph is not the *autokopros* we have been given to believe (*JA*, 17), the typical nobody whose story the novel usually tells,⁴⁷ the mere brother of Pamela. His virtue is inbred, born of gentility.

But much remains puzzling about the inclusion of the Wilson story. Not only do we not need such a detailed digression to establish Joseph's genealogy, but the character of Wilson is exemplary in a way that demands accounting. The clearest indication of his unusual status is his capacity for hospitality, otherwise almost absent from the novel. Wilson can take the travelers in and provide for them. But why is this possible for him and not others? If modernity makes hospitality irrational, even unthinkable, Wilson earns his exemption by discreetly but firmly opting out of the commercial economy:

> Here was variety of Fruit, and every thing useful for the Kitchin, which was abundantly sufficient to catch the Admiration of *Adams*, who told the Gentleman he had certainly a good Gardener. Sir, answered he, that Gardener is now before you; whatever you see here, is the Work solely of my own Hands. Whilst I am providing Necessaries for my Table, I likewise procure myself an appetite for them. (*JA*, 196)

Because Wilson has everything he needs, and does not have to depend on others or view them through the lens of profit and loss, forms of acting become available to him that are hardly possible in a commercial society.⁴⁸ Although it will always be open to us to act generously, charitably, hospitably in individual instances, a profound structural transformation is necessary if these ways of acting are to become systematic and pervasive practices.

Wilson's solution to modernity's ills is undoubtedly utopian. The description of his life in the country is in fact an embedded mini-utopia, drawing on tropes from an already well-established utopian tradition. But if we should be obtuse enough to overlook the generic markers, Adams calls our attention to the experiment in utopian writing we have just witnessed: "They then departed, *Adams* declaring that this was the

Manner in which the People had lived in the Golden Age" (*JA*, 199). To call something utopian is usually a dismissive gesture, but scoffing at the utopia at the heart of *Joseph Andrews* would prevent our understanding the most fundamental operation the novel hopes to perform. *Joseph Andrews* locates the capacity for judgment as the decisive remedy for the seemingly ineluctable advance of modernity; it means to develop a narrative practice that encourages the reader's judgment against the various forms of quasi-instinctual behavior that are portrayed as inescapable (self-interest, sentimentality, ridicule, common sense). Ultimately, Wilson's utopia opens the space of judgment in the novel, because it allows us to imagine an alternative to the modernity that seemed so inevitable. It, or something like it, is the fictive standard or internal difference that offers us some vantage from which modernity is to be judged and perhaps found wanting. It, or something like it, is the utopia to which we will have to commit ourselves if our critique of modernity is to be more than mere whining, reflexive ridicule, and the infinite play of irony.[49] If we refuse to imagine utopian alternatives that might solicit our allegiance, then we will have surrendered our capacity to judge. Unlike sentimental or aesthetic "judgments," which rely on immediate, almost instinctive responses, the novel becomes for Fielding the privileged vehicle for the exercise and development of judgment, precisely because its narratives offer such rich possibilities for exploring alternatives.

Fielding's novel gives us an important insight into the nature of judgment. A judgment is not the mere assertion of private or personal opinion, any more than it constitutes a form of knowledge; it is not just a variety of vague wish or idle speculation. A judgment—against modernity, in this case—requires us to commit ourselves to the material and structural transformations that would be necessary to change it, and that commitment is to the ideality of a utopian vision. Utopia underwrites the ideality of judgment, as judgment anticipates the materiality of utopia. The necessarily fictive grounds of judgment, here the commitment to a utopian vision, must not be mistaken for an arbitrary or dogmatic assertion of faith, belief, or opinion. If it is to be a judgment, then it also implies a commitment to giving reasons, offering justifications, making one's vision ever more articulate, defending one's position, and always holding open the possibility of abandoning the commitment itself if it is found to be untenable, and this deliberative work should take place as much with oneself as with others (see Shaftesbury's "Soliloquy"). Such is the precarious and elusive difference between a judgment and an opinion.

Two of the signal features commonly attributed to the novel are its capacity for psychological introspection and sociological observation; Richardson is often regarded as the progenitor of the former strain and Fielding of the latter.[50] Indeed, there is much to be said for such a view. If, for convenience, we consider Mandeville one of the earliest to practice a distinctly modern form of sociological thinking, then it is clear that *Joseph Andrews* emerges in close dialogue with early conceptions of "the social." The preface even remarks on the novel's sociological vocation of "introducing a greater Variety of Characters" into novelistic narrative (*JA*, 4). But to characterize Fielding's novel as concerned with the social misses its polemic against nascent forms of social theory in the eighteenth century that were already in thrall to a sense of inevitability and to the disqualification of judgment that marks a later sociology.[51] But this does not imply that Fielding's concern for judgment is a reversion to a Richardsonian mode of introspection or Shaftesburian aesthetic discrimination. Rather, although Hannah Arendt views the modern novel as concerned with the social against the epic's political ambition,[52] *Joseph Andrews* is better understood as political in Arendt's precise sense of the term, with its characteristic concerns of freedom, judgment, and the desire to transcend the social realm of necessity and inevitability.[53] Fielding's novel of judgment, then, opens the way to a third kind of novel, the political novel, which, no matter how rarely it is instantiated, remains one of the most thrilling possibilities of the form.

Notes

1   For recent assessments of the importance of judgment in Austen's novels, see Hina Nazar, *Enlightened Sentiments: Judgment and Autonomy in the Age of Sensibility* (New York: Fordham University Press, 2012), 116–46; Karen Valihora, *Austen's Oughts: Judgment after Locke and Shaftesbury* (Newark: University of Delaware Press, 2010); Vivasvan Soni, "Committing Freedom: The Cultivation of Judgment in Rousseau's *Emile* and Austen's *Pride and Prejudice*," *Eighteenth Century: Theory and Interpretation* 51, no. 3 (2010): 363–87; Vivasvan Soni, "Preface: Jane Austen's Critique of Aesthetic Judgment," in *Jane Austen and the Arts: Elegance, Propriety, Harmony*, ed. Natasha Duquette and Elisabeth Lenckos, xi–xxi (Bethlehem, PA: Lehigh University Press, 2013). This essay has been adapted from an article published in *MLQ* 76.2, pp. 159–80. © 2015, University of Washington. All rights reserved. Republished by permission of the copyright holder and Duke University Press.

2   See Hannah Arendt, *On Revolution* (New York: Viking, 1965), 40–52; Isaiah Berlin, "Historical Inevitability," in *Liberty*, ed. Henry Hardy (Oxford:

Oxford University Press, 2004), 94–165. Arendt develops her signature account of judgment in part as a response to this sense of historical inevitability. See Hannah Arendt, *Lectures on Kant's Political Philosophy*, ed. Ronald Beiner (Chicago: University of Chicago Press, 1992), 5. Pfau does not address the problem of inevitability directly, but his account confirms the elision of agency associated with it in this period. See Thomas Pfau, *Minding the Modern: Human Agency, Intellectual Traditions, and Responsible Knowledge* (Notre Dame, IN: University of Notre Dame Press, 2013), 185–413. On the way that causal inevitability can dialectically reverse itself into a sense of radical contingency, see Christian Thorne, *Dialectic of Counter-Enlightenment* (Cambridge, MA: Harvard University Press, 2009), 289.

3   See Aristotle, *Nicomachean Ethics*, 1112a 17–b 11, 1139a 14, 1141b 8–12 in *The Complete Works of Aristotle: The Revised Oxford Translation*, vol. 2, ed. Jonathan Barnes (Princeton, NJ: Princeton University Press, 1984).

4   Frankfurt and Dennett have challenged this fundamental assumption of moral philosophy found in Aristotle and Kant, among others, and a debate has ensued in analytic philosophy. See Harry G. Frankfurt, "Alternate Possibilities and Moral Responsibility," *Journal of Philosophy* 66, no. 23 (1969): 829–39; Daniel C. Dennett, "I Could Not Have Done Otherwise—So What?" *Journal of Philosophy* 81, no. 10 (1984): 553–65. But their arguments are not persuasive, since they are premised on the conflation of final and efficient causation, a distinction crucially at issue when it comes to the problem of judgment, and on a refusal of judgment in relation to what *otherwise* might mean. The debate is uncannily similar to the one between Hobbes and John Bramhall in the seventeenth century, so lucidly analyzed by Kramnick. See Jonathan Kramnick, *Actions and Objects from Hobbes to Richardson* (Stanford, CA: Stanford University Press, 2010), 27–38. *Joseph Andrews* is strongly positioned on one side of this debate.

5   There is no *a priori* guarantee that there is such a thing as judgment, but if there is not, then responsibility and much else in human life would not make *sense*.

6   There is by now a long and distinguished tradition of criticism that has recognized the importance of judgment, especially the reader's judgment, in Fielding. See John Bender, *Ends of Enlightenment* (Stanford, CA: Stanford University Press, 2012), 28; William Empson, "*Tom Jones*," *Kenyon Review* 20, no. 2 (1958): 217–49; Wolfgang Iser, *The Implied Reader: Patterns of Communication in Prose Fiction from Bunyan to Beckett* (Baltimore, MD: Johns Hopkins University Press, 1974), 50–55; Scott MacKenzie, "'Stock the Parish with Beauties': Henry Fielding's Parochial Vision," *PMLA* 125, no. 3 (2010): 606–21; Robert James Merrett, "Empiricism and Judgment in Fielding's *Tom Jones*," *Ariel: A Review of International English Literature* 11, no. 3 (1980): 3–21; John Preston, *The Created Self: The Reader's Role in Eighteenth-Century Fiction* (London: Heinemann, 1970), 114–32; Malinda

Snow, "The Judgment of Evidence in *Tom Jones*," *South Atlantic Review* 48, no. 2 (1983): 37–51; Raymond Stephanson, "The Education of the Reader in Fielding's *Joseph Andrews*," *Philological Quarterly* 61, no. 3 (1982): 253–55; Ian Watt, *The Rise of the Novel: Studies in Defoe, Richardson, and Fielding* (Berkeley: University of California Press, 2000), 288; Alexander Welsh, *Strong Representations: Narrative and Circumstantial Evidence in England* (Baltimore, MD: Johns Hopkins University Press, 1992), 44–76. Bender expands the argument to the early novel more broadly (*Ends of Enlightenment*, 21–37). My argument differs from these earlier approaches in a number of ways. It is not simply that most studies focus on *Tom Jones*. More importantly, judgment is treated as an epistemological problem, even when moral issues are at stake, eliding an important dimension of Fielding's contribution. See Bender, *Ends of Enlightenment*, 25; MacKenzie, "'Stock the Parish with Beauties,'" 613, 614; Merrett, "Empiricism and Judgment," 3, 20; Preston, *Created Self*, 114; Snow, "Judgment of Evidence"; Welsh, *Strong Representations*, 55. Empson is the exception here ("*Tom Jones*"). That is why I am careful to distinguish rigorously between judgment and knowledge. In addition, these studies tend not to focus on the process of judgment or on the fictive grounds of judgment, as I do. But on the latter, see Bender, *Ends of Enlightenment*, 29–30, 50; Welsh, *Strong Representations*, 13.

7   On this distinction, see Vivasvan Soni, "Introduction: The Crisis of Judgment," *Eighteenth Century: Theory and Interpretation* 51, no. 3: 282–83; Vivasvan Soni, *Mourning Happiness: Narrative and the Politics of Modernity* (Ithaca, NY: Cornell University Press, 2010), 76, 109, 135.

8   It should go without saying that there are epistemological claims that can be evaluated according to these criteria.

9   Other examples of such paradoxes and infinite regresses that affirm the inevitability of judgment include: How do I know the right time to make a judgment? And how do I know that this is the appropriate situation in which to apply a particular rule for judgment?

10 On the novelty of this strategy of "overwriting" a character from another novel, see Paul Baines, "Joseph Andrews," 56 in *The Cambridge Companion to Henry Fielding*, ed. Claude Rawson (Cambridge: Cambridge University Press, 2007), 50–64.

11 Henry Fielding, *The History of the Adventures of Joseph Andrews and of His Friend Mr. Abraham Adams; An Apology for the Life of Mrs. Shamela Andrews*, ed. Douglas Brooks-Davies (Oxford: Oxford University Press, 1999), 3. Hereafter cited parenthetically as *JA*.

12 Watt finds that "the epic influence on Fielding was very slight" (*Rise of the Novel*, 259). But Fielding rewrites the *Odyssey*'s topos of hospitality to important effect. On this point, see Martin C. Battestin, *The Moral Basis of Fielding's Art: A Study of "Joseph Andrews"* (Middletown, CT: Wesleyan University Press, 1959), 87; Baines, "Joseph Andrews," 58.

13 See Deidre Shauna Lynch, *The Economy of Character: Novels, Market Culture, and the Business of Inner Meaning* (Chicago: University of Chicago Press, 1998), 4; Thorne, *Dialectic of Counter-Enlightenment*, 283; Watt, *Rise of the Novel*, 251. On the complex and fraught relationship of the nineteenth-century novel, especially George Eliot's *Middlemarch*, to sociology, see Gage McWeeny, "The Sociology of the Novel: George Eliot's Strangers," *Novel* 42, no. 3 (2009): 538–45.

14 Empson observes that Fielding offers a moral response to Hobbesian egotism in *Tom Jones*, but claims that Fielding only comes to this position well after *Joseph Andrews*. See Empson, "*Tom Jones*," 224. But if anything, the response to Hobbes is more systematic and pointed in *Joseph Andrews*.

15 Lynch argues that social circulation in eighteenth-century novels usually restores social harmony (*Economy of Character*, 81–82), but in *Joseph Andrews* it exposes social divisions caused by the commercial economy.

16 On the way that the psyche is construed as a reactive automatism, without the capacity to judge—that is, to reflect on its desires and thereby to alter them—in Hobbes, Locke, and Mandeville, see Pfau, *Minding the Modern*, 185–269. Of course, even when characters decide according to calculations of self-interest, they cannot avoid making judgments. Indeed, the choice to act according to these algorithms is itself a judgment. However, they act *as if* they had no judgment: the reflective practices of judgment are concealed, and the burden of and responsibility for judging evaded.

17 As Hunter rightly argues, in the stagecoach scene Fielding "insists on a scale of values that places social obligation highest," but how to ensure the flourishing of this value remains unclear in this scene. See J. Paul Hunter, *Occasional Form: Henry Fielding and the Chains of Circumstance* (Baltimore, MD: Johns Hopkins University Press, 1975), 109. See also Battestin, *Moral Basis of Fielding's Art*, 53, 55, 76, on Fielding's alignment with the Latitudinarians against Hobbes and Mandeville.

18 Morris Golden, *Fielding's Moral Psychology* (Amherst: University of Massachusetts Press, 1966), 3, 6, 21, 24.

19 See especially, Louis Dumont, *From Mandeville to Marx: The Genesis and Triumph of Economic Ideology* (Chicago: University of Chicago Press, 1977); Michael Sandel, *What Money Can't Buy: The Moral Limits of Markets* (New York: Farrar, Straus and Giroux, 2012).

20 Though there is much to disagree with in his rejection of rights, Milbank offers a cogent diagnosis of the corrosive nature of legalistic, rights-based individualism in early modernity. See John Milbank, "Against Human Rights: Liberty in the Western Tradition," *Oxford Journal of Law and Religion* (2012), 1–32. Of course, Fielding was himself a lawyer and a justice of the peace. See Linda Bree, "Henry Fielding's Life," 10, 13 in *The Cambridge Companion to Henry Fielding*, ed. Claude Rawson (Cambridge: Cambridge University Press, 2007), 3–16. On Fielding's hostile

relationship to the law of damages, see Sandra Macpherson, *Harm's Way: Tragic Responsibility and the Novel Form* (Baltimore, MD: Johns Hopkins University Press, 2010), 103–05.

21 See Pfau, *Minding the Modern*; Thorne, *Dialectic of Counter-Enlightenment*, 279.
22 See Soni, *Mourning Happiness*, 293.
23 See Aristotle, *Nicomachean Ethics*, 1142a 11–15 in *Complete Works*.
24 For my purposes, it is sufficient that Fielding treats commercial inns as emblematic of the problems of modernity, without trying to date their advent. They are also an important feature of *Don Quixote*, the text on which *Joseph Andrews* is modeled. On the difficulties of specifying a date for modernity, see Fredric Jameson, *A Singular Modernity: Essay on the Ontology of the Present* (London: Verso, 2002). Like Fielding I am interested in a longer trajectory of modernity extending beyond and before the eighteenth century, though the problem of judgment comes into focus in this period for intellectual-historical reasons easily specified.
25 For the argument that monetization of a good can corrupt the institution it serves, see Sandel, *What Money Can't Buy*, 93–130.
26 C. B. Macpherson, *The Political Theory of Possessive Individualism: Hobbes to Locke* (London: Oxford University Press, 1964).
27 See Battestin, *Moral Basis of Fielding's Art*, 61.
28 Ibid., 52.
29 On Fielding's complicated proximity to the sentimental tradition, see Golden, *Fielding's Moral Psychology*, 147, 151; Macpherson, *Harm's Way*, 110, 125.
30 Samuel Richardson, *Pamela; or, Virtue Rewarded*, ed. Thomas Keymer and Alice Wakely (Oxford: Oxford University Press, 2001), 7.
31 Of course, we will always have the ability to judge, but the narrative does not encourage this. Although Arendt's "enlarged thinking" resembles sentimental sympathy, it seeks to restore the capacity for judgment by refusing the constricting perspective and affective conditioning of sentimentalism. See Arendt, *Lectures on Kant's Political Philosophy*, 71.
32 See Nazar, *Enlightened Sentiments*, 59–80; Valihora, *Austen's Oughts*, 159–91; and, with respect to Jean-Jacques Rousseau's *Julie*, Thomas Pfau, "The Letter of Judgment: Practical Reason in Aristotle, the Stoics, and Rousseau," *Eighteenth Century: Theory and Interpretation* 51, no. 3 (2010): 289–316.
33 See Preston, *Created Self*, 116, 121; Stephanson, "Education of the Reader," 253. Virno, following Sigmund Freud, argues that the three-person structure is necessary both for jokes and for Aristotle's conception of *phronesis*. See Paolo Virno, *Multitude: Between Innovation and Negation*, trans. Isabella Bertoletti, James Cascaito, and Andrea Casson (Los Angeles: Semiotext(e), 2008), 79–97. Given that his narrative is often structured as a

joke, Fielding appears to share this intuition when he insists on separating character, narrator, and reader. The necessity of the third perspective for judgment is highlighted in the example where two men give Adams two conflicting characterizations of the same person and he cannot judge without the assistance of the innkeeper's third perspective (*JA*, 83–84).

34 See William B. Warner, *Licensing Entertainment: The Elevation of Novel Reading in Britain, 1684–1750* (Berkeley: University of California Press, 1998), 263.

35 On the importance of second reading for judgment, see Soni, "Committing Freedom."

36 On the "economic" nature of character portrayal in neoclassical writing, see Lynch, *Economy of Character*, 23–24.

37 Paknadel describes the image prefacing Shaftesbury's "Soliloquy" as follows: "The main theme of the emblem is the mirror in which Man should look at his true self." See Felix Paknadel, "Shaftesbury's Illustrations of *Characteristics*," *Journal of the Warburg and Courtauld Institutes* 37 (1974): 307. Preston and Stephanson also have recourse to the mirror metaphor when describing Fielding's judgment. See Preston, *Created Self*, 117; Stephanson, "Education of the Reader," 248.

38 Iser shows how insistently Fielding implicates his readers in his texts and compels them to judge for themselves (*Implied Reader*, 29–56). Hunter also argues that Fielding's interfering narrators prompt the reader to self-reflection and judgment (*Occasional Form*, 8, 12). See also Empson, "*Tom Jones*," 239; Golden, *Fielding's Moral Psychology*, 28, 39; MacKenzie, "'Stock the Parish with Beauties,'" 610, 611, 614; Merrett, "Empiricism and Judgment"; Preston, *Created Self*, 114–32; Snow, "Judgment of Evidence," 37, 48; Stephanson, "Education of the Reader"; Warner, *Licensing Entertainment*, 237, 241, 246, 257, 259; Welsh, *Strong Representations*, 44–76. Macpherson finds Fielding more concerned with character and interiority than scholars of the novel usually do, but her analysis does not focus on the reader or on questions of judgment (*Harm's Way*, 98–132).

39 In his *Champion* paper of March 27, 1740, Fielding explains more directly that the sentimentalism of the man of good nature (his capacity to care for the happiness of others) has to be supplemented with judgment: "That as Good-nature requires a distinguishing Faculty, which is another Word for Judgment, and is perhaps the sole Boundary between Wisdom and Folly; it is impossible for a Fool, who hath no distinguishing Faculty, to be good-natured." See Henry Fielding, *The Champion: Containing a Series of Papers, Humorous, Moral, Political and Critical*, vol. 2. (London, 1741), 40.

40 The essays "Sensus Communis" and "Soliloquy" appear in Anthony Ashley Cooper, Third Earl of Shaftesbury, *Characteristics of Men, Manners, Opinions, Times*, vol. 1 (Indianapolis, IN: Liberty Fund, 2001), hereafter cited parenthetically as *Characteristics*.

41 Dickie recognizes the moral function of laughter in *Joseph Andrews*, but he wants to draw attention to the way laughter becomes unruly, cruel, and patrician in the episode depicting the roasting of Adams. See Simon Dickie, *Cruelty and Laughter: Forgotten Comic Literature and the Unsentimental Eighteenth Century* (Chicago: University of Chicago Press, 2011), 156–89. See also Empson, "*Tom Jones*," 230, on the way Fielding's unusual double irony allows us to appreciate multiple moral codes.

42 On Fielding's relationship to Shaftesbury, see Battestin, *Moral Basis of Fielding's Art*, 12, 62. On his important role in the emerging discourse of common sense, see Sophia Rosenfeld, *Common Sense: A Political History* (Cambridge, MA: Harvard University Press, 2011) 39–41.

43 On Shaftesbury's ultimately modern view of politics, and the difficulty of reconciling this with the "virtue ethics" he proposes, see Douglas J. Den Uyl, "Shaftesbury and the Modern Problem of Virtue," *Social Philosophy and Policy* 15, no. 1 (1998): 275–316. Hunter finds Fielding similarly caught between modern and ancient views, though I argue that the alignment of virtue ethics and a classical republican politics is more straightforward in *Joseph Andrews*. See Hunter, *Occasional Form*, xi, 4, 9, 14.

44 As MacKenzie points out, recent criticism has not sufficiently attended to Fielding's deployment of Shaftesbury's method of ridicule in *Joseph Andrews* ("'Stock the Parish with Beauties,'" 614). But unlike MacKenzie, who argues that "Fielding adopts [ridicule] as a key mechanism of judgment for readers of *Joseph Andrews*" ("'Stock the Parish with Beauties,'" 608), I show that Fielding recognizes the shortcomings of Shaftesbury's intuitive and aesthetic model and provides an alternative based on novelistic narration.

45 Battestin, *Moral Basis of Fielding's Art*, 119.

46 On the privilege of circumstantial evidence over eyewitness testimony in Fielding, see Welsh, *Strong Representations*, 57.

47 Catherine Gallagher, *Nobody's Story: The Vanishing Acts of Women Writers in the Marketplace, 1670–1820* (Berkeley: University of California Press, 1994).

48 MacKenzie finds Fielding privileging the disciplinary institutions of the parish over the manor but does not take into account the Wilson episode, whose politics are undoubtedly more manorial ("'Stock the Parish with Beauties,'" 609, 617).

49 On the relation of critique to utopianism, and the priority of concrete over abstract utopianism, see Vivasvan Soni, "Modernity and the Fate of Utopian Representation in Wordsworth's *Female Vagrant*," *European Romantic Review* 21, no. 3 (2010): 363–81.

50 Lynch, *Economy of Character*, 4.

51 See Leo Strauss, *Natural Right and History* (Chicago: University of Chicago Press, 1953), 40.

52 Hannah Arendt, *The Human Condition* (Chicago: University of Chicago Press, 1958), 39.

53 Watt also recognizes some of this when he speaks of "Fielding's realism of assessment," though realism is perhaps a misnomer in reference to judgment and utopianism (*Rise of the Novel*, 290–91). For Watt, the assessment or judgment is that of the narrator rather than of the reader (288). On "the act of judgment that formed such an essential part of Fielding's pedagogical goal," see also Hamilton, *Accident*, 159.

Bibliography

Arendt, Hannah. *The Human Condition*. Chicago: University of Chicago Press, 1958.
Arendt, Hannah. *Lectures on Kant's Political Philosophy*. Edited by Ronald Beiner. Chicago: University of Chicago Press, 1992.
Arendt, Hannah. *On Revolution*. New York: Viking, 1965.
Aristotle. *The Complete Works of Aristotle: The Revised Oxford Translation*, Vol. 2. Edited by Jonathan Barnes. Princeton, NJ: Princeton University Press, 1984.
Baines, Paul. "Joseph Andrews." In *The Cambridge Companion to Henry Fielding*, edited by Claude Rawson, 50–64. Cambridge: Cambridge University Press, 2007.
Battestin, Martin C. *The Moral Basis of Fielding's Art: A Study of "Joseph Andrews."* Middletown, CT: Wesleyan University Press, 1959.
Bender, John. *Ends of Enlightenment*. Stanford, CA: Stanford University Press, 2012.
Berlin, Isaiah. "Historical Inevitability." In *Liberty*, edited by Henry Hardy, 94–165. Oxford: Oxford University Press, 2004.
Bree, Linda. "Henry Fielding's Life." In *The Cambridge Companion to Henry Fielding*, edited by Claude Rawson, 3–16. Cambridge: Cambridge University Press, 2007.
Dennett, Daniel C. "I Could Not Have Done Otherwise—So What?" *Journal of Philosophy* 81, no. 10 (1984): 553–65.
Den Uyl, Douglas J. "Shaftesbury and the Modern Problem of Virtue." *Social Philosophy and Policy* 15, no. 1 (1998): 275–316.
Dickie, Simon. *Cruelty and Laughter: Forgotten Comic Literature and the Unsentimental Eighteenth Century*. Chicago: University of Chicago Press, 2011.
Dumont, Louis. *From Mandeville to Marx: The Genesis and Triumph of Economic Ideology*. Chicago: University of Chicago Press, 1977.
Empson, William. "*Tom Jones*." *Kenyon Review* 20, no. 2 (1958): 217–49.
Fielding, Henry. *The Champion: Containing a Series of Papers, Humorous, Moral, Political and Critical*. Vol. 2. London, 1741.
Fielding, Henry. *The History of the Adventures of Joseph Andrews and of His Friend Mr. Abraham Adams; An Apology for the Life of Mrs. Shamela Andrews*. Edited by Douglas Brooks-Davies. Oxford: Oxford University Press, 1999.
Frankfurt, Harry G. "Alternate Possibilities and Moral Responsibility." *Journal of Philosophy* 66, no. 23 (1969): 829–39.

Gallagher, Catherine. *Nobody's Story: The Vanishing Acts of Women Writers in the Marketplace, 1670–1820*. Berkeley: University of California Press, 1994.

Golden, Morris. *Fielding's Moral Psychology*. Amherst: University of Massachusetts Press, 1966.

Hamilton, Ross. *Accident: A Philosophical and Literary History*. Chicago: University of Chicago Press, 2007.

Hunter, J. Paul. *Occasional Form: Henry Fielding and the Chains of Circumstance*. Baltimore, MD: Johns Hopkins University Press, 1975.

Iser, Wolfgang. *The Implied Reader: Patterns of Communication in Prose Fiction from Bunyan to Beckett*. Baltimore, MD: Johns Hopkins University Press, 1974.

Jameson, Fredric R. *A Singular Modernity: Essay on the Ontology of the Present*. London: Verso, 2002.

Kramnick, Jonathan. *Actions and Objects from Hobbes to Richardson*. Stanford, CA: Stanford University Press, 2010.

Lynch, Deidre Shauna. *The Economy of Character: Novels, Market Culture, and the Business of Inner Meaning*. Chicago: University of Chicago Press, 1998.

MacKenzie, Scott. "'Stock the Parish with Beauties': Henry Fielding's Parochial Vision." *PMLA* 125, no. 3 (2010): 606–21.

Macpherson, C. B. *The Political Theory of Possessive Individualism: Hobbes to Locke*. London: Oxford University Press, 1964.

Macpherson, Sandra. *Harm's Way: Tragic Responsibility and the Novel Form*. Baltimore, MD: Johns Hopkins University Press, 2010.

McWeeny, Gage. "The Sociology of the Novel: George Eliot's Strangers." *Novel* 42, no. 3 (2009): 538–45.

Merrett, Robert James. "Empiricism and Judgment in Fielding's *Tom Jones*." *Ariel: A Review of International English Literature* 11, no. 3 (1980): 3–21.

Milbank, John. "Against Human Rights: Liberty in the Western Tradition." *Oxford Journal of Law and Religion* (2012): 1–32.

Nazar, Hina. *Enlightened Sentiments: Judgment and Autonomy in the Age of Sensibility*. New York: Fordham University Press, 2012.

Paknadel, Felix. "Shaftesbury's Illustrations of *Characteristics*." *Journal of the Warburg and Courtauld Institutes* 37 (1974): 290–312.

Pfau, Thomas. "The Letter of Judgment: Practical Reason in Aristotle, the Stoics, and Rousseau." *Eighteenth Century: Theory and Interpretation* 51, no. 3 (2010): 289–316.

Pfau, Thomas. *Minding the Modern: Human Agency, Intellectual Traditions, and Responsible Knowledge*. Notre Dame, IN: University of Notre Dame Press, 2013.

Preston, John. *The Created Self: The Reader's Role in Eighteenth-Century Fiction*. London: Heinemann, 1970.

Richardson, Samuel. *Pamela; or, Virtue Rewarded*. Edited by Thomas Keymer and Alice Wakely. Oxford: Oxford University Press, 2001.

Rosenfeld, Sophia. *Common Sense: A Political History*. Cambridge, MA: Harvard University Press, 2011.

Sandel, Michael. *What Money Can't Buy: The Moral Limits of Markets*. New York: Farrar, Straus and Giroux, 2012.
Shaftesbury, Anthony Ashley Cooper, Third Earl of. *Characteristics of Men, Manners, Opinions, Times*. Vol. 1. Indianapolis, IN: Liberty Fund, 2001.
Snow, Malinda. "The Judgment of Evidence in *Tom Jones*." *South Atlantic Review* 48, no. 2 (1983): 37–51.
Soni, Vivasvan. "Committing Freedom: The Cultivation of Judgment in Rousseau's *Emile* and Austen's *Pride and Prejudice*." *Eighteenth Century: Theory and Interpretation* 51, no. 3 (2010a): 363–87.
Soni, Vivasvan. "Introduction: The Crisis of Judgment." *Eighteenth Century: Theory and Interpretation* 51, no. 3 (2010b): 261–88.
Soni, Vivasvan. "Modernity and the Fate of Utopian Representation in Wordsworth's *Female Vagrant*." *European Romantic Review* 21, no. 3 (2010c): 363–81.
Soni, Vivasvan. *Mourning Happiness: Narrative and the Politics of Modernity*. Ithaca, NY: Cornell University Press, 2010d.
Soni, Vivasvan. "Preface: Jane Austen's Critique of Aesthetic Judgment." In *Jane Austen and the Arts: Elegance, Propriety, Harmony*, edited by Natasha Duquette and Elisabeth Lenckos, xi–xxi. Bethlehem, PA: Lehigh University Press, 2013.
Stephanson, Raymond. "The Education of the Reader in Fielding's *Joseph Andrews*." *Philological Quarterly* 61, no. 3 (1982): 243–58.
Strauss, Leo. *Natural Right and History*. Chicago: University of Chicago Press, 1953.
Thorne, Christian. *The Dialectic of Counter-Enlightenment*. Cambridge, MA: Harvard University Press, 2009.
Valihora, Karen. *Austen's Oughts: Judgment after Locke and Shaftesbury*. Newark: University of Delaware Press, 2010.
Virno, Paolo. *Multitude: Between Innovation and Negation*. Translated by Isabella Bertoletti, James Cascaito, and Andrea Casson. Los Angeles: Semiotext(e), 2008.
Warner, William B. *Licensing Entertainment: The Elevation of Novel Reading in Britain, 1684–1750*. Berkeley: University of California Press, 1998.
Watt, Ian. *The Rise of the Novel: Studies in Defoe, Richardson, and Fielding*. Berkeley: University of California Press, 2000.
Welsh, Alexander. *Strong Representations: Narrative and Circumstantial Evidence in England*. Baltimore, MD: Johns Hopkins University Press, 1992.

10 THE LINGUISTIC CONDITION OF JUDGMENT: KANT'S "COMMON SENSE"

Claudia Brodsky

1 Verbal action in Kant

It is fair to say there is not a lot of talking, whether first-hand or cited, within the comprehensive "composition"[1] of Kant's tripartite *Critique*, and that its confounding, founding hypothesis, that empirical knowledge is not only valid but inevitable when "empirical" is understood not to be empirical but representational—that is, that our ability to know depends first on our rethinking what "knowledge" is—it is fair to say that such a non-normative (or, as it commonly dubbed, "counterintuitive") hypothesis relies on nothing resembling "common sense."[2] There is so little talking, and so little talk about talking, whether in itself or in relation to knowledge and action, across the expansive discursive universe of the *Critique*, that Kant's open dependence upon verbal utterance at key moments in his analyses of the distinctly "human"[3] "faculties" is indeed easy to overlook. Unremarkable until remarked upon, Kant's essential reliance upon verbal practices within the intensively logical "construction"[4] of his project resembles nothing so much as its apparent vernacular opposite, the vital utterances, largely ignored in themselves, within and upon which our daily lives are built.

When, having proven that a logical "concept" of "freedom"—"keystone"[5] of the entire "building" ("Gebäude"[6]) of his critical philosophy—is itself, necessarily, logically unavailable to proof, Kant must attempt to demonstrate its all-critical "possibility" by other means, it is neither to empirical and physical *data* nor to abstract formal categories, but to specifically *verbal* actions that his analysis turns. Asserting that, "experience, too, confirms this [*a priori*] ordering of concepts in us" ("Aber auch die Erfahrung bestätigt diese Ordnung der Begriffe in uns"[7]), Kant offers, in lieu of logic, a brief, hypothetical narrative of one such "experience:" the story of an everyman whose sovereign "demands" he "bear false witness against an honest man" upon "threat" of immanent death. In keeping with the actions leading up to it, the dénouement of Kant's experiential narrative is entirely verbal in kind, as Kant poses of its putative subject a final hypothetical "question:" "Ask him however, whether, if his prince demanded, under threat of execution, that he bear false witness against an honest man, whether he then, no matter how great his love of living may be, holds it for possible that he may well overcome it" ("Fragt ihn aber, ob, wenn sein Fürst ihm, unter Androhung der . . . Todesstrafe, zumutete, ein falsches Zeugnis wider einen ehrlichen Mann . . . abzulegen, ob er da, so gross auch seine Liebe zum Leben sein mag, sie wohl zu überwinden für möglich halte . . ."[8]).

"Frag ihn aber, ob . . ." ("*ask* him, however, whether . . .") he "*holds it for possible*" that, even upon "*threat*" of death, he may "*refuse*" to "*lie*" upon "*demand*:" what these narrated acts—*discursive acts* all—serve (in yet another verbal act) to "*confirm*" ("bestätigt") is the priority of the concept of "freedom" "within us" ("bestätigt diese Ordnung der Begriffe in uns"[9]), which is to say, the ability to act in independence (of the causal ordering of concepts) that is definitive of free action itself. The absence or presence of a "gallows" "erected" on the spot may prove decisive to the subject's—this or any such subject's—ability to withstand a personal inclination: "Given that someone asserts he would be unable to withstand his most pleasurable inclination if the desired object and opportunity presented themselves together; [ask him] whether, if a gallows were erected in front of the house in which he encountered this opportunity, he would then not overcome his inclination" ("Setzet, dass jemand von seiner wollüstigen Neigung vorgibt, sie sei, wenn ihm der beliebte Gegenstand und die Gelegenheit dazu vorkämen, für ihn ganz unwiderstehlich: ob, wenn ein Galgen vor dem Hause, da er diese Gelegenheit trifft, aufgerichtet ware, um ihn sogleich nach genossener Wollust daran zu knüpfen, er alsdenn nicht seine Neigugng bezwingen würde"[10]). Yet, what the subject of Kant's hypothetical narrative demonstrates, in finding it "possible" that he might indeed "overcome his love of living" rather than condemn to death another man through his own lie, is that he identifies his own *life*—what it is in itself, in absolute distinction from its empirical conditions—with his own *relation to the words he says*, with the truth or falsity of the words he employs in relation to any subject whatsoever, rather than to any empirical set of conditions. By contrast, neither his personal like or dislike of the "honest man" about whom he has been ordered to lie, nor his sovereign's threat that refusal to do so will issue in his own death, may prove similarly decisive to this subject at all. Insofar as he cannot "ensure" he "would or would not [bear false witness]" against an "honest" man, even supposing that the refusal to do so will result in his own physical demise, such a subject "must" (by yet another verbal act) "concede" it is "possible" he may so refuse, and, we, by extension, that he is what Kant calls "free:" "Whether he would do it or not, he will perhaps not trust himself to ensure; that it is, however, possible for him he must concede without compunctions" ("Ob er es tun würde, oder nicht, wird er vielleicht sich nicht getrauen zu versichern; dass es ihm aber möglich sei, muss er ohne Bedenken einräumen"[11]).

That the verbal actions composing this pivotal moment in the *Second Critique*, and the centrality of discursive operations to the *Critique* in general, do not figure prominently, if at all, in the historical reception of Kant's project may owe simply to the fact that, unlike the hypothetical narrative scenario to which Kant's own unimpeachable logic gives way, such "inclinations" rarely "find the desired object and opportunity" to "present themselves" within the "architectonic" logic of the *Critique*.[12] Yet rarity may itself mean everything in the *Critique*. If talk is cheap, Kant implies, blame it on the cheapness, the meretriciousness or lack of real value of what is said by those who make it appear so, not on the value of language, as a mode of meaning, or its common purveyor—the value-neutral, proverbial "phone company," or nominal, discursive knowledge we all rely on—let alone our ability *to form* discursive hypotheses and "*synthetic judgments a priori*"[13] in the first place, or that of any man to decide at any time *not* to lie.

2 Judgment and "Indeterminacy"

As foundational as the concept of "freedom" to the *Critique* is the noncognitive act of judgment that, separate subject of the *Third Critique*, is already described in the First Preface to the *First Critique* as that action whose exercise—"the mature power of judgment of the age" ("der gereiften Urteilskraft des Zeitalters")—defines its time as the *Age of Critique*.[14] Indeed, even the crucial, final paragraph of §6 of the *Second Critique* just cited, ends with an act of "judging" upon which, first, the "recognition" of "freedom" and, second, that of a "moral law" itself dependent on the recognition of freedom, depend: "Thus he [someone] *judges* that he can do something because he is conscious that he should, and recognizes in himself the freedom which without the moral law would otherwise remain unknown to him" ("Er *urteilet* also, dass er etwas kann, darum, weil er sich bewusst ist, dass er es soll, und erkennt in sich die Freiheit, die ihm sonst ohne das moralische Gesetz unbekannt geblieben wäre.")[15] But "judgment" itself is theorized for the first time in the history of philosophy as an active *a priori* faculty—indeed, the most critical of all faculties—in Kant's *Critique of Judgment*. And judgment is said in the *Third Critique* to be based, most unusually—and for the first time in Kant—on what he calls, despite his acerbic critique of the term as a feinting usurpation of logic,[16] "common sense."

Indeed, given his equation of "common sense" with an antiphilosophical "call to the judgment of the herd,"[17] no single statement in Kant's critical philosophy may be met with greater disappointment or incomprehension than the assertion made without further conceptualization or explanation in the *Third Critique* (§20), that the "power of judgment" (*Urteilskraft*)—and with it, the entire philosophical project whose coherence and possibility that power alone ensures—itself relies on the operation of something that Kant, as if simply following common parlance, calls "common sense" (*Gemeinsinn*):

> If judgments of taste (like cognitive judgments) had a definite objective principle, anyone rendering them according to this principle would claim the unconditional necessity of his judgment. If they were without any principle, like those of merely sense-based taste, no one would allow the necessity of them into their thoughts. Thus they must have a subjective principle that determines, only through feeling and not through concepts, but nonetheless generally, what pleases or displeases. Such a principle however can only be seen as a *common sense*, which is essentially different from the common understanding that people sometimes also call commons sense (sensus communis): for the latter does not judge according to feeling but always according to concepts, even if these are commonly only obscurely represented principles.

[Wenn Geschmacksurteile (gleich den Erkenntnisurteilen) ein bestimmtes objektives Prinzip hätten, so würde der, welcher sie nach dem letztern fället, auf unbedingte Notwendigkeit seines Urteils Anspruch machen. Wären sie ohne alles Prinzip, wie die des blossen Sinnengeschmacks, so würde man sich gar keine Notwendigkeit derselben in die Gedanken kommen lassen. Also müssen sie ein subjektives Prinzip haben, welches nur durch Gefühl und nicht durch Begriffe, doch aber allgemengültig bestimme, was gefalle oder misfalle. Ein solches Prinzip aber könnte nur als ein *Gemeinsinn* angesehen werden; welcher vom gemeinen Verstande, den man bisweilen auch Gemeinsinn (sensus communis) nennt, wesentlich unterschieden ist: indem letzterer nicht nach Gefühl, sondern jederzeit nach Begriffen, wiewohl gemeiniglich nur als nach dunkel vorgestellten Prinzipien, urteilt.[18]]

Limiting knowledge of things to a coordination of concepts and perceptual representations, and basing aesthetic judgment on perceptions shorn of conceptual content, Kant's critical "revolution"[19] in metaphysics makes no concessions to and no mention of the rule of common sense—intellectual and cultural norms or assumptions of the very kind his "Copernican" *Critique* defied. Even as it appears to appeal to the very kind of platitudinous belief Kant criticized in Scottish common sense philosophy, Kant's introduction of "common sense" into German letters, in distinction from "healthy," "sound," or "common human understanding" (*gesunder* or *gemeiner Menschenverstand*)— popular terms more commonly employed, including, on occasion, by Kant himself—remains consistent with the critical rigor of his own project, or, what is the same, with a supreme lack of common sense on his part. For Kant ends §20 by admitting there is nothing whatsoever commonsensical, nothing anyone, let alone each of us, can presume to know about the effectivity, existence, or basis of the capacity for "common sense" (*Gemeinsinn*) on which his central theory of judgment rests. Unlike every other "sense," "common sense" is not an "external" medium through which we experience sensuous objects; but neither is it a hypothetical medium originating solely within the subject. "Common sense" functions instead on the shared or general "presupposition" that it is "given," a "presupposing" defined by Kant, in §22, as "really" rather than merely theoretically enacted: "only under the presupposition that there 'is' [or, more accurately, 'would be:' *gebe**[20]] common sense (by which we do not understand an external sense, but the effect resulting from the free play of our powers of cognition), only, I say, under the presupposition of such a common sense can judgment of taste be rendered;" "This undetermined norm of a common sense is really presupposed by us: our presumed ability to make judgments of taste proves it" ("nur unter der Voraussetzung, dass es einen Gemeinsinn gebe [wodurch wir aber keinen äussern Sinn, sondern die Wirkung aus dem freien Spiel unserer Erkenntniskräfte, verstehen], nur unter Voraussetzung, sage ich, eines solchen Gemeinsinns kann das Geschmacksurteil gefällt warden"); ("Diese unbestimmte Norm eines Gemeinsinns wird von uns wirklich vorausgesetzt: das beweiset unsere Anmassung, Geschmacksurteile zu fallen"[21]).

As extraordinary as Kant's introduction of "common sense" into critique is his verbal act of direct self-reference in doing so. Interposed between clauses describing, on the one hand, our "presupposition" of an undefined "common sense" "resulting from the free play of our powers of cognition," and, on the other, an ability to judge said both to "prove" the "reality" of what we presuppose and to depend upon it, is Kant's statement of the origin of these propositions, his own speaking self, "I:" "I say" ("ich sage"). As noted above, when indicating the presupposed existence of "common sense," Kant employs the mood of the German subjunctive that serves to indicate reported speech and alleged facts ("would be" [*gebe*]), the same verbal tense and grammatical equivalent of quote marks with which he will refer to "common sense" thereafter. Yet, nowhere else in the *Critique* does Kant declare, as befits the grammatical function and context of that tense, the actual fact that he is not hypothesizing, or theorizing, but, quite literally, *saying* this. As if openly enacting the act of presupposition on which "common sense" and "judgment" are based, Kant verbally indicates the indistinguishability of its proposition from the presupposition of that proposition itself by speaking of "common sense" *as a speaker speaking in the first person*. Kant, in other words, does what he says as he is saying it, and, in so doing, renders explicit the verbal form his proposal of "common sense" and the common "presupposition" of it share. The logically entailed, temporal, or sequential cognitive distinction between proposition and presupposition is eclipsed here by a statement indicating that, like what it proposes, such a proposition is "really" ("wirklich") taking place, in a particular speaker's words. Thus Kant's proposition of a fundamental "common sense" defies what we assume common sense to be by declaring itself to be in fact and indeed nothing more nor less than *a fact of speech*, one alleged by a subject ("I") engaged at that moment in the very act of enacting or presupposing it. The difference, in short, between proposing in theory and presupposing in practice the existence and effectivity of what Kant calls "common sense" is limited by Kant to the verbal equivalent of diacriticals: a reporting of speech by a subject himself engaged in the act of presupposition which that speech ("would be" [*gebe*]) describes.

That the pathbreaking ability to bridge the primary analytic division between theoretical and practical uses of reason and their respective objects, limited knowledge and free moral action, on which his own *Critique* depends, should itself depend on the "presupposed," that is, critically unanalyzed faculty that Kant, speaking in uncharacteristic *propria persona*, calls "common sense," appears a conspicuous, if not fatal flaw in the "building" (*Gebäude*) of Kant's "system," an exception, as evident as it is inexplicable, to the regularity and autonomy of its logical, "architectonic" exposition.[22] Yet, the analytic weakness unambiguously articulated by Kant's introduction of "common sense" at the close of the First Analytic of the *Third Critique*, may also be seen to reveal the rigor and integrity of Kant's analytic procedure overall, his refusal either to derive an analytic definition of "common sense" from its commonplace conception or to circumvent the need for analysis in the name of the commonsensical, the assumed rather than articulated presupposition of "Gemeinsinn" first named in the course of that analysis itself.

In refusing to define "common sense" as "just" "common sense," something beyond, or before, but, in any case, independent of analysis in that it is, simply, naturally given, without relation to anything else, Kant distinguishes "common sense" from the purely verbal assertion of sense with which it may most easily be confused, tautology. Tautology, verbal truncheon of all pretenders to the mind's supposed "throne,"[23] compels the surrender of reason not to a power greater or essentially different from itself—the unforeseeable intellectual event, say, of "a happy notion" ("ein glücklicher Einfall"),[24] to which all "revolutions" in "mode of thought" ("Revolutionen der Denkart") are attributed in the Second Preface to the *First Critique*, or, oppositely, to the "feeling" ("Gefühl"[25]) from which the *Third Critique* specifies all aesthetic judgments spring—but, rather, to nothing and no power at all but that of stating itself. Equating truth with a willed act of repetition purposed to usurp analysis, and as exactly opposite to the critical clarity of what Kant elsewhere calls "discursive thinking"[26] as any single predicative utterance can be, tautology employs the form of predication so as to render any form a redundancy, pretending to include within its limits, and so preclude, not merely all necessary but all possible thought. Just as the age-old advertisement for brutality, "might makes right," seeks to supplant all basis for the analyses of right *and* might by dressing the two, disconnected concepts in nearly tautological garb, linking them on no other basis than the pronouncement of a succinct narrative rhyme, so positive logical tautology, an identity statement identifying only itself, represents not self-evidence but the aim to enact, in language, total sovereignty over language, over difference of any kind: the difference between thoughts and things, as between thinking and tautology; the verbal assertion of nothing and destruction of everything but the pure, context-shorn repetition of a word, "itself." Stated so as to abrogate every action of perception, along with the temporality all such acts require, tautological statements are not the result but the reductio ad absurdum of "common sense," not its end but its termination. Tautology negates common sense by presuming at once to be, to speak for, and to surpass it, to pass off its own purposeful verbal redundancy as the supposed self-evidence and givenness of reality.

Rather than define "common sense" as itself self-evident, a sense definable by and as tautology, Kant instead relates it, without explicating it, to an analytic definition of judgment, and thus to the very possibility of specifically *critical* (or traditionally anti-"commonsensical") thought. Surprising in that it occurs at all, let alone in the voice of the first person, and describing "common sense" to be as central to the *Critique* as its own demonstration, let alone definition by the *Critique*, must remain inconclusive, what Kant's reference to "common sense" demonstrates is that "common sense" could never be sufficiently defined as common sense "itself," another dumb redundancy dependent, like all tautology, upon its own enforced echo, the appropriation within it, in the guise of merely being "itself," of all that is not it, just as every echo dissembles the Narcissus at its source. For, if stated instead as a tautological "given," "common sense" would preclude all it does not already include as "given," every statement that differs from or refers to something other than its own formal self-mirroring, including, most significantly, the fact of its own essential vacuity.

Like every tautology asserted as a statement referring only and sufficiently to "itself," a statement, in short, whose predicate "is" its subject, "common sense" defined *as* common sense could do nothing but assert successive assertions of its own success; like every tautology, its truest—most effective and empty—translation is the familiar affirmation, "nothing succeeds like success." Kant's reference to "common sense" succeeds in remaking "common sense"—most commonly cited "authority" of anti-intellectual tautology—into a singular object of intellectual inquiry by stating, in unsubordinated addition to it, what that reference does not contain: an adequate account of what "common sense" is. At the close of the Fourth (and final) Moment of the Analytic of the Beautiful (*Critique of Judgment* §22), Kant acknowledges the failure of his analysis of judgment to account fully for itself, the nonconformity of the formative capability—or, as he calls it, "faculty" ("Vermögen")—of "common sense" with the formality of the analysis that requires it, including the division of our mental abilities into "faculties" themselves. Unlike reason, imagination, and understanding, the principle faculties or capabilities of the mind whose alternating configurations Kant delineates across the divisions (figuratively speaking, the wings) of the "building" composing his *Critique*; and unlike the different capacities of experience primarily associated with these faculties, that is, logic, sensation, and representation, respectively, "common sense" neither has nor could have any clearly defined status or function, and so can be subordinated neither to the "hypothetical" and "theoretical" nor "real" and "practical" conditions of knowledge or of action analyzed in the *First* and *Second Critiques*. Further questioning "whether" such a "constitutive principle of the possibility of experience" as "common sense" even "in fact exists," and "judgments of taste are thus original and natural," or "whether" the "possibility" of "common sense," of a sensible feeling ascribed by each to all, is "the idea" of a faculty whose "artificial" "acqui[sition]" and "regulation" of experience is "require[d]" by a "higher principle of reason" instead—in short, whether common sense is "original" or is a posteriori to "the possibility of experience" itself—Kant leaves that fundamental question, and with it, the very credibility of "common sense," undecided. With the negative assertion that he has neither the "ability" nor "desire" to answer it "for now," and positive demurral of any logical need to do so, the last paragraph of §22 and the entire series of deductive Moments[27] comprising Kant's Analytic of the Beautiful ends:

> Whether there "is" [or "would be:" *gebe*] in fact such a common sense as a constitutive principle of the possibility of experience, or whether a yet higher principle of reason only "makes" [*mache*] producing a common sense with higher aims into a regulative principle for us; whether taste "is" [*sei*] an original and natural faculty or only the idea of an artificial one to be acquired, so that a judgment of taste, with its presumption of general determination, "is" in fact only a demand of reason that such a

unanimity in the mode of sense be brought forth, and whether the ought, i.e., the objective necessity of the confluence of the feeling of any one man with the particular one of every other man only "signifies" [*bedeute*] the possibility of arriving at this agreement, and judgment of taste only "exhibits" [*anstelle*] an example of the application of this principle: this we here neither want nor can investigate as of yet, but rather propose now only to break down the faculty of taste into its elements and unite them finally within the idea of a common sense.

[Ob in der Tat einen solchen Gemeinsinn, als konstitutives Prinzip der Möglichkeit der Erfahrung gebe, oder ein noch höheres Prinzip der Vernunft es uns nur aum regulativen Prinzip mache, allerest einen Gemeinsinn zu höhern Zwecken in uns hervorzubringen; ob also Geschmack ein ursprüngliches und Natürliches, oder nur die Idee von einem noch zu erwerbenden und künstlichen Vermögen sei, so dass ein Geschmacksurteil, mit seiner Zumutung einer allgemeinen Bestimmung, in der Tat nur eine Vernunftforderung sei, eine solche Einhelligkeit der Sinnesart hervorzubringen, und das Sollen, d. i., die objective Notwendigkeit des Zusammenfliessens des Gefühls von jedermann mit jedes Seinem besondern, nur die Möglichkeit, hierin einträchtig zu werden, bedeute, und das Geschmacksurteil nur von Anwendung diese Prinzips ein Beispiel aufstelle: das wollen und können wir hier noch nicht untersuchen, sondern haben vor jetzt nur das Geschmacksvermögen in seine Elemente aufzulösen, und sie zuletzt in der Idee eines Gemeinsinns zu vereinigen.[28]]

The investigation of its own nature signaled as wanting and that lack, as one that Kant himself does not even wish to attempt to repair as of yet, "common sense" names whatever it is that makes judgment a general capacity or faculty, rather than an individually contingent operation of taste, disposition, or opinion, in Kant. A universal subjective capacity that renders possible the linking of the "pure" "practical reason" of "free" (or "moral") action in the *Second Critique* with the "practical" and applied nature of "pure (or 'theoretical') reason" in the *First*, judgment is not another mode of reason introduced to supplement those between which it mediates. In terms of the different modalities accorded practical and pure reason by Kant, judgment neither "legislates" the activity of the mind nor conforms to intellectual "laws," whether these are logical, phenomenal-perceptual and causal, or noumenal and moral. Its operation depends instead on an ability whose very normativity renders it immediately at odds with the project of critique. Small wonder, then, that Kant's unadumbrated introduction of "common sense," an appeal unprecedented and unprepared for in the analytic sequence preceding it, has attracted little scrutiny (with the important exception of Arendt in her late *Lectures on Kant's Political Philosophy*[29]) in the separate developments of philosophy and aesthetic theory ever since.[30] The same is true for more recent analyses devoted to re-evaluating and resuscitating "common sense" *in opposition to* philosophy, efforts in which Kant's introduction of the "faculty" into philosophy plays an understandably minimal, consistently negative role."[31]

By the same token, an adherence to Kant that questions his own judgment, in invoking "common sense" as a first "principle" without demonstrable origin, would demonstrate nothing so much as a failure to understand the critical significance of the act such questions serve to dismiss. Rather than subordinate it to the guiding critical "hypothesis" clearly stated in the Second Preface to the *First Critique*, Kant raises a series of incontrovertible questions ("whether ... or whether ..." [*ob* ... *ob*[32]]) regarding the nature of this "common" critical capability—a capability and not a content, a "possibility" ("Möglichkeit") and not a logical necessity or rule—not only refusing thereby to comprehend "common sense" under any prior, logical or hypothetical "principle" whatsoever, but implying in addition that, whether dismissive, skeptical, or simply unquestioning in orientation, the failure to reflect critically on the significance of "common sense" will obscure its effectivity both within the *Critique* and ourselves. Such acts of distortion or neglect are entirely understandable (if in a distinctly non-Kantian sense); indeed, the singularly "real" "effectivity" Kant ascribes to "common sense" seems to invite them. It is the very prosaic, unexceptional, indeed, apparently negligible assumption of a common turn of mind—of something shared, in the undergoing of a certain experience, by one with all—that has made the capability Kant defined as the most important to judgment and thus the entire "building" of the *Critique* also appears the weakest in his architectonic design: a mere commonplace that, not submitted, like other social conventions (like "taste" itself) to critique, is made to do too much with too little. An appeal to "common sense"—verbal last resort and refuge from analysis of epistemological and cultural chauvinists alike—would indeed appear most out of place in Kant, whose powers of analytic scrutiny and comprehensive originality made his tri-partite

Critique self-critical like no other philosophical work before it, a theory which every theory of knowledge, aesthetics, or moral action has had to consider since.

Taken alone, in the way it is commonly asserted, "common sense" is a term for what does, or should, "go without saying," an ability enacted and relied upon by every practically reasonable mind. It boasts no particular capacities or components but its own, a self-sufficiency that, "knowing"—like a practiced physical motion—what it is about, renders any additional effort of critical analysis or introspection superfluous, if not injurious, to its execution. This would appear true of Kant's provocative invocation of the term as well, his stated refusal to attempt to answer just those question, regarding the existence and origin of this particular "faculty," as he directly proposes himself, the pronounced disengagement from further speculation with which his discussion of this "presupposed" faculty comes to an end: "this we neither can nor want to investigate here as of yet" ("das wollen und können wir hier nocht nicht untersuchen").

Yet, unlike conventional gestures toward self-evidence, Kant's appeal to a "faculty" he calls "common sense" is part of the final step of a categorical analysis said to have depended, in every preceding step, upon it. And unlike most appeals to "common sense," Kant's serves rather than impedes the development of a course of critical reflection. Here "common sense"—less defined than it is left undescribed by its broad identification as "effect of the free play of our powers of cognition" ("die Wirkung des freien Spiels unserer Erkenntniskräfte")—is introduced in response to an exacting formal examination of the felt intangibles of judgment and aesthetic experience in general, acts and experiences that, while unmistakably specific, have defied definition at least since Plato's isolation of truth and beauty, conceived as eternal "ideas," from the changing manifestations of mimesis. Thus, before dismissing its reference to "common sense" as a retreat from critical reason into banality, it is to the *Analytik*, out of whose positive steps the "necessary" but no less negative "condition" ("notwendige Bedingung") and "undefined norm" ("unbestimmte Norm") of "common sense" are shaped, that we must look if we are to make sense of rather than read past it, confusing "common sense" with the "hollow" ("schal"), "confident" ("getrost") notion of "common human understanding" Kant criticized, or mistaking it for the disproof of the entire preceding analytic procedure which it underpins.[33] For if Kant's invocation of "common sense" highlights a banality, it does so consciously, indicating that, just as it participates in judgment, "common sense" is an intellectual "effect" in which we all participate, a common practice on which, whether or not analytically inclined, we all unconditionally, if inexplicably, rely.[34]

3 Speech

That common practice, so common as to go unnoted, is the way in which judgment at once takes place and, in addition, makes itself known. The medium of the power of judging in the *Third Critique*, unlike that of any other purported "faculty" or "capacity," is not only specifically described but described specifically to be that of speech. Already in his attribution of the feeling of freedom to the apperception of a subject who judges ("the person who judges feels himself fully *free*") ("sich . . . völlig *frei* fühlt"[35]) and of "generality" ("Allgemeinheit") to the feeling of pleasure judged ("he [who judges] must believe he has reason to attribute a similar pleasure to everyone") ("muss er glauben Grund zu haben, jedermann ein ähnliches Wohlgefallen zuzumuten"[36]), Kant states that it is only in the act of "speaking" that such an experience of freedom and generality of feeling articulates itself and makes itself known. Judgment *speaks* ("says," "names," "calls," "describes," "communicates" or "publishes"[37]) and what it says does not name but qualifies, describing an unknown nominative subject ("it") by a simple predicative complement ("is beautiful;" "is sublime"). It is because the "subject" of judgment can find no "personal," as he can no "objective," basis for his "feeling"[38] that he "speaks" in the first place, and it is *as speech*, the mode of manifestation shared by all, that judgment indicates its general, nonprivative nature:

> Since [judgment] does not base itself on any inclination of the subject (nor on any other dominating interest), but rather *because* he who judges feels himself fully *free* in view of the pleasure he attributes to the object, so can he discover the grounds of this pleasure in no personal conditions that would depend upon his subject alone, and thus must regard it as grounded in that which he can presuppose of everyone else; consequently he must believe he has reason to attribute a similar pleasure to everyone. He will thus so *speak of the beautiful, as if* beauty were a quality of the object and judgment, logical (constituting a cognition of the object through concepts) . . . . For

[aesthetic judgment] has this similarity with logical judgments, that we can suppose its validity for everyone.

[Denn da es sich nicht auf irgend eine Neigung des Subjekts (noch auf irgend ein anderes überlegtes Interesse) gründet sondern *da* der Urteilende sich in Ansehung des Wohlgefallens, welches er dem Gegenstande widmet, völlig *frei* fühlt; so kann er keine Privatbedingungen als Gründe des Wohlgefallens auffinden, an diese sich sein Subjekt allein hinge, und muss es daher als in demjenigen begründet ansehen, was er auch bei jedem andern voraussetzen kann; folglich muss er glauben Grund zu haben, jedermann ein ähnliches Wohlgefallen zuzumuten. Er wird daher *vom Schönen so sprechen, als ob* Schönheit eine Beschaffenheit des Gegenstandes und das Urteil logisch (durch Begriffe vom Objekte eine Erkenntnis desselben *ausmache*) wäre . . . darum, weil es doch mit dem logischen die Ähnlichkeit hat, dass man die Gültigkeit desselben für jedermann daran vorasussetzen kann.[39]]

The assumption of the general validity of judgment is reflected in the fact of its verbal articulation: it is the specifically *verbal* mode, and not "mode of thought" ("Denkungsart") of judgment, its enactment in an utterance understood to be comprehensible and attributable to all, that lends it the "logical" quality "constituting" the constative form of "cognition," even though what it says says nothing about either that generality or the subject's "relation" to the object that occasions it, but is limited to "speak[ing]" merely "as if" speaking of a "quality of the object" itself. The relationship of judgment to logic implied by its exclusive realization in verbal form, the very form whose rules of comprehension are required for the exercise of logic generally, remains one of implication rather than identity, causing judgment to appear at once universal and particular, its "real" meaning both self-evident and covert, "objective" and "subjective"—a speech act, in short. The expression of a feeling (pleasure or displeasure) in words that *do not express that feeling*, the experience of a feeling subject, but something else instead, something of which it states, "it is beautiful," "it is sublime," and nothing more, appears both sufficiently empty of particularity to resemble statements that are logical, that is, statements constating the knowable existence or state of something and nothing more, *and* "free" of the cognitive content given shape by logical statements, and thus logical—if one can say so much—only *in part*.

The confusion of logic with "feeling" that his analysis of the specifically verbal mode of judgment describes is one Kant neither advances nor avoids, and if it seems as unsuited to the rigor of his distinctions between "faculties of reason" as does his final (and avowedly ungrounded) appeal to "common sense," closer inspection reveals the grounds of that confusion to be those that determine the rigor of Kant's analysis itself. For in describing judgment as a "feeling" in a subject (i.e., an "I" who feels pleasure or displeasure) translated into a logical, universally valid statement about an object (i.e., "It is beautiful," "It is sublime"), Kant describes—and must describe—an experience that is *neither theoretical nor practical but otherwise expressible*: a "feeling" that produces neither knowledge nor action but *words*; a statement, uttered by someone who could be anyone, "logically" constating *not that feeling* but a quality of something, anything, outside ourselves. The subject who, in judging, "speaks of the beautiful as if beauty were a quality of the object and judgment were logical" neither knows anything nor acts in any physical or moral sense, *but says*; and, consistent with saying the speech act it speaks—sole act the "power of judgment" effects—the specifically verbal production of judgment must owe to an experience neither cognitive nor moral "reason" can define, one unencompassed by their separate, "object" "realms"[40] of sensory objects and the Good, respectively. Rather than representing or enacting any object, any subject who, in the experience of "feeling," "feels himself free," is free to speak of something *in the place of feeling itself*. Judgment speaks "as if" what it says "were *constitutive* of a cognition of the object through concepts of the same" even while employing no such concepts and constituting no such cognition. Rather than expressing a personal sense or feeling of a subject, judgment is spoken as a *general* statement about an unnamed but *specific object*, and it is in its expression, *in the form of a definition, rather than subjective judgment, of an object* it does not know, that judgment effectively passes for something else, a constative statement that "possesses this resemblance to the logical, that we can presuppose its validity for everyone."

The deductive circle described here by Kant's identification of judgment with its pronouncement, the empirical indistinguishability of the subjective experience of feeling from the general verbal or speech act in which judgment consists, is as irresolvable as it is plain. Its "validity" as a disinterested illocution performable by anyone, or, as Kant calls it, defined by its own "general communicability" ("allgemeine Mitteilbarkeit"[41]), endows the speech act that is judgment with the universal quality of logic just as its constative, logical form, in speaking of an "it" rather than for an "I," makes judgment that particular kind of speech act ascribable to everyone else. Does the "general communicability" defining acts of judgment make judgment part of discourse or part of action, and its language, that of "merely nominal" conceptual logic or the "real being" and "first basis of the possibility" of things? In theorizing the particular power of judgment Kant renders that very opposition—organizing principle of his entire critical project and strict methodological division drawn between "nominal" and "real definitions" in his *Logik*[42]—a distinction itself merely nominal in scope, dependent only on the end of the reversible definition of judgment, as enactable only in speaking and as speech act, with which one chooses to begin.

As in his refusal to speculate on the bases of "common sense," Kant makes no attempt here to resolve the rational puzzle of the identity of the mental capability he proposes, to disentangle the premises from the consequences of its circular definition, nor even to decide which is which, so as to order premise and consequence into a logically consecutive deductive chain. The "Moments" of Kant's *Analytik*—like the organizational categories they employ—are descriptive, not hypothetical or speculative. Refusing to arrive at a single, "real" *or* "nominal," origin of judgment by playing Solomon to the general capacity for "common sense" on which it is based, he chooses instead to emphasize that, while judgments "resemble" logical procedures in their constitutive "validity"— which is to say, their "communicability"—for all *subjects*, that validity and that resemblance rest on no sensory concepts, and so no logical constitution and cognition of *objects* at all.

The categorically descriptive speech act, "it is beautiful," can and will only be uttered in reference to an object capable of occasioning the kind of "feeling" its subject believes he or she can "attribute" to "everyone." Yet because judgment consists of no knowledge of an object, either de facto or de jure (a logical distinction effectively effaced by the activity of judgment itself), it remains, despite the *form* of logical, constative language it takes, an *act* of speech and nothing more: nothing more, that is, than speech standing for the feeling "attributable to every and any subject"[43] by translating it into a "quality constitutive of an object," a substitution of object for subject, and of a referential copular statement for the report of an action ("feeling"), spoken without any personal "interest" in performing that speech act at all.

Kant's description of an internal power of judgment whose universality stems from being externally identifiable with speech reminds us that, like speech acts themselves, language as a whole depends on concepts but not concepts alone. The language that enables logical procedures also enables the replacement, in the act of articulation, of inarticulate "feeling," and the confusion of the two, logic and the mere appearance thereof, may prove as critically productive as it is misleading. The fact that any single judgment no less than the singular qualities that define all acts of judgment are both made available to us only through speech, indicates that, just as a truly "private language" is not a language but an oxymoron—a notion of "language" invented by a subject who himself could never remember it because, unexpressed or externalized, it cannot be received by anyone as extant—so without speech there would be no judgment, insofar as we can understand and imagine it.

The question, however, which the reversible structure of the foundation of judgment raises as its result, is *whether without judgment, there could be speech*: whether language, repository of all discursive concepts, definitions, and logical relations, and thus of all knowledge in Kant, originates with the noncognitive faculty of aesthetic judgment itself, an inarticulate "feeling" *disguised in being articulated* as a constative statement—the, strictly speaking, illogical birth of language and of logic that makes the movement or "transition" within the *Critique* (as within every subject) between the limits of logical, phenomenal cognition and the "practical" realization rather than merely "technical" imitation of "free" action (described by Kant in the first draft of the Preface to the *Third Critique*) possible.[44] Like the *a priori* forms of time and space, the conceptual content of language appears fully formed within the *Critique*, just as the linguistic basis of all possible epistemology is given by its founding "hypothesis." Yet in the *Third Critique* language is instead the unique modality of a noncognitive ascription to an object. What is ascribed to that object, to any object, perceived as if for the first time—which is to say, as a "free" form or even "not-form" ("Unform"[45]), something apparent but without content, severed from any preexisting knowledge of or interest in it on our part—is a quality predicative not of its conceptualization but of its nonconceptual and thus unstated experience: the experience, free even from the fundamental operations of schematism, of how that perception makes the subject "feel."

"It is beautiful"—which is to say, I feel pleasure in the mere perception of it, in the "free play of imagination and understanding" that it occasions in me—is the speech act that does not speak for itself, but for "it," and for "it" as it is perceived, without constitutive knowledge, not by an "I" but by all. The aesthetic perception that occasions feeling and the feeling that occasions judgment first occur as judgment in a speech act, a specifically noncognitive use of speech. Thus it is that this particular origin of judgment, in a feeling so impersonal or general that only language can express it, indicates at the same time the unique generality attributable to language, any language, itself. Judgment, that "power" which is "merely contemplative," which is "indifferent as regards the existence of an object," which is "not directed to concepts," not "*based* on concepts, nor has concepts as its purpose," may in turn share not only the generality of language with regard to its own formal expressive mode, but indicate how such an inherently disinterested, general form of expression could have been formed to begin with.

For, how could language, which includes the possibility of speech acts, that is, acts taken in independence of the cognitive and persuasive measures of speech language provides, ever "free" itself from such limited, "technical" aims so as to act with the disinterest of a *techne*? Or, by the same token, in what merely contemplative experience—the experience by a subject of an unknown object, "it"—can language, repository of knowledge, instrument for the formulation and pursuit of interests, *and* expression of merely contemplative experience alike, disengage itself from the captive language we use and so allow a disinterested power, that of judgment, to articulate itself in the first place?

The combined feeling of freedom and pleasure experienced in view of an object is communicated by its subject, but in words that neither state those feelings nor say anything about the particular subject nor object of perception at all. Instead, the speech in which the "free" experience of "pleasure" in perception results, "resembles" statements "sprung from logic" in that, like logic, it "presupposes" its "validity" for "everyone."[46] The universal "validity" "presupposed" in and by the speech act of aesthetic judgment is, however, void of specific content: no "concepts"— the discursive purveyors of content—are articulated by judgment (not even those of beauty or sublimity themselves), just as no object is named by it, "for from concepts there is no passage to the feeling of pleasure displeasure" ("denn von Begriffen gibt es keinen Übergang zum Gefühle der Lust oder Unlust"[47]), no "passage" and passage alone of the kind only judgment without content other than a non-object-specific, predicative quality provides. By extension, the "claim" of judgment to interpersonal "validity" stems not from any sense of "generality" ("Allgemenheit") "placed in objects" themselves but is instead "bound to a claim to subjective generality itself" ("es muss damit ein Anspruch auf subjective Allgemeinheit verbunden sein").[48]

As if to indicate how far from Kant's critical sense of "common sense" our own thinking about the aesthetic has come, we now call such judgments "objective" even though they replace the identity of the object with a single, non-object-specific adjective ("It is beautiful;" "it is sublime"). For Kant, they are, instead, "subjective" in a specifically "general" sense precisely because, while explicitly verbal, they leave, along with the object, the particular subject of speech out of the picture: any utterances of judgment would, indeed, be "laughable," Kant states, that included the referral of their content to the identity of the subject who speaks them. Defining such qualifying acts as "self-justifications" based on merely "pleasant" sensations, whose working "principle"—"everyone has his *own* taste (of the senses)"—is directly contrary to the theory of judgment he describes here, Kant writes:

> In the case of the beautiful, things are entirely different. Indeed, it would, on the contrary, be laughable, if someone who was somewhat proud of his taste thought to justify himself in saying: "this object (the building that we see, the dress that one is wearing, the concert that we are hearing, the poem that is posited for judging), is beautiful *for me*. For he must not name it *beautiful* when it pleases merely him; but when he pronounces something beautiful so he attributes to others just the same pleasure: he judges not only for himself, but for everyone, and thus speaks of beauty as if it were a quality of things. He says, the *thing* is beautiful; and does not thereby more or less count on the agreement of others in his judgment of this pleasure, because he found them frequently in agreement with his, but *demands* it from them.
>
> [Mit dem Schönen ist es ganz anders bewandt. Es wäre (gerade umgekehrt) lächerlich, wenn jemand, der sich auf seinen Geschmack etwas einbildete, sich damit zu rechtfertigen gedächte: dieser Gegenstand (das Gebäude, was wir sehen, das Kleid, was jener trägt, das Konzert, was wir hören, das Gedicht, welchers zur Beurteilung aufgestellt ist) ist *für mich* schön. Denn er muss es nicht *schön* nennen, wenn es bloss ihm gefällt . . .; wenn er aber etwas für schön ausgibt, so mutet er andern eben dasselbe Wohlgefallen zu: er urteilt nicht bloss für sich, sondern für jedermann, und spricht alsdann von der Schönheit,

als ware sie eine Eigenschaft der DInge. Er sagt daher, die *Sache* ist schön; und rechnet nicht etwa darum auf anderer Einstimmung in sein Urteil des Wohlgefallens, weil er sie merhmalen mit dem seinigen Einstimmung befunden hat, sondern *fordert* es von ihnen.[49]]

What kind of voice speaks neither of the "feelings" of a subject nor bases what it says on the spoken "agreement" of "other subjects" ("anderer Einstimmung") with its words, no matter how "frequently" ("mehrmalen") individually voiced instances of agreement may be "found" ("befunden")? What kind of voice speaks so "objectively" as to say nothing about a particular object that *could* be subject to disagreement because what it says "depends" neither on the object spoken of nor on the subjects who speak it? What kind of voice, in short, can never say "I"?

4 The "postulation" of "a general voice"

This "voice" ("Stimme"), as Kant calls it, neither gives voice to "rules" that can override or generate our and others' experience of "feeling," nor articulates "reasons and propositions of reason" capable of persuading individuals to experience feelings, nor names particular empirical "sensations" ("Empfindungen") on which still other subjects may believe their "pleasure depends." The voices which say as much are the voices of speakers and not judgment itself, the stated views of so many subjects, so many individual "I's," who can and do naturally disagree because they misconstrue aesthetic experience as a subject of, and so subject to, private conviction, and thereby confuse "judgment" with taste. Among these figure all self-appointed arbiters and social regulators of "good" taste; positivist rationalizers of the pleasure afforded by "having" taste; and those who conflate "taste" with the physical sensation for which it is falsely named. Just as judgment does not rely on, indeed excludes "concepts" of its object, it speaks with a voice independent of any of the individual voices from which these various conceptions of it emerge:

> When we judge objects merely according to concepts, so all perception of beauty is lost. Thus there can also be no rule according to which someone can be compelled to acknowledge something as beautiful. Whether a dress, a house, a flower would be ("sei") beautiful: no one lets his judgment be cajoled by reasons and principles of reason to that

conclusion. Some people want to submit the object to their own eyes, just as if their pleasure depended on the sensation; and nevertheless, when one names an object beautiful, one believes one has a general voice, and makes claim to the accession of everyone, since otherwise every private sensation would only decide for him and his pleasure alone.

Here we can now see that in the judgment of taste nothing is postulated other than such a *general voice*. . . .

[Wenn man Objekte bloss nach Begriffen beurteilt, so geht alle Vorstellung der Schönheit verloren. Also kann es auch keine Regel geben, nach der jemand genötigt werden sollte, etwas für schön anzuerkennen. Ob ein Kleid, ein Haus, eine Blume schön sei: dazu lässt man sich sein Urteil durch keine Gründe oder Grundsätze beschwatzen. Man will das Objekt seinen eigenen Augen unterwerfen, gleich als ob sein Wohlgefallen von der Empfindung abhinge; und dennoch wenn man den Gegenstand alsdann schön nennt, glaubt man eine allgemeine Stimme für sich zu haben, und macht Anspruch auf den Beitritt von jedermann, da hingegen jede Privatempfindung nur für ihn allein und sein Wohlgefallen entscheiden würde.

Hier ist nun zu sehen, dass in dem Urteile des Geschmacks nichts postuliert wird, als eine solche *allgemeine Stimme* . . .[50]]

In this important first formulation and reformulation of "a general voice" of judgment, the problem of "common sense" already comes into view. In "naming" an "object" "beautiful," "one believes one has a general voice"— that is, one believes the utterance of that speech act does not, indeed, could not speak for one's self alone—and, in naming such a "belief," Kant judges or generalizes from it, redefining such "a general voice" as the sole "postulate" of the act of judgment itself. The (not quite) formal act of postulating from action rather than causal logic—"Here is now to be seen, that in judgment nothing is postulated but such a *general voice*"—is echoed in the initial and then reformulated mention of "common sense" already cited at the opening of this analysis:

Such a principle (that "determines" [or, "would determine:" *bestimme*] what pleases and displeases only through feeling and not through concepts but nonetheless generally) can only be seen as a *common sense*; which is essentially different from the common understanding that one sometimes also names common sense (sensus communis) . . .

Thus only under the presupposition that there "is" [or, "would be:" *gebe*] common sense (by which we do not understand an external sense, but the effect resulting from the free play of our powers of cognition), only, I say, under the presupposition of such a common sense can judgment of taste be rendered. . . .
This undetermined norm of a common sense is really presupposed by us: our presumed ability to make judgments of taste proves it. Whether in fact such a common sense . . . "exists" [or "would exist:" *gebe*]. . . .

[Ein solches Prinzip (welches nur durch Gefühl und nicht durch Begriffe, doch aber allgemengültig bestimme, was gefalle oder misfalle) aber könnte nur als ein *Gemeinsinn* angesehen werden; welcher vom gemeinen Verstande, den man bisweilen auch Gemeinsinn (sensus communis) nennt, wesentlich unterschiden ist . . .

Also nur unter der Voraussetzung, dass es einen Gemeinsinn gebe (wodurch wir aber keinen äussern Sinn, sondern die Wirkung aus dem freien Spiel unserer Erkenntniskräfte, verstehen), nur unter Voraussetzung, sage ich, eines solchen Gemeinsinns kann das Geschmacksurteil gefällt werden . . .

Diese unbestimmte Norm eines Gemeinsinns wird von uns wirklich vorausgesetzt: das beweiset unsere Anmassung, Geschmacksurteile au fallen. Ob in der Tat einen solchen Gemeinsinn . . . gebe . . .[51]]

The "common sense" which may or may not in fact "exist" and on which the execution of judgment depends, speaks in the "general voice" that is the sole "postulate" of the theory of judgment itself. "A general voice"— only voice that never says "I"—must speak to and for every subject by speaking, instead, of an object. The voice of every subject translates, into speech qualifying an object, something "generally communicable" among subjects. That quality has no "objective" content, nor does it contain, or in any semiotic sense, represent the experience of a subject. Contingent, transitory, and formally unpredictable by definition, "feeling," the individual experience of an individual subject *in the absence of a sign*, is as little "communicable" in itself to the subject in which it occurs. Whether speaking or silent, feeling requires an "I." Yet the subject of "feeling" in Kant "feels himself fully free" from "private conditions" to translate his "feeling," in the "general voice" of judgment, into language about an object: to "name" something by a "generally communicable" quality alone. Each subject is subject to "himself," "his" or "her"[52] changing experience and interests, but the subject of judgment, speaking subject of "a general voice" that says of an object, "it is beautiful," "it is sublime," speaks of something whose particular name and identity, like his own, he, in judging, no longer knows. In judging he speaks the principle of speech, "general communicability," with every translation from object to subject (in disinterested perception and feeling), subject to object (in impersonal or third-person expression) and subject to subject (in "a general voice") he makes, without any one of which "communicability" could never be "general," and what we call "language" would not be language at all.

The "general voice" is language spoken without reference to an "I" and without knowledge of which it speaks. "General communicability," as independent of any particular subject and object as it is dependent upon every possible object and subject, substitutes for the "feeling" of a subject a definitive statement about an object—definitive not because it defines that object's content but because spoken as if speakable by "every and any subject."[53] Judgment speaks in "a general voice," and "common sense"— "condition," "faculty," and "capability" for "general communicability," that, alone among all such conditions hypothesized in the *Critique*, "cannot" be defined as either *a priori* or *a posteriori* by Kant—allows us to judge by allowing us *to speak in general*. Its "presupposition" is the linguistic condition on which not only the explicitly verbal act Kant calls "judgment," but the necessary internal "communicability"—between knowledge and action, limitation and freedom—that judgment alone grants the *Critique* depend. Neither incidental nor merely rhetorical across the course of Kant's *Critique*, specifically linguistic practices are instead literally and theoretically central to the historically and philosophically transformative argument it makes, that is, *a "positive[ly]" "negative"*[54] *argument not for logical necessity but logically necessary "possibility."*[55] For like the fact of language, which, while amenable to use by logic, is not a subset of logic itself, and like the acts of speech on which the apparently paradoxical logic[56] of his own anti-metaphysical metaphysical project turns, Kant's "critical" philosophy provides the "limited" formal means for constructing the commensurate human version of the noumenal or "unlimited." This "unlimited" is no metaphysical realm of the "supersensible" unavailable, by definition, to both understanding and sensuous perception, but the realm of "possible" understanding and perception that language both is and represents. Yet this is also no less than to say, non-commonsensically, that the "free" linguistic "capacity"

Kant called "common sense," and which the "universal communicability" defining "judgment" must "presuppose," is and represents that of agency itself.

Notes

1 "Composed" (or "compositional" [*ein Zusammengestztes*]) is the very first term Kant employs to designate "our knowledge of experience" as described by the working "hypothesis" of his *Critique*, namely that empirical knowledge is as much a product of our own, internal "capacity for cognition" as of our passive "reception" of external "sensory impressions." This essay uses it here to draw an opening analogy between Kant's account of experience and the empirical content of his *Critique* itself. See Kant, *Werkausgabe*, Hrsg. William Weischedel, XII Bde. (Frankfurt: Suhrkamp, 1968), III: 45, B 1–2, 28, B XXIII; all translations form the German in this essay are my own.

   This essay is a condensed version, concentrating solely on Kant's primary text, of a longer scholarly argument about language and action in the Age of Critique developed in full in a forthcoming book on poetics and judgment in Kant and eighteenth-century literature.

2 Kant, X: 157, *KU* §20–21, B 65–66.

3 Kant, III: 51, *KrV*, B 9.

4 The geometrical and architectonic notion of "construction"—Kant's early term for the simultaneously internal and external, and thus cognitively "revolution[ary]" realization of the self-defining isosceles triangle—is both *analogical* in significance to the formation of "synthetic *a priori* judgments" (i.e., those combining intellect with experience) whose "possibility" lies at the foundation of Kant's own "revolution in mode of thought," and descriptive *in kind* of what Kant repeatedly calls the "architectonic" "logic" and "systematic" "building" of his *Critique*. See Kant, III: 22–62 (*KrV* B XI–25).

5 Kant, III: 107, *KpV*, A 4).

6 Kant, III: 51, 64, *KrV*, B 9, 27, et. al.

7 Kant, VII: 140, *KprV*, A 54.

8 Ibid.

9 Ibid.

10 Ibid.

11 Ibid.

12 Kant, IV: 693–998, *KrV*, B 859–64.

13 "*Whether it is possible*" to form "*synthetic judgments a priori*" in our cognition of experience akin to geometrical propositions, such as

"the shortest distance between two points is a straight line," and all arithmetic propositions in which a distinct predicate is understood to be already contained in our conception of its subject, is the all-critical question Kant raises in the Introduction to the *First Critique* (III: 59, B 20 [emphasis in text]). In Kant's affirmative answer to that question is contained what might be called the essential syntactic principle on which Kant's entire grammar of cognition rests. See Kant, III: 52–62, *KrV* B 11–B 25: "On the Difference between Analytic and Synthetic Judgments;" "In all Theoretical Sciences of Reason Synthetic Judgments *a priori* are Contained as Principles;" "The General Task of Pure Reason").

14 Kant, III:13, *KrV* A XI,

15 Kant, VII: 140, *KprV* A 54.

16 For Kant's exclusion of essentially "tautological," so-called "common sense" statements from logic, and equation of what he calls, by contrast, the "logic of common reason (*sensus communis*)" ("Logik der gemeinen Vernunft [*sensus communis*]") with "actually no logic, but an anthropological science" ("eigentlich keine Logik, sondern eine anthropologische Wissenschaft"), see especially Kant, *Logik* A 223, VI: 526, and A 12, VI: 430, respectively.

17 For Kant's explicit distinction between "common sense" and "common understanding" based not in "feeling" but in "concepts," see *KU*, B 65, X: 157. For his refutation of the easy assumption of a "common human understanding," in important contrast to his own foundation of judgment on a "faculty" of "common sense," see his *Prolegomena* A11–12, *Werkausgabe*, VI: 117–18. Refusing to take for granted such a "comfortable means" of circumventing careful thought, and representing the recourse to "calling upon common human understanding" as nothing more than a "subtle invention of modern times," one deceptively permitting "the hollowest enthusiasts to affiliate confidently with exacting minds," Kant cautions that, "while there is still even a small remainder of insight, one will do well to prevent oneself from grasping at this emergency assistance," whose own "appellation." he concludes, is "nothing other" than a "calling upon the judgment of the herd" ("sich auf den gemeinen Menschenverstand zu berufen, das ist eine von den subtilen Erfindungen neuerer Zeiten, dabei es der schalste Schwätzer mit dem gründlichsten Köpfe getrost aufnehmen... So lange aber noch ein kleiner Rest von Einsicht da ist, wird man sich wohl hüten, diese Nothülfe zu ergreifen... diese Appellation nichts anders, als eine Berufung auf das Urteil der Menge" [VI: 117–18]).

18 Kant, X: 157 (*KU*, B 65).

19 Kant, III: 22–62 (*KrV* B XI–25).

20 The German, *gebe*, here conjugates the third-person impersonal expression, *es gibt* ("there is," "there are") in the "first subjunctive" tense used for indirect, imputed, and reported speech.

21 Kant, X: 159 (*KU*, B 68).

22 See endnote 6, this essay.

23 Cf. Kant, on the "death of philosophy" at the hands of those who, presenting themselves as "superior" to analytic "discursive" labor, instead incant the words of ancients they "[en]throne" out of their own "incapacity to think," in "Of a newly elevated, superior tone in philosophy" ("Von einem neuerdings erhobenen Ton in der Philosophie"), *Werkasugabe* VI: 383, 389–90n (A 309, 412–13).

24 Kant, III: 22 (*KrV* B XI).

25 Kant, X: 97 (*KU* B XL), et passim.

26 See Kant, VI: 380 (A 394). Pertinent to the particularity of Kant's undisclosed concept of "common sense" is its relation, as the basis of judgment, to our capability for "discursive thought." For an opposite view advocating a nondiscursive reliance on common sense *beliefs*, see Nicholas Rescher, *Common-Sense: A New Look at an Old Philosophical Tradition* (Milwaukee: Marquette University Press, 2005), 32: "A common-sense belief . . . is a nondiscursive and nonreflective belief of which one is certain—and as *reasonably* certain—as one can be of anything."

27 Unlike Hegel's use of "moments" to designate discrete temporal and dialectical steps in the development of thinking as he understands it, the four "moments" of Kant's "Analytic of the Beautiful" openly employ Aristotle's primary analytic categories ("quality," "quantity," "relation" and "modality") to define what constitutes a "judgment of the beautiful" *as* a "judgment" (rather than a [representational] cognition or free [moral] action), and distinguishes it from the experiences and expressions with which it is instead regularly confused, such as personal impressions, opinions, likes and dislikes, and feelings.

28 Kant, X: 159 (*KU* B 68).

29 The salient exception to this history of near neglect, Arendt's interpretation of Kant's reference here to "common sense," in *Lectures on Kant's Political Philosophy*, ed. Ronald Beiner (Chicago: University of Chicago, 1982), makes it the basis of a Kantian theory of political *sensus communis*. While Arendt's recognition of the critical function of "common sense" in Kant speaks to her distinctive ability to read philosophy meaningfully, with regard for the conditions and practices that distinguish specifically human activity, her expansion of Kant's inclusion of "common sense" to the *polis* effectively displaces its situation or status within the *Critique* itself. A direct attempt to build upon Arendt's discussion is offered in Anthony Cascardi's, *Consequences of Enlightenment* (Cambridge: Cambridge University Press, 1999); see especially 80–86, 161–64. Acknowledging Adorno's skirting of the singularity of "common sense" in Kant (77, 83) as well as Arendt's important "vacillat[ion]" on the "aporia" or logical circle it presents (85), Cascardi refers the unprecedented quality of Kant's "common sense" to our very capability for cognizing precedence, or "memory"—a "lost knowledge" implicitly reminiscent of Plato's theory of the recollection (*anamnesis*) of the Beautiful (85–86).

30 See, for example, the passing reference to "common sense" in relation to "judgment" in Susan Meld Shell's exhaustive analysis of epigenetic, organistic, hypochondriacal, and other bodily themes in Kant, in *The Embodiment of Reason* (Chicago: University of Chicago Press, 1996), 208. See also the brief, initial definition of "common sense" as "a kind of *feeling*, namely the feeling of a certain or, as it were, instinctively correct choice" and its tautological restatement as "a feeling of *sensus communis*" rather than "obscure conceptuality" in Jan Kulenkampff's otherwise careful analysis of the relation between aesthetic judgment and rationality, *Kants Logik des aesthetischen Urteils* (Frankfurt a. M.: Klostermann, 1978), 99. The obscurity of its conception is the main conclusion of Brent Kalar's discussion of "common sense," in his generally excellent analysis, *The Demands of Taste in Kant's Aesthetics* (London: Continuum, 2006), see especially 138–40. Christian Helmut Wenzel's, *Introduction to Kant's Aesthetics: Core Concepts and Problems* (London: Blackwell, 2005) offers a helpful review of philosophical uses of "common sense" before Kant, and concludes, like Kalar, by identifying it as an "effect of free play," before associating that effect, as Kant does not, both with the pseudoscientific view, inherited from the Greeks, of "an inner sense or faculty that unites our five senses," and the moral "duty to develop a taste for beauty" (see 80–85 especially). By contrast, in *Kant and the Claims of Taste* (Cambridge: Cambridge University Press, 1996), Paul Guyer begs the question of what, if anything, the mention of "common sense" is doing in the *Third Critique* in the first place, concluding, simply, that its "basic meaning... for Kant is... the faculty of taste itself" (405n42). For an excellent critique of Guyer's approach to the *Third Critique*, and Kant in general, as a case of mistaken identity, in which the central "revolution in mode of thought" constituted by Kant's founding "hypothesis" is replaced by Humean, empiricist notions of predictability and agreement, see Kalar, *The Demands of Taste in Kant's Aesthetics*, 19–36.

31 This includes the full spectrum of positive and negative evaluations of "common sense" philosophies. Contrast, for example, the argument for common sense and against Kant (and "neo-Kantians") in Stephen Boulter, *The Rediscovery of Common Sense Philosophy* (London: Palgrave, 2007), especially xi, 98–117, with the indictment both of Kant and all appeals to common sense, considered complicit with "disciplinary" stagings of "humiliation," in Paul Saurette, *The Kantian Imperative: Humiliation, Common Sense, Politics* (Toronto: University of Toronto Press, 2005), 12–14 especially. Conflating "common sense" with "common sense recognition," Saurette identifies the contemporary persistence of this "subterranean Kantian logic" in "Rawls, Habermas, Taylor, and many others" (11, 46–48).

32 See endnote 28, this essay.

33 Kant, VI: 117–18 (*Prolegomena* A11–12).

34 Kant's analysis of judgment as a uniquely human "faculty" or "capacity" inextricable from its linguistic medium, and of "common sense" as the "ground" (of "universal" "communicability") defining language as such,

the precise temporal and circumstantial origin of which must remain indeterminable to him (and, presumably, anyone else), dovetails perfectly with Chomsky's theory of the "language faculty," or "capacity for language in our species" (54), as the "internal mental tool" (81) primarily responsible for human history and the possibility of action as such, an "internal language of thought" that is "fundamentally a system of meaning" (101) rather than "reference" (86), whose finite formal rules allow for unlimited or "infinitely many" (66) "structured expressions" (87) and whose mode of development of "human concepts" (87) in particular remains "completely unknown" (87) to us. See Noam Chomsky, *Why Only Us* (Cambridge, MA: MIT Press, 54, 81, 101, 101, 86, 66, 87, 87).

35 Kant, X: 124 (*KU* B 18).
36 Ibid.
37 These are the verbs—denoting exclusively verbal actions—by which Kant defines the enactment and identity of aesthetic judgment itself. See Kant, X: 117 (*KU* B 7;) X: 124, B 18; X: 126, B 20; X: 127, B 22; X: 130, B 26; X: 157, B 65; X: 170, B 82; X: 179, B 95; X: 185, B 105; X: 186, B 106; X: 196, B 119; X: 208, B 133, et. al.
38 Kant importantly distinguishes between the "subjective" experience that "we commonly call by the name of feeling" and the "objective" product of the "senses" "describe[d]" by the "word" "sensation." Whereas "sensation" cannot result in "judgment," but merely individually and biologically contingent "enjoyment," "feeling" is what we produce, and undergo, when perceiving merely the "free" "delineation" of something what we don't know (X: 118–21 [*KU* B 9–14]).
39 Ibid.
40 Kant, X: 82–85 (*KU*, B xviii–xxii).
41 Kant, X: 158 (*KU* B 66 [emphasis added]).
42 See Kant, VI: 576 (*Logik* A 221–22).
43 Kant, X: 101 (*KU,* B XLVI).
44 Kant, X: 13–14. (*KU*).
45 Kant, X: 104 (*KU* B XLIX).
46 Kant, X: 124 (*KU,* B 18).
47 Kant, X: 126 (*KU* B 20).
48 Kant, X: 130 (*KU* B 26, X: 130).
49 Ibid (original emphasis).
50 Ibid (original emphasis).
51 Kant, X: 167–69 (*KU* B 65–68 [original emphasis]).
52 The use of the masculine pronoun and possessive adjective, here and elsewhere throughout this essay, reflects both the colloquial difficulty of expressing in English (unlike German and the Romance languages) a

general, non-gendered subject (in the nominative or any other case) and the grammatical impossibility of coordinating the gender of adjectives of possession with that of the thing possessed rather its possessor, and thus the absence of a generally accurate linguistic mode for representing any subject speaking in judgment's specifically "general voice."

53 Kant, X: 101 (*KU* XLVI).
54 Kant, III: 29–30, X: 165, 195, 201–02 (*KrV* B XXIV, KU B 76, 118, 125–26 et. al.)
55 Kant, X: 83, 101–02, 135–36; *KU* B XX, XLVI–VII, 33–35, et. al.
56 Kant, III: 27, B XX.

Bibliography

Arendt, Hannah. *Lectures on Kant's Political Philosophy*. Edited by Ronald Beiner. Chicago: The University of Chicago Press, 1982.
Berwick, Robert C., and Noam Chomsky. *Why Only Us*. (Cambridge, MA: MIT Press, 2016).
Boulter, Stephen. *The Rediscovery of Common Sense Philosophy*. London: Palgrave, 2007.
Cascardi, Anthony. *Consequences of Enlightenment*. Cambridge: Cambridge University Press, 1999.
Descartes, René. *Oeuvres philosophiques*. 3 vol., Edited by Ferdinand Alquié. Paris: Garnier, 1963.
Gregoric, Pavel. *Aristotle on the Common Sense*. Oxford: Oxford University Press, 2007.
Guyer, Paul. *Kant and the Claims of Taste*. Cambridge: Cambridge University Press, 1996.
Kalar, Brent. *The Demands of Taste in Kant's Aesthetics*. London: Continuum, 2006.
Kant, Immanuel. *Werkausgabe*. XII Bde., Hrg. Wilhelm Weischedel. Frankfurt: Suhrkamp, 1974.
Kulenkampff, Jan. *Kants Logik des aesthetischen Urteils*. Frankfurt, a. M.: Klostermann, 1978.
Rescher, Nicholas. *Common-Sense: A New Look at an Old Philosophical Tradition*. Milwaukee: Marquette University Press, 2005.
Saurette, Paul. *The Kantian Imperative: Humiliation, Common Sense, Politics*. Toronto: University of Toronto Press, 2005.
Savi, Mariana. *Il concetto di senso comune in Kant*. Milano: FrancoAngeli, 1998,
Shell, Susan Meld. *The Embodiment of Reason*. Chicago: The University of Chicago Press, 1996.
Wenzel, Christian Helmut Wenzel, *Introduction to Kant's Aesthetics: Core Concepts and Problems*. London: Blackwell, 2005.

INDEX

Adorno, T. W.   129 n.46, 250 n.29
"Age of Critique"   1, 2, 3, 9, 10,
   248 n.1
Alkmene   24–5
allegorization
  vs. "lively present-tense" writing,
   in *Clarissa*   126
allegory   6, 143
  in *Clarissa*   112, 114, 115,
   116, 118, 127–8 n.27,
   128 n.28
  defined by Paul de Man   116, 118
  of didactic status of literature, in
   reception of Aristotle's
   Poetics   143*ff.*
  Platonic, as represented by
   Diderot   6, 87, 88, 89,
   90, 91, 102, 104, 105, 106
Althusser, Louis   2, 161, 167 n.31
Amphitryon
  story of, adapted by Kleist   24–5
architectonic
  logic of construction of Kant's
   Critique   152, 227, 231,
   235, 248 n.4
Arendt, Hannah   2, 12, 214–15,
   218 n.31, 220 n.52, 235,
   250 n.29
Aristotle   2, 215 n.4
  analytic categories of   5, 250 n.27
  on category of "sex"   5, 57, 63,
   73 n.21, 74 n.34, 75 n.39
  on deliberative judgment   202
  Lessing's retranslation of   7
  Nicomachean Ethics of   11, 215 n.3,
   218 n.23

  Poetics of   7–8, 134–44, 146 n.30
  theory of predication of   63
Armstrong, J. M.   138, 141, 142,
   143, 146
Auerbach, Erich   131 n.76, 132
Austen, Jane   201, 214, 218 n.32, 223

Baines, Paul   216 nn.10, 12, 221
Battestin, Martin   216 n.12
Baudelaire, Charles   1
Bender, John   198 n.19, 215 n.6,
   216 n.6, 221
Berlin, Isaiah   214 n.2, 221
Borges, Jorge   1
Boulter, Stephen   251 n.31, 253
Boulukos, George   43, 49 n.35, 50
Bowen, Elizabeth   30, 32, 36, 46, 50
Bree, Linda   217 n.20, 221
Brodsky, Claudia   26 n.1, 146, 151,
   152, 165 n.8, 168
Burke, Kenneth   40, 41, 49 n.32, 50

Callirhoé   90, 84, 85, 92, 93, 94, 97,
   101, 105
Cascardi, Anthony   250 n.29, 253
causality   5, 6, 8, 9, 121
  experiential   149
  and mediation   159
  narrative   7, 109, 118–21
  natural (*see* Newtonian
   mechanics)
  structural   153, 157
  in tragedy   8, 140–1
Cervantes, Miguel de   1
Chandler, James   196 n.9, 198
Clare, John   4, 20, 21, 26 n.7, 27

common sense 13, 220 n.42, 222,
    253, *see also sensus
    communis*
  anti-theoretical rhetoric of 37
  Kant's reconception of 12, 228-33,
    235-7, 239-40, 243,
    245-8, 249 n.16,
    249 n.17, 250 nn.26,
    29, 251 n.30
  Scottish philosophy of 229
  in Shaftesbury 11, 204, 207,
    210-11, 213
  as "universal" linguistic "faculty,"
    in Kant's Analytic of the
    Beautiful 246-7
communicability 13
  as "general" "condition" of judg-
    ment in Kant 239-40,
    247-8, 251
"Copernican Revolution"
  Kant's own 18, 229
  in mathematics and science, as
    described by Kant 4
Corésus 84-5, 92, 93, 94, 97, 100,
    101, 102, 104, 105,
    107 n.7

Dasein 21, 23, 151
  in der Zeit 8-9, 150-3, 159, 163
Davis, Lennard J. 174, 175, 194 n.1,
    195 n.4, 197 n.16, 198-9
de Beauvoir, Simone 73 n.23
Defoe, Daniel 49 n.26, 198 n.17,
    199, 203, 223
deixis 110, 115
  in Hegel's *Phenomenology of
    Spirit* 116
de Man, Paul 116, 118, 128 n.34,
    150, 165 n.5
Dennett, Daniel C. 215 n.4, 221
Descartes, René 3, 4, 17, 18, 19, 21,
    24, 25, 26, 26 n.2, 27,
    27 n.18
  "cogito" of 2, 4, 17, 18, 24, 27
Deslauriers, Marguerite 63, 74,
    75, 77

Deutsch, Helen 174, 194 n.1,
    195 n.2, 198 n.16, 199
dialectical materialism 9, 149, 150,
    161, 163, 164, 166 n.30,
    169
Dickie, Simon 221 n.41, 221
Diderot, Denis de 2, 6
  his account of (unseen) painting
    by Fragonard 85-9,
    93, 95-105, 106 n.2,
    106-7 n.6, 107 n.7
  on theatricality of history
    depicted in Fragonard
    painting 6, 85-7, 95-6
  his "dream" of Plato's allegory of
    the Cave 86-91, 94
  works by
    Salons of 1765 84, 92, 107 n.8
    Salons of 1767, entry on
      Vernet 107 n.7
difference 1, 2, 6, 10, 28
  constituted by utopian
    fiction 213
  constitutive of painting according
    to Diderot 87, 94, 96
  constitutive of speech acts
    73 n.25
  constitutive of surplus value of
    labor according to
    Marx 168 n.53
  and disability 175, 183, 191,
    194 n.1, 195 n.2,
    199, 200,
  of epistolary form 115
  historical, 116
  and identity 2, 6
  linguistic 40
  referential 118
  between "sensation" with and
    without "knowledge"
    according to Keats 22
  sexual 2, 52-3, 55-7, 60, 62, 65,
    67-8, 71, 75 n.40
  sovereignty over, asserted by
    tautology 232
  in species 63-4

256 INDEX

between subject and predicate in
    Hegel 117, 153
supposed categorical, between
    sexes 5, 51–7, 60, 62,
    65, 67–8, 70–1, 75 n.40
between synthetic and analytic
    judgments according to
    Kant 249 n.13
temporal 112, 114, 115, 119, 125
between theory and practice
    according to Kant 231
disability
    and/as "deformity," "physical"
    and "moral" 176,
    179–80, 182–4, 187, 189,
    190, 197 n.13
disenfranchisement
    of disabled 192
Dumont, Louis 217 n.19, 220

Eagleton, Terry 36, 44, 46 n.12,
    50, 127 n.21, 132,
    198 n.18, 199
eliminativism
    of sexual categorization of the
    subject 67, 69
Ellison, Julie 196 n.12, 199
emplotment 109, 114, 121
Empson, William 215–16 n.6, 217
    n.14, 219 n.38, 220 n.41,
    221
epistolary novel 7, 110, 113, 114,
    115, 127 n.33, 208
equalization
    of sexual difference 56–8
exercitive(s)
    in J. L. Austin 60
externality, viz. externalization
    19, 125, 147
    as interiority in Watt 38, 42
    as non-determinative of delib-
        erative judgment in
        Aristotle 11
    of other to self traversed by
        judgment according to
        Kant 12, 239, 241

in relation to interiority in
    Hegel 33–4, 47–8 n.20,
    150, 153, 157, 159, 162
its relation to internal experi-
    ence as sole basis of
    temporal perception in
    Kant 149, 151–2

Farneth, Molly 153, 169
Ferrari, G. R. F. 8, 138–43, 145 n.12,
    146 n.30, 147
Ferris, David 142–4, 146 n.32, 147
Fielding, Henry 2
    and Hobbesian social
        psychology 201, 204–5
    on mimetic reflection of moral
        "deformity" 209
    and modernity 206
    novels by
        Joseph Andrews 202ff.
        Tom Jones 37–43
    psychology of his characters
        207
    according to Watt 37–9
    and sentimental novel 203–4,
        208–9
    and Shaftesbury 11, 181, 197 n.14,
        198–200, 201, 207, 209,
        210, 211, 220 n.42
    and utopian fiction 11, 212–13,
        221 n.53
Flaubert, Gustave 2, 6
    exchange of objects for subjects in
        narratives of 124–45
    mitigation of plotted causality
        by 119–21
    objectivization and spatialization
        of time in narratives
        of 121–4
    "Un coeur simple" by 7, 125ff.
    use of imperfect tense in narratives
        of 109, 118–19, 122,
        123, 129 n.37
Force, Pierre 196 n.9, 199
Forman-Barzilai, Fonna 198 n.20,
    199

Foucault, Michel 76 n.41, 77, 197, 198 n.19, 199
Fragonard, Jean-Honoré, *see* Diderot, Denis de
Frankfurt, Harry 215 n.4, 221
Frazer, Michael L. 196 n.9, 199
Fried, Michael 87, 106 n.4, 107 n.9, 108

Goethe, Johann Wolfgang von 1, 2, 4, 46 n.18
  works by
    Faust 23
    Wilhelm Meister 27 n.15
Gournay, Marie de
  on Aristotelian theory of essential form 63–4, 74 n.34, 76 n.39
  on contradiction between categories of sex and the human 5, 52–8, 63–9
  and Montaigne 55, 72 n.12, 75 n.40
  and phyrronic skepticism 5, 55–7, 73 n.15
  on social *vs.* natural sexual categorization 51–2, 54–72
Gregoric, Pavel 253
Grimm, Melchior 6, 46–7, 50, 86–7, 92–3, 94–5
Griswold, Charles L. 196 n.9, 199
Guyer, Paul 251 n.30, 253

Hamilton, Ross 221 n.53, 222
Hardy, Thomas 30, 32, 214
Haslanger, Sally 60, 65–7, 70, 74–7
Hegel, G. W. F. 2, 7–9, 30, 33–43, 46–50, 121–4
  on fictionality of empiricist "assumptions" *vs.* logic of "negation" 39–42
  his conception of "interiority" 40–3
  works by
    Lectures on Aesthetics 36, 128 n.32
    Lectures on the History of Philosophy 41, 46 n.17, 49 n.31
    Logic of 158
    Phenomenology of Spirit 19, 115, 117, 128 n.29, 137 nn.73, 75, 153–5, 159–60, 164 n.3, 166 nn.21, 28, 167 nn.32, 35, 36, 44
    Chapter on "Sense-Certainty" in 115–18, 154
    dialectical model of lord-bondsman in 156–7
    dialectical-ethical analysis of agency in Sophocles' *Antigone* in 9, 158, 160
Heidegger, Martin 4, 17, 24
historicism 1, 202
Hobbes, Thomas 11, 203–7, 199–201, 215
Hobbesianism
  anti-, Fielding's 11, 206–7, 209
Hölderlin, Friedrich 208
humanism 5, 48, 53–4, 56, 67, 69, 72, 78
Hume, David 180, 196–7, 199, 251
Hunter, Paul 217 n.17, 219 n.38, 220 n.43, 222
Hutcheson, Frances 181, 197 n.14, 199, 206

"impartial spectator"
  Smith's theory of 10, 177–9, 183–4, 188, 189, 190, 193–4
interiority 4, 10, 29–39, 41–4, 44 nn.1, 3, 45 nn.4, 9, 46 n.12, 46–7 n.18, 47–8 n.20, 125, 147, 153, 176, 180, 219 n.38
Irigaray, Luce 68
Iser, Wolfgang 215 n.6, 219 n.38, 222

Jakobson, Roman   130 n.57, 132
James, William   2
    his redefinition of "interiority" in
        Principles of Psychology
        (1890)   30-2
    adopted by 20th-cent. critics
        of the English "realist"
        novel   32-44, 45 n.5,
        46-7 n.18, 50
Jameson, Frederic   218 n.24, 222
Jauss, H. R.   118
Jenkins, Katherine   67, 69, 75 n.47,
        75 n.58, 78
judgment   9-13, 83-4, 202-3,
        215 nn.2, 5, 216 nn.7, 9,
        217 n.16, 218 nn.24, 31,
        32, 219 nn. 33, 35, 37,
        38, 221 n.53
    "age of"   9-10
    and Cartesian "cogito"   18
    defined as "universal faculty"
        by Kant   12, 228, 231,
        233-7, 241, 251 n.30
    in Diderot   88, 96, 104
    enlightenment theories of moral
        and aesthetic   174, 196
        n.9, 215-16 n.6, 218 n.24
    and "feeling" in Kant   231, 237-9,
        242-7, 252 n.38
        varying accounts of   250 n.30
    in Fielding   11, 201, 207-9, 213-14,
        219 n.39, 220 n.44
    "general communicability" of, in
        Kant   240, 248, 251 n.30
    "general voice" of, in Kant   244-7
    in Gournay   55
    in Hegel   158, 166 n.20
    Hobbesian exclusion of   204-6,
        215 n.4
    and Kant's conception of
        "common sense"   230-7,
        246-7, 249 n.17, 256 n.9
    logical form of, in Kant   238
    as noncognitive subject of Kant's
        Third Critique   227-9

    in relation to conceptions of
        Being   17-18
    in Shaftesbury   210-11
    similarity of Kant's "universal"
        conception of, to
        Chomsky's theory of
        "universal" "language
        faculty"   251-2 n.34
    in Smith   10, 177-85,
        189, 193
    as speech act, in Kant   237,
        240-3, 247
    "synthetic *a priori*" in Kant   227,
        248 n.4, 248-9 n.13
    verbal form of, in Kant   13, 238-9
Justman, Stuart   196 n.12

Kalar, Brent   251 n.30
Kant, Immanuel   1-4, 8-9, 12-17,
        18, 21, 23, 26 n.2, 31, 41,
        44-5 n.3, 148-55, 157,
        164, 215 n.4, 225-48
    works by
        Critique of Judgment (*Third
            Critique*)   12, 228, 231,
            237, 241, 251 n.30
        "Analytic of the Beautiful"
            in   233-48
        Critique of Practical Reason
            (*Second Critique*)
            12, 225-7, 228, 233-4
        Critique of Pure Reason (*First
            Critique*)   3, 9, 12, 149
        Logic   240, 249 n.16, 251 n.30,
            252 n.48
        "On a newly elevated, superior
            note in philosophy"
            22, 231, 250 n.23
        *Prolegomena to Any Future
            Metaphysics*   21, 228,
            249 n.17
        "What is Enlightenment?"   83,
            106 n.1, 119, 129 n.47
katharsis   135-7, 141, 143,
        146 n.30

Keats, John 2, 4, 22, 110, 113
Kelleher, Paul 197 n.14
Klein, Lawrence E. 197 n.14
Kleist, Heinrich von 2, 4, 24–5
Kramnick, Jonathan 215 n.4
Kuhlenkampff, Jan 251 n.30

Laqueur, Thomas 64, 75 n.41
Leidhold, Wolfgang 197 n.14
Lessing, G. E. 2, 8, 134–7, 143–4 n.3, 144 nn.4, 5
Locke, John 202, 206, 208, 210, 227 n.16
Lukács, Georg 122, 130 nn.57, 58
Lynch, Deirdre Shana 217 nn.13, 15, 219 n.36, 220 n.50

MacKenzie, Scott 215–16 n.6, 219 n.38, 260 n.44
Macpherson, C. B. 206, 217–18 n.20, 219 n.38
McWeeny, Gage 217 n.13
Mandeville, Bernard 202, 206–7, 211, 213, 217 n.16
Manne, Kate 53, 72 n.3
Marinella, Lucrezia 54
Marshall, David 183, 198 n.17
Marx, Karl 2, 8, 9, 149–50, 153, 155, 161–4
Mendelssohn, Moses 138
Merrett, Robert James 215–16 n.6, 219 n.38
Mikkola, Mari 65–6, 74 n.28, 75 n.44, 76 n.60
Milbank, John 217 n.20
Mitchell, David T and Sharon L. Snyder 195 n.6
Montaigne, Michel de 55, 72 n.12, 75 n.40
Motooka, Wendy 196 n.12

Nazar, Hina 196 n.9, 214 n.1, 218 n.32
Newtonian mechanics 5, 202
Nicot, Jean 58

Nussbaum, Felicity 174, 194 n.1, 198 n.16
Nussbaum, Martha 137, 145 n.9

O'Neill, Eileen 62–3, 72 n.1, 74 n.34
ontology 1, 24, 52, 74 n.29

Paknadel, Felix 219 n.37
Pausanias 84, 94, 106 n.3
performative
 assignments of sexual
  categorization 60–1
 theatrical, of the historical
  (in painting) 85
Pfau, Thomas 215 n.2, 217 n.16, 218 n.21
Pinkard, Terry 166 n.28, 167 n.35
Pippin, Robert 153, 166 n.26
Plato, viz. Platonic 1–2, 61, 63, 236
 allegory of the Cave 6, 87–91, 94, 97–8, 102–6
 Forms 138
 theory of anamnesis 250 n.29
plot, viz. emplotment 6, 23
 construction of, in tragedy 8, 134, 136–44, 145 n.12
 narrative 7, 109–19, 121, 126, 128 n.28, 129 n.45, 209, 212
positivism, viz. positivist 1, 4, 43, 244
 psychological, empiricist
  determination of, in
  James, Watt 38–44
pragmatism, viz. pragmatic 4, 70, 71, 76 n.65
Preston, John 215–16 n.6, 218 n.33, 219 n.37
Protestantism 35, 43, 49–50 n.37
Proust, Marcel 7, 107, 119, 129 n.47, 131 n.78
psychology 32, 34–9, 41–2, 136, 204, 207

Querelle des femmes, la   52, 54,
    71, 72 n.1
realism   5, 39, 42, 49 n.28, 114–15,
    129 n.45, 221 n.53
Rescher, Nicholas   250 n.26
Richardson, Samuel   2, 6, 7
    his "Author's Preface" to
        Clarissa   7, 9, 11
    novels by
        Clarissa, or, the History of a
            Young Lady   109–11,
            112, 115, 116, 118,
            126 n.1
        Pamela   201–2, 207, 210
Rosenfeld, Sophia   220 n.42
Rousseau, Jean-Jacques   2, 4, 18, 21,
    22, 23, 179, 196 n.10

Sandel, Michael   217 n.19, 218 n.25
Saurette, Paul   251 n.31
Savi, Mariana   253
sensus communis   11, 204, 207,
    209, 210, 219 n.40,
    228–9, 245–6, 249 n.16,
    250 n.29, 251 n.30,
    see also common sense
Shaftesbury, Anthony Ashley, Third
    Earl of   2, 11, 181,
    197 n.14, 198 n.17, 201,
    207–11, 213, 219 n.37,
    220 nn.42, 43, 44
Shakespeare, William   36, 45, 49 n.22
Shapiro, Joseph P.   174–5, 198 n.3
Shell, Susan Meld   251 n.30
Siebers, Tobin   196 n.11
Smith, Adam   2
    works by
        Theory of Moral
            Sentiments   10,
            175–91, 193
        Wealth of Nations   10
Snow, Malinda   215–16 n.6,
    219 n.38
Socrates   61

space, viz. spatialization
    as metaphor for internal
        experience   3–4, 11,
        29, 31–5, 38, 42, 125,
        128 n.43, 159–60, 203,
        205, 209, 213
    as representation of time   121–3
speech   40
    as action   60, 124, 238–43, 245
    figures of   151
    its "general voice," in Kant   246–7
    judgment as, in Kant   237
    reported, verbal tense of   230–1,
        249 n.20
Stephanson, Raymond   216 n.6,
    218 n.33, 219 n.37
Stout, Jeffrey   166 n.28, 167 n.44
Strauss, Leo   221 n.51
Suchon, Gabrielle   54
Sveinsdóttir, Ásta   60, 74 n.27
sympathy,   53, 141, 203, 207–8,
    218 n.31
    Hume's theory of   197 n.13
    Smith's theory of   10, 174–8,
        187, 190, 193–4, 195 n.6,
        196 n.9, 198 nn.17, 20
Szondi Peter   134, 144 n.1

tautology   231–3
techne   242
theatricality
    of Diderot's prose   86–7, 106 n.4
    of psychic landscape in James   33
    of Smith's conception of
        sympathy   198 n.17
Thorne, Christian   215 n.2, 216 n.13,
    218 n.21
tragedy
    theories of   7–8, 136–42, 145 n.9,
        146 n.30
Trousset, Alexis   55
Turner, David M.   174, 176, 194 n.1,
    195 n.8

Uyl, D. J. Den   220 n.43

Valihora, Karen 214 n.1
Vann, Gerald 26, 33–8, 41–4,
  46 nn.10, 13, 15, 48 n.22
Veloso, C. W. 8, 137, 143, 145 n.7
verdictive(s) 60, 74 n.26
Virno, Paolo 218 n.33

Warner, William B. 219 nn.34, 38
Watt, Ian 36–44, 49 nn.24, 28, 30,
  49, 31, 127 n.23, 216 n.6,
  217 n.13, 221 n.53
 empiricist "realism" of, *vs.* Hegel's
  dialectical logic of
  the real 39–43

mimetic theory of "interiority"
  of 42–3
pseudo-Hegelianism
  of 39–41, 43
Welsh, Alexander 216 n.6, 219 n.38,
  220 n.46
Wenzel, Christian 251 n.30
White, Hayden 144, 146 n.34
Wittig, Monique 2, 67–8, 70,
  75 n.53
Wordsworth, William 2, 4, 18–19,
  21, 26 nn.3, 6

Žižek, Slavoj 153, 155, 166 n.30

www.ingramcontent.com/pod-product-compliance
Lightning Source LLC
Chambersburg PA
CBHW062127300426
44115CB00012BA/1843